INVEST DIVA'S GUIDE TO MAKING MONEY IN FOREX

How to Profit in the World's Largest Market

KIANA DANIAL

New York Chicago San Francisco Athens London Madrid
Mexico City Milan New Delhi Singapore Sydney Toronto

1 2 3 4 5 6 7 8 9 0 DOC/DOC 1 9 8 7 6 5 4 3

ISBN 978-0-07-181873-5
MHID 0-07-181873-1

e-ISBN 978-0-07-181874-2
e-MHID 0-07-181874-X

Library of Congress Cataloging-in-Publication Data

Danial, Kiana.
Invest Diva's guide to making money in Forex : how to profit in the world's largest market / by: Kiana Danial.
pages cm
Includes bibliographical references and index.
ISBN 978-0-07-181873-5 (alk. paper) — ISBN 0-07-181873-1 (alk. paper)
1. Foreign exchange market. 2. Foreign exchange futures. I. Title.
HG3821.D26 2013
332.4'5—dc23
2013007681

This book is printed on acid-free paper.

To my wonderful Mom and Dad:
Who always believed in me and supported my most rebellious choices.

To the women of Iran:
Whose bravery empowered me.

To the women of Japan:
Whose dedication inspired me.

And a BIG thank you to my amazing coach, David Parke, who kept me on track.

CONTENTS

PART 2
Technical Stuff

PART 3
Winning Diva Stuff

INTRODUCTION

What is a woman worth? Should we kiss our feminine gifts goodbye just because a certain field is currently male-dominated? Women in Japan certainly don't think so. Japanese housewives have been pioneers in stay-at-home currency trading, followed by many other women in Asia. According to an article in *Wall Street Daily*, some of the so-called Mrs. Watanabes earn an average of $150,000 a year and, according to Japan Inc., Japanese housewife traders have been a stabilizing force in currency markets and at times are the force behind the movements of the Japanese currency, the yen.

Whether we're a trendy fashionista, a career babe, or a trophy wife, we all aspire to be unique and to have an enriched lifestyle. We want to have enough wealth to stay chic and splurge on weekend travel. Wouldn't it be nice if we could earn our own pleasure and improved lifestyle, even if we are financially secured by our family or a daytime job? I'm talking about living the fab life without guilt.

In today's world, it's just too hard to keep our style up to date while also balancing the budget. Even if we somehow manage to save up extra cash, we often waste it frivolously without getting the most for our money, or we simply have a guilty feeling about spending our spouse's cash or the family budget. Time goes by, and the next thing we know, we just can't afford the lifestyle of our dreams. We fear the title "gold digger." We wish people could see our true capabilities. So what is a girl to do?

Become a Forex Diva. Invest easily in the largest market in the world, which wasn't available to retail traders until the late 1990s: the currency market.

Many recent studies, including the one conducted by Richard Peterson, MD, show that women make better investment decisions than men. A study by Barclays Wealth and Ledbury Research found that women were more likely to make money in the market, mostly because they didn't take as many risks.

Trading currencies, or so-called forex, can be easy, fun, and enriching if it is done wisely after having undergone the essential education.

In this book, I have brought together all the forex trading material from my online Invest Diva videos and classes, and added tips and tricks from real women who have attended my seminars. This book will teach you how to be practical in managing, saving, and investing money that you would otherwise consider expendable income. Together, we will learn a great deal about the educational techniques and essential basic knowledge that you need in order to successfully invest in the forex market to make your dreams come true.

> Become educated to invest your extra income in the forex market.

And anyone who thinks that forex trading can only be a man's job is either delusional or quite honestly uninformed. If there were ever a battle of the sexes in the world of forex trading, I have no doubt that women who were properly trained in my trading methods would always come out on top. Women in the forex arena are not handicapped by stereotypical male power egos. In other words, men trade to win, but women trade to invest.

Am I suggesting feminism, or that you should turn into a man, act like a man, or even think like a man? Not at all! In fact, I'm proposing the exact opposite. We adore men and have learned a great deal from them about trading techniques. But as mentioned before and discussed in detail in Chapter 1, women genetically have better heads on their shoulders when it comes to managing risks in investing and trading. Furthermore, adding forex trading to your list of hobbies will help you achieve your goal of being different, unique, and a "Creature Unlike Any Other," as the great book *The Rules* by Ellen Fein and Sherrie Schneider puts it. You won't believe how men are instantly intrigued when I casually mention that I trade forex in my free time. They usually say something like, "This is the most unexpected thing I've heard," and then they just can't stop talking! Now, instead of boring guys to death with the story of my previous heartbreak, I get them crazy about talking to me regarding something we can both relate to.

"You rarely have a losing trade?" they will ask. And of course I don't give away my Invest Diva secrets of successful investments—and even if I did, they usually wouldn't follow them. Boys will be boys, and old habits are slow to die. So why bother? Just be that sexy, smart, mysterious girl who has the keys to an exciting friendship, bonding, and financial success. At best, this can be something you can do together with your boyfriend, husband, or male friends and have the best of both worlds: their appetite for risk and your talent of risk management.

By carefully understanding the necessary steps and dynamics of forex trading, and by tapping into and utilizing the hidden powers of the feminine mind, I can help to guide you step by step from the ground level and onward to climb the ladder of financial success. In this book, we argue that women can become superstar forex traders.

Q: Can men read this book?

A: Absolutely! We would love it if men could also learn to earn money in forex and to manage their risks properly. Just be prepared to go through a lot of feminine metaphors and women's secrets of risk management and patience.

As a graduation reward for learning these special techniques for forex trading, you can stop just dreaming about taking that family trip to Disneyland or buying that iconic Louis Vuitton wallet.

How I Got Into Forex Trading

First, please answer the following question: have you ever been the only woman in a group of men? If you haven't, just use your imagination! When you are the only girl in a group of boys, one of the following things may happen to you:

1. You are treated like the princess you deserve to be.
2. All the guys hit on you and you get frustrated.
3. The guys start fighting over you, and you feel important.
4. The guys start punching each other because of you, and you get annoyed.
5. All the guys around you are too shy to talk to you, and you feel ignored.

Maybe you guessed it, but in my case, the last was what happened. I went to Japan on a Japanese government scholarship to study electrical engineering, and I was both the only girl in my class and the only foreigner. And at that time, I didn't even speak the language very well.

As for my classmates . . .

First, think about engineering students: they're known for being studious—but not necessarily being the life and soul of the party. Then think Japanese guys: they're known for being respectful—but not necessarily being smooth-talking Romeos. Now combine "male engineering student" and "Japanese guy" and put yourself in my shoes as the only girl in a group of them.

It wasn't so much fun, and I was competing with computers—and losing as potential girlfriend material! And forget about trying to get any of my classmates to solve my math problems just because I was a cute girl.

Yes, I could have given up because of the stereotype that engineering is for men, but I'm happy that I did not. I also could have found a sugar daddy to marry me so that I wouldn't ever have to study or work if I didn't want to. Maybe I'll do that one day! But for now it's time to reach my full potential as a woman.

Engineering and forex trading have at least one thing in common: they are both male-dominated industries.

I first started forex trading while I was a college student. It was mid-September 2008, exactly when the collapse of Lehman Brothers shocked the world. At that point, I had never even heard the name of Lehman Brothers and didn't know the meaning of a "financial crisis," either in Japanese or in English. But I could hear people saying that the Japanese yen was strengthening because of it, and that now was a good time to buy dollars.

So my mind started working overtime thinking that I had to take advantage of all the things that were going on in the world. I began checking the Japanese yen currency rates against the U.S. dollar on my neighborhood ATM machine, and I noticed that in fact, the prices were changing every day. The dollar's price against the yen went from 110 to 105, 103, 100, 99, 98 . . . ! This seemed *amazing*! I should start selling my yen before the prices went back up again! But wait a minute, maybe I should trade only a small part of my money at first and wait for the market reaction, so that if the prices continued to drop, I would still have some yen to sell.

I started to get addicted to checking the prices on the ATM machine on my way to work (and later on my way to school after my internship was over), during lunchtime, and on my way home. I would buy more dollars using my yen as the dollar's price continued to go down against the yen, and I would get more upset about the yen that I had sold the day before for a cheaper price. I could more or less sense that the prices were going to drop even further, but I didn't want to risk an opportunity or the danger of the prices going back up. If only there was a system that would let me set the point at which I would buy dollars.

Just out of nowhere, I started talking about this with my "Japanese mom," a lady who with her family had taken responsibility for my emotional support in Japan. "I'm thinking of exchanging my yen for dollars because I think I'm moving to the United States soon, and I want to get the timing right. I think now is a good time because the dollar is getting cheaper and cheaper against the yen, but I don't know when it is going to hit its lowest point. I don't have time to check the prices all the time because I'm at school. I wish I could hire someone or write a computer program that could do this for me automatically while I'm not by an ATM machine! Do you think there is a way?"

Guess what? There *is* a way!

"Open an online forex account, and you can not only set stops and limits for your trades, but also multiply your gains by up to 50 times because of the leverage!" she said.

I had no idea what leverage was, but it all sounded very cool!

I transferred $10,000 worth of yen to a forex account right away at an exchange rate of 100. That was an exchange of about 1 million yen. Leverage (which is something that you will learn about in Chapter 3) was available below 50:1 with the Japanese broker that I had opened my account with. I chose 14:1, which made my position $140,000, the equivalent of 14 million yen! That was an outrageous leverage for a beginner, but I was young and rebellious. I would never advise such a high leverage for forex beginners. But the wise thing I did was set my stop and limit carefully:

I set my profit limit order at USD/JPY = 93, which would enable my account to automatically close with a profit when the price of the dollar against the yen went down to 93. I set my stop loss order at USD/JPY = 102 to prevent extreme losses in case the prices started to move against me.

Less than a month later, the price did fall all the way to 93, and even further to 91 or so. The rest is history. My account was automatically closed while I was sleeping at the exchange rate of 93, where I had originally set the limit order. I wasn't able to take advantage of the further declines that followed in the market, but the bottom line is that I more than doubled my money in less than a month in October 2008 without doing anything special and just by giving the currency market some time to move.

My Trading Action	USD	JPY	Amount of USD/JPY with 14:1 leverage
I opened an account worth 1,000,000 yen at the USD/JPY exchange rate of 100	-10,000	+1,000,000	140,000[a]
Less than a month later, I exchanged my 1,000,000 yen for U.S. dollars at the exchange rate of 93	+10,752[b]		150,528[c]
Profit	752[d]		10,528[e]
Total money in my account			**20,528[f] USD**

[a] 10,000 × 14 = 140,000.
[b] 1,000,000/93 = 10,752.
[c] 10,752 × 14 = 150,528.
[d] 10,752 - 10,000 = 752 (without leverage).
[e] 150,528 - 140,000 = 10,528. (Also, 752 × 14 = 10,528, so it can be calculated either way.)
[f] Initial $10,000 + new leveraged profit 10,528 = 20,528.

Here is a different version of this table:

My Trading Action	USD	JPY
I opened an account worth 1,000,000 yen at the USD/JPY exchange rate of 100	-10,000	+1,000,000
I set the leverage at 14:1	-140,000	+14,000,000
Less than a month later, USD/JPY hit an exchange rate of 93	+150,528	
Profit	10,528	
Total money in my account	**20,528**	

Now, who says that just because I am a woman, I cannot dominate the wonderful world of forex trading?

CHAPTER 1

Why Women Can Be Great Forex Traders

Women in Japan are pioneers in at-home forex trading. While forex has an image of being risky, Japanese housewives, or the so-called Mrs. Watanabes, have found ways to invest in currencies that have eliminated risk. They have found a balance between their savings and their investment capital, and they manage their risk properly. Is successful trading limited to Japanese women, or is it a gift that has been given to all women around the globe?

First of all, having taught both men and women from different backgrounds, I have discovered that women in general make better investment decisions than men and therefore are better candidates for forex trading. Additionally, the increasing numbers of female traders all around Asia, the Middle East, and Europe give us a green light. Interestingly enough, even male traders admit to this—not to mention the research and university studies that have also backed me up on the reasons why women can be great forex traders:

1. **Women Have More Patience**

   Being patient is one of the keys to success in forex trading, and women in general are more patient. The hardest thing for men to do is to sit and watch the screen when there is no signal. Women, however, can keep their cool. This arises from women's unique talent for multitasking. It's very easy for a woman to wait for the next forex signal (and to avoid missing it!) while doing her manicure, chatting on the phone, cooking, or reading her favorite fashion magazine.

2. **Women Admit When They Are Wrong More Quickly and Easily**
   In general, women have an easier time admitting that they are wrong or that they have made a mistake. For men, "I made a mistake" or "You are right" is a very hard thing to say. Realizing that you are wrong and admitting it is very important in forex trading. If the prices are going against you and you are tempted to move your stop, the possibility of your losing an even larger amount of money gets higher.

3. **Women Are More Teachable**
   Just because they don't have as many ego issues as men, women pay more attention to forex education and are better at following the rules. Following your gut works only 10 percent of the time in forex trading, and, as we will discuss later, women actually even have better "guts" than men. Forex education is absolutely necessary for traders, as are learning about money management, position sizes, how the system works, and the general discipline and trading psychology.

4. **Women Don't Have the "Alpha Male Complex"**
   There is a difference between having pride in your work and wanting to prove that you are the king of the markets. For men, trading is mostly about being better than other men (an alpha male competition). This leads men to take unnecessary risks and to feel extremely bad when they don't make large gains.

   Conversely, men get excited when they make some money and, just to prove their majesty, they may enter a huge position without analyzing the markets carefully, just because they think that they have already beaten the markets and they know best. Something interesting to know is that *most of the losses in forex trading come after a huge success.*

Women, on the other hand, don't get too proud and won't start doubling their trade size. Pride in a trade can easily go against you. While making continuous successful trades for a long period of time is generally not likely in forex trading, women's ability to let go of their pride and let the price hit the stop can prevent a huge loss.

5. Women Are More Risk-Averse

Women are simply more risk-averse than men, which can be another advantage in trading risky markets. According to an article published in the *New York Times* on March 14, 2010, this has to do with pornography, motherhood, and the caveman brain. Researchers have found that activating the nucleus accumbens—a brain region that is stimulated when you eat delicious food or look at an attractive person—can affect financial risk taking. When young Stanford men were shown pictures of partially clothed men and women kissing, that region of their brains was activated. And when they were then given financial tests, the men became more likely to make high-risk gambles. Women didn't respond much to the same pictures.

According to Alexandra Bernasek, a professor of economics at Colorado State University, before the dawn of history, aggressive risk taking might have given men an advantage in finding mates, while women might have become more risk-averse to protect their offspring.

6. Women Invest Better in General

A study of 100,000 portfolios showed that women's investment returns outperform men's, 18 percent to 11 percent. This could be because women are typically more cautious with their investment decisions and think longer term. According to a new study, during the financial crisis, men were more likely to sell stocks at the bottom of the market than women were, based on IRA account activity in 2008–2009 at Vanguard, the mutual fund company. This happens for the same reason that men have to ask women out on dates and never stop to ask for directions (and other universal truths about men and women).

"There's been a lot of academic research suggesting that men think they know what they're doing, even when they really don't know what they're doing," says John Ameriks, head of Vanguard Investment Counseling and Research and a coauthor of the study. Women, on the other hand, appear more likely to acknowledge when they don't know something—like the direction of the stock market or of the price of a stock or a bond.

PART 1

Basic Forex Stuff

CHAPTER 2

What Is Forex?

Have you ever traveled to a foreign country? If you have, you probably had to find a currency exchange counter at the airport, and you probably noticed a screen with a lot of numbers and strange-looking currency names that you may never have heard of.

You give the nice lady at the counter $100, and you receive a 10,000-yen bill in return. *Ten thousand yen!* You now probably get all excited and think to yourself, "I'm rich!! I can easily become a millionaire in Japan!"

You may even post a photo of you and your 10,000-yen bill on your Facebook page.

Of course, this excitement dies down quickly when you take a cab to your hotel and all of a sudden half of your money is gone. But the bottom line is that by doing this, you have essentially participated in the forex market! You didn't see that coming, did you?

Forex is actually a combination of the words *foreign* and *exchange* (see Figure 2-1).

So it's perfect for wannabe foreigners or for foreigners in general.

It has nothing to do with your "ex," and you are not doing anything special "for" him if you trade forex. Trading forex simply means exchanging one currency for another.

FIGURE 2-1

Now, going back to your imaginary visit to Japan, if you have any money left in your pocket after spending some time in Tokyo (which I would doubt, because Tokyo is brutally expensive!), you will go back to the currency exchange counter and notice that the rates have changed.

Let's take an extreme example of a rate change, and say that the rates changed from 100 to 80 in a mere two weeks (see Figure 2-2).

FIGURE 2-2

This means that for every 10,000 yen you exchange, you will now get $125, and that means that you have made $25 on those yen during your time in Japan, without doing anything special and just by giving the currency market some time. It's that easy.

But don't get too excited yet. These changes in the currency markets sometimes allow you to make money, but other times they "allow" you to lose money; just as in any other kind of investing and trading.

Are you still thinking about what the differences are between forex and stocks? This is an indicator that you should keep on reading this book.

CHAPTER 3

Top Advantages of Trading Forex Versus Trading Stocks

When I bring up the topic of online trading, the first thing that comes to the minds of many people is trading stocks. While the fluctuations of the two markets can be interconnected, and following the movements of these markets and analyzing the charts share a massive amount of similar techniques, the forex market has a number of solid advantages over the stock market.

The Forex Market Is Open 24 Hours a Day, Nonstop

Yes, you can trade when you're having a sleepless night, or during your coffee breaks on your mobile phone. You can discuss the market with your family and friends in the evening and place orders at the same time. You can even trade while you are waiting for your children to get out of school.

While stock trading allows you to trade only when the stock markets are open, the forex market does not stop at four o'clock. It's a nonstop 24-hour market, starting on Sunday at 5 p.m. in New York and closing five days later on Friday at 4 p.m. And of course, with today's technology, it is available on your iPad and your mobile devices.

Why does it start on Sunday night in New York, you ask? Because that is when the Sydney and Singapore markets open. That's their Monday morning. Then you can trade around the clock and basically follow the market openings in Tokyo, London, Europe, and other places.

The Forex Market Is the Largest and Most Liquid Financial Market in the World

Are you ready to hear this? The foreign exchange market is on average 53 times bigger than any stock exchange (see Figure 3-1).

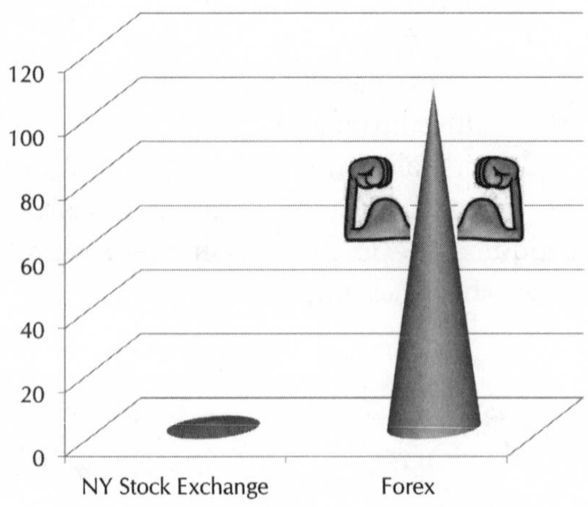

FIGURE 3-1: The Global Forex Market Is 53 Times Bigger Than the NYSE Euronext

But the tiny little stock markets such as NYSE Euronext are the markets that people are making all that noise about every day on Bloomberg and MSNBC, which makes nonfinancial-savvy people like you and me want to switch the channel as soon as we accidently get there.

The liquidity of the forex market is about $4 trillion every day, around the globe. What is liquidity, you ask? It is the degree to which an asset can be bought or sold without affecting its price.

The secret to the huge size and liquidity of the forex market is that this huge amount of liquidity includes the entire global currency exchange market. You can make money trading a foreign country's currency without having to leave your apartment. Talk about the global village! It also means that you can get in and out of trades of almost any size at almost any time. This market is deep, baby!

There Are Only a Few Major Currencies Compared to Thousands of Stocks

There are only seven major currency pairs that you can follow nonstop, whereas there are thousands of stocks listed on the New York Stock Exchange or Nasdaq alone. How are you going to decide which stock to follow?

I mean, come on. It's practically impossible to follow all the thousands of stocks listed on the NYSE and Nasdaq and decide which is the best stock to invest in.

Equal Opportunity for Bears and Bulls

Have you heard of equal opportunity employers? The forex market is something like that. It's an equal opportunity market for both bears and bulls.

Bulls are investors who make money when they expect the stock markets to go up. Bears are considered pessimistic investors; if they don't get out of the markets in time when stocks are going up, they are going to lose money. Instead, they make money when they expect the markets to go down, which can lead to getting bullied by the bulls, because it is considered "un-cool."

Bears and bulls basically fight every day in the stock market to see which one wins during the trading day. If you have ever traveled to New York or have watched the movie *Hitch*, *Inside Man*, or *Arthur*, you may be familiar with the Wall Street Bull, the bronze sculpture of a bull that stands at the heart of the financial district in downtown New York.

The statue of the bull speaks for itself. On Wall Street, stock traders favor *only* the bulls. There is a great deal of discrimination against bears.

But the forex market is fair; the bears can also be the winners! That's because in the forex market, trading opportunities exist regardless of which way the market moves. You will be the ultimate champion whether you make money by being a bull or bear. Whether you are short or long, you still have equal potential for profit and risk. To sum it up, there is no shame in short selling. (By the way, for those of you who don't know what the terms *short* and *long* mean in trading, please be patient until you get to Chapter 8.)

Get a Bigger Fish with a Smaller Bait

You gotta love this one, especially if you are a savvy person. In the forex market, you can "get a bigger fish with a smaller bait." In other words, you can get more by giving less than you have to give in the stock markets. Who wouldn't like this? I think your face looks like a huge question mark right now, so allow me to explain more.

In the forex market, you need a smaller deposit (or bait) to control a larger contract value (or fish). How is that possible? It's because of leverage.

Leverage is basically a loan that brokers give to traders, so that they have the ability to control a large amount of money using very little of their own money.

In the forex market, the allowed leverage is much higher than in the stock market. In stock trading, your maximum leverage is only 2:1. But in the forex world, it can be 50:1 or even 200:1.

For example, if you want to have a $200,000 position, you can put in only $1,000 of your own, and your broker will give you the ability to control the $200,000 account with your mere $1,000. That means that if you make a 1 percent return, or $2,000, on your $200,000 investment, that is going to be much more than a 1 percent return on the $1,000 you put in, right?

I know that you are now all amazed and excited and probably on your way to open a forex account, but please, listen carefully to what I'm about to say.

While you can get a significant return, leverage has the potential to bring you equally significant losses. It enlarges losses and profits by the same magnitude. So be careful. Please.

Minimal or No Commissions

Most forex brokers charge no commissions or additional transaction fees to trade currencies online or over the phone. Instead, most brokers are compensated for their services through the bid/ask spread. Since these spreads are tight, consistent, and fully transparent, forex trading costs are lower than those in any other market.

Focus on One Thing and It Will Expand

Why do people engage in trade in general? Why does anyone sell anything? I know you are smarter than that and you know the simple answer: to make money.

People generally trade in order to make money, right? Now if you can answer one other question for me, we will be right on track. Do you know, what is traded in forex trading?

The answer is the same: money!

So basically, forex trading means trading money to make money. What's better than that? This is literally following the Law of Attraction to its core: like attracts like; money attracts money; make more money by focusing on money and trading money.

Now this does *not* mean that if you stare at your $1 bill for 10 hours, it will turn into a $100 bill. I am also not encouraging you to put all your money in a forex account and trade all of it for another currency.

I'm just suggesting that after you have finished this book, have become a Forex Diva, and have made your husband (or your boyfriend or your parents) very proud, then there is a strong possibility that you are making more pips than you are losing (discussed in Chapter 7), and that you can eventually even buy a private jet and fly over to your castle in Malibu.

Forex trading can be a lot of fun, and I am sure that with your special feminine skills and ability to manage risks, you actually can become a Forex Diva, but please keep this in mind:

> *Forex trading involves a substantial risk of loss. Forex trading is not a piece of cake. Forex education is crucial for beginners. Use only money that you can afford to lose to trade forex.*

On the bright side, with a lot of studying and practice on free demo accounts on the web, you can easily become a successful trader and make money from the convenience of your bedroom, your kitchen, or even your bathtub. (Don't try the last unless you have a super-cool, waterproof laptop.)

CHAPTER 4

How to Make Money by Trading Money

As we said before, forex trading means trying to make money by trading money. This simply means that you buy or sell different currencies on a forex trading platform, expecting that the prices will change so that the currency that you bought will become more valuable compared to the one that you sold.

It all comes down to the basic element of any trading:

> Buy low and sell high.

The Risk!

Here is an internal conversation among I, myself, and me:

I: Is forex trading risky?

Myself: It kind of feels like trading currencies involves a lot of risk . . .

Me: You bet it does! Depending on the currency movements and your level of education, forex trading can be very risky!

I: What?! Very risky? What if I lose all my money trading forex?

Me: Well, that is why you are reading this book! There are ways to avoid the risk before it gets you. But before you can avoid a risk, you need to understand it.

So why can forex trading be risky? The first reason that comes to mind is the *risk of currency movement*. (See Figure 4-1 for the different risks you face in the currency market.) Just like the stock market, the currency market sometimes moves in a direction opposite to what you expected. That can result in your losing the money you invested in the market.

Currency Movement Risk

Don't put all your eggs in one basket. Invest in different currencies. Don't set your leverage too high.

Global Risk

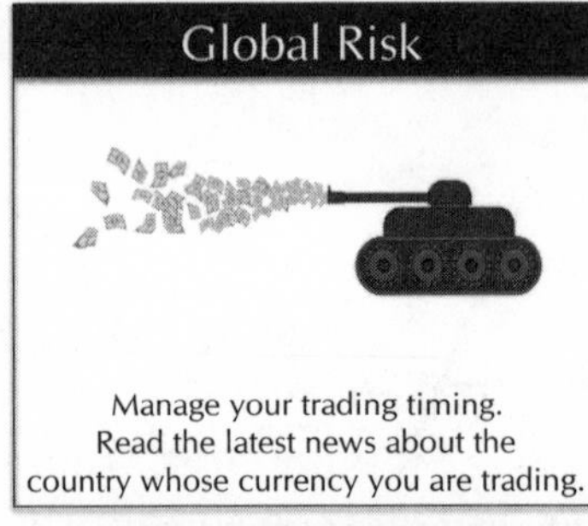

Manage your trading timing. Read the latest news about the country whose currency you are trading.

Liquidity Risk

Try to avoid the minor currency pairs and stick to the majors, which have more volume and liquidity.

Reliability Risk

Do your homework before choosing a forex broker. Invest with a broker that has a stable financial reputation.

Systems Risk

Practice for free on different forex platforms before opening a real account. Choose the platform that works best for you and runs smoothly.

Other Risks

Beware of hackers. Choose passwords that include letters, numbers, and symbols. Change your password regularly.

FIGURE 4-1

The biggest cause of risk in forex trading is the tempting *leverage*. As we said before, leverage is a double-edged sword. While it enables you to multiply your profits, it also multiplies your losses. If you are 100 percent confident that your trade will be profitable, you may use a high leverage to expand your return, but you need to know that when you do this, you are also expanding your risk of losing all your money and more!

This is just the beginning. The *world* can also add risk to forex trading. You heard me, the world! Natural disasters, wars, terrorism, and politics can all have an immediate impact on the forex market. So at least for the sake of your forex account, you may want to put more energy into achieving world peace. But before that happens, the least you can do is listen to the news and be aware of what is going on around the globe. I mean, watching the Kardashians over and over again may be fun, but it won't do you any good when it comes to your forex account and your future life of luxury.

Lack of liquidity can also create risk. If you trade currencies with very low volume, you may not be able to close your trade because the pairs just won't move! This usually happens in the minor currency pairs. You will learn all about them in the next chapter.

What else? The last but not least of the risky stuff in forex trading is your *forex broker*. In addition to the risk of the broker's going *bankrupt* or having a total *system breakdown*, your broker can also screw you up behind the scenes and work against your trades. That is why it is very important to choose a reliable broker. You will learn about that in Chapter 20.

Invest Diva's Guide to Risk Management

The Sword of Leverage

It may take you to heaven, but most likely it will send you to hell first. We talked about how leverage can be higher in the forex market, and how this will give you the opportunity to multiply your profit. But we also mentioned leverage in our discussion of risk. So let's get it straight once and for all.

Leverage is a double-edged sword. When you start trading in a real account, you usually start by investing a small amount of money. Some brokers even let you open accounts with just $25. Here is where you want to be careful, because trading in a small account can mean that you are using a giant amount of leverage that will eventually kill you. And by doing that you are basically cooperating with the sword to commit a suicide by hara-kiri.

Leverage is money borrowed from your broker that gives you the ability to control a large amount of money using none or very little of your own money. Should you fall for the fairy-tale story that just popped into your mind?

No!!

You first need to understand the types of accounts you can open, which depend on the amount of money you want to invest. The basic ones are a *standard account*, a *mini account*, and a *micro account*. You can invest less money in a micro account than in a mini or standard account, and each gives you different choices for leverage and *lots*.

For example, a micro lot is equivalent to 1,000 units of the base currency, whereas a mini lot is equivalent to 10,000 units and a standard lot is equivalent to 100,000 units.

> Remember, no matter what the forex broker tells you, don't ever open a standard account with just $5,000 or a mini account with just $500. Start with a demo account where you can trade with fake money, and then move on to a micro account. Manage the leverage properly!

For example, let's say you have $1,000 and you are trying to trade the euro. Figure 4-2 shows you the effects of leverage.

To sum it up, using leverage enables you to trade big with a small amount of money, but it can also result in a bigger loss . . . and it doesn't end here! The sword of leverage has other deadly powers as well that will kill you on a slower pace, kind of like dying from a thousand cuts.

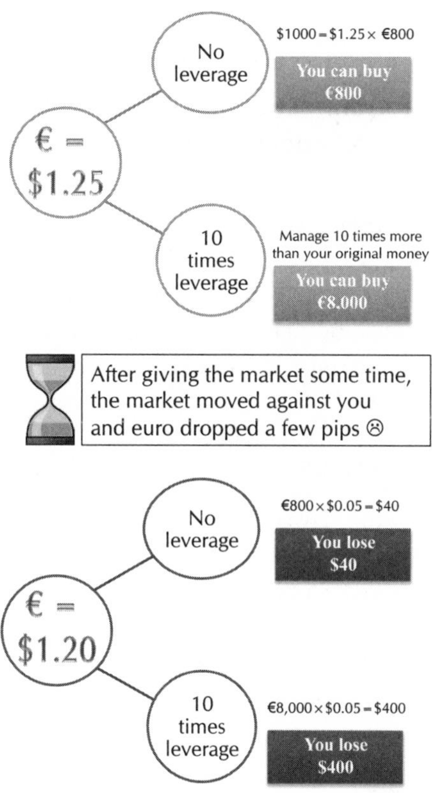

FIGURE 4-2

> Leverage amplifies your transaction cost as a percentage of your account.

Did you think you can just borrow all this money from your broker and not get charged for it? Wishful thoughts, my lady! The higher your leverage, the higher your transaction cost will be. This cost definitely differs depending on the broker, and therefore it is a very important factor to check before choosing a broker.

Margin

So what does the term *margin* mean? That's an excellent question.

Let's go back to the earlier example.

To let you control a $100,000 position, your broker will set aside $1,000 from your account. Your leverage, which is expressed as a ratio, is now 100:1. You're controlling $100,000 with $1,000.

The $1,000 deposit is the *margin* you had to give in order to use leverage.

Margin is the amount of money you need to provide as a "good faith deposit" before you can open a position with your broker. Your broker uses it to maintain your position.

What Happens if There Is a Humongous Loss in Your Account?

Now, you know that trading forex carries a high level of risk. What happens if you lose your lucky charm and the whole forex market moves in a way that screws you? How would you deal with the shock of opening your account and noticing that your balance has become zero?

Don't worry. Most forex brokers have a mechanism called a *margin call* that will alert you if your margin (or the amount of money you *haven't* borrowed) decreases past a certain point. For example, if you're controlling $100,000 with $1,000 and your overall position decreases to $99,500, the margin you have remaining is $500 because you still have $99,000 borrowed.

No matter how much you like people to call you up, a margin call is one thing that you want to avoid. If you get one, there is one thing you need to do immediately: restart reading this book from the beginning and go back to demo trading.

All traders fear the dreaded margin call. (Remember the movie *Margin Call*?) While trading on margin can be a profitable investment strategy, it is important that you take the time to understand the risks.

Make sure you fully understand how your margin account works, and be sure to read the margin agreement between you and your broker. Always ask questions if there is anything in the agreement that is unclear to you.

CHAPTER 5

Forex Party

It's now time to dig in and see what the forex world is all about. If you are a party girl, you can relate to this very well. If you don't like to party, well, I'm sorry, but I have to notify you of something.

It's Time to *Party*!

Imagine that you have a foreign boyfriend, someone who is not of your ethnicity.

So if you are Asian, your boyfriend may be European. If you are American, he can be British, Portuguese, or even a hot Japanese man. The point is, you can*not* have a date who comes from your own country at this party.

So, you and your international partner enter a party and start dancing.

Oops! It seems that you two are not entirely compatible. Every time you make a good move, your partner screws up. Every time he picks up the rhythm, you are stuck in your previous move. Obviously you draw some attention, and a bunch of your friends who are watching you start betting on which one of you is going to screw up next.

They keep track of each of your moves, and they keep betting. In the first round, some of your friends make money and some others lose. Then your friends will get even more excited and will probably start predicting and betting on which one of you guys is going to make better moves the next time. After all, this could be an easy way to make money, right?

This party is exactly what the forex world is all about. The international couple can be a metaphor for the currency pairs. The dance party is a metaphor for a forex trading platform. The audience members who are betting on your performance are the forex traders.

In your romantic vision, maybe two is better than one. Most of us are constantly looking for our soulmate. That is exactly the bright side of forex trading: there are no single ladies!

In forex trading, currencies *always* come in pairs. There will be no parties where singles can mingle. The parties are always filled with couples—international ones.

The downside of this fairy-tale international love story is that the currencies in each pair are in constant competition. One of them will always outperform the other one, and the traders bet on which side will win. It is definitely not a healthy relationship, but it is what it is, and some smart people—aka Forex Divas—can start making money out of the pairs' competition.

Now let's get the party started. There are different parties going on, and you can attend whichever one you like.

For the venue, you have:

- The major currency pairs party
- The major cross-currency pairs party, or the so-called minor currency pairs party
- The exotic pairs party

Disclaimer: Exotic pairs may sound sexy, but my recommendation to you is this: hold your horses.

Major Currency Pairs Party

There are seven currency pairs that are called the majors. You can find them at Forex Diva's major currency pairs party.

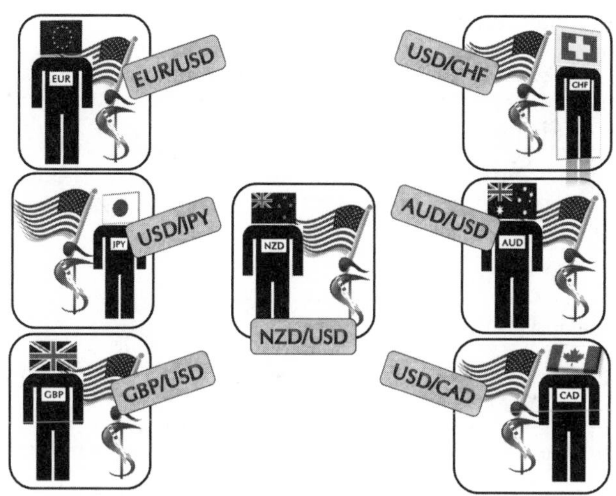

FIGURE 5-1: Ms. USA Dancing with Other Currencies

Now guess where the party is located. If you said the United States, you are just about right. Each of the major currency pairs contains the U.S. dollar.

Imagine this: the currencies from areas such as the United Kingdom (British pound), Europe (euro), Japan (yen), Switzerland (Swiss franc), Canada (Canadian dollar), and New Zealand (New Zealand dollar) are a bunch of guys, and they decide to go to a party and find a dancing partner.

Then they realize that in order to be called a major couple, they need to pair with the currency of the United States (U.S. dollar). Let's pretend that the currency of the United States is a female (we will call it Ms. USA from now on), and the other major currencies all have to dance with her.

In the major currency party, the "one and only" Ms. USA pairs as a dancing partner with all the other major currencies (see Figure 5-1).

> The moral of the major forex party is this: if you consider the U.S. dollar to be the prom queen, in order to become part of a major pair, you have to dance with her.

TABLE 5-1: Major Currency Pairs Party

Currency Pair	FX Nickname	Symbol
Mr. Euro and Ms. USA	Euro-Dollar	EUR/USD
Ms. USA and Mr. Japan	Dollar-Yen	USD/JPY
Mr. UK and Ms. USA	Pound-Dollar	GBP/USD
Ms. USA and Mr. Switzerland	Dollar-Swissy	USD/CHF
Mr. Australia and Ms. USA	Aussie-Dollar	AUD/USD
Ms. USA and Mr. Canada	"Dollar-Cad" or "Dollar-Loonie"	USD/CAD
Mr. New Zealand and Ms. USA	Kiwi-Dollar	NZD/USD

Table 5-1 gives a list of those present at the major currency pairs party and their nicknames.

In the forex world, even if the pairs get into a serious relationship and eventually get married, the females will never change their last name.

Minor Currency Pairs Party

One day the major currencies realized that they were fed up with Ms. USA. They were actually kind of jealous of her because she wasn't letting the other currencies get to know each other. So the currencies from Europe, Japan, Switzerland, New Zealand, Australia, and Canada decided that each of them would throw a party of his own, and that they would invite the major currencies other than Ms. USA to come and dance with them.

They were told by the Organization of Currency Pair Parties (OCPP—this organization is not real) that if they did this, they would no longer be called major currency pairs, but they didn't care. After a lot of negotiation, their new name was decided on: "minor currency pairs."

They are also called the "major cross-currency pairs," but to be honest with you, I think this second name was given

TABLE 5-2: Euro Crosses

Currency Pair	FX Nickname	Symbol
Ms. Euro and Mr. Switzerland	Euro-Swissy	EUR/CHF
Ms. Euro and Mr. UK	Euro-Pound	EUR/GBP
Ms. Euro and Mr. Canada	Euro-Loonie	EUR/CAD
Ms. Euro and Mr. Australia	Euro-Aussie	EUR/AUD
Ms. Euro and Mr. New Zealand	Euro-Kiwi	EUR/NZD
Ms. Euro and Mr. Japan	Euro-Yen	EUR/JPY

TABLE 5-3: Japan Crosses

Currency Pair	FX Nickname	Symbol
Mr. Europe and Ms. Japan	Euro-Yen or Yuppy	EUR/JPY
Mr. UK and Ms. Japan	Pound-Yen or Guppy	GBP/JPY
Mr. Switzerland and Ms. Japan	Swissy-Yen	CHF/JPY
Mr. Canada and Ms. Japan	Loonie-Yen	CAD/JPY
Mr. Australia and Ms. Japan	Aussie-Yen	AUD/JPY
Mr. New Zealand and Ms. Japan	Kiwi-Yen	NZD/JPY

to them only so that they didn't feel discriminated against when compared with the U.S. dollar.

The Organization of Currency Pair Parties created new rooms, and one of the major currencies threw a party in each room. Each room got its very own name, too. The party hosted by the European currency was called Euro Crosses, for example. As you can see in Table 5-2, Ms. Euro bonds with other major currencies like the Swiss franc, the British pound, and the Canadian dollar.

And so all the other major currencies threw their own cross parties.

Table 5-3 shows Japan's cross party.

Table 5-4 shows the pound crosses.

TABLE 5-4: Pound Crosses

Currency Pair	FX Nickname	Symbol
Ms. UK and Mr. Switzerland	Pound-Swissy	GBP/CHF
Ms. UK and Mr. Japan	Pound-Yen	GBP/JPY
Ms. UK and Mr. Europe	Pound-Euro	GBP/EUR
Ms. UK and Mr. Canada	Pound-Loonie	GBP/CAD
Ms. UK and Mr. Australia	Pound-Aussie	GBP/AUD
Ms. UK and Mr. New Zealand	Pound-Kiwi	GBP/NZD

TABLE 5-5: Random Minor Currency Pairs

Currency Pair	FX Nickname	Symbol
Ms. Australia and Mr. Switzerland	Aussie-Swissy	AUD/CHF
Mr. New Zealand and Ms. Canada	Kiwi-Loonie	NZD/CAD
Mr. Europe and Ms. Japan	Euro-Yen	EUR/JPY
Ms. UK and Mr. Australia	Pound-Aussie	GBP/AUD
Ms. Switzerland and Mr. Canada	Swissy-Loonie	CHF/CAD
Mr. Australia and Ms. New Zealand	Aussie-Kiwi	AUD/NZD

Finally, the very open-minded international currencies decided to throw a random party where no matter where they are from and what their sex is, they can just join and enjoy pairing up with whomever they feel like. Table 5-5 is a sample of currency pairs in the random minor currency party. I bet Pitbull and Chris Brown were inspired to write their famous song "International Love" after attending this party.

These parties can now be found on almost any currency trading platform.

Exotic Pairs Party

If you are already bored with the minors and majors, allow me to introduce you to the exotic pairs. You obviously would find different people "exotic" depending on where you are from. In Japan, a blond white guy with blue eyes is pretty exotic, whereas American girls (stereotypically) find British or tanned Middle Eastern guys attractive and exotic.

In the forex world, exotic pairs are made up of one major currency paired with the currency of an emerging economy, such as Brazil, Mexico, or Hungary, or an ancient country, such as Iran.

The exotic pairs in the currency market have a pretty fair relationship, because each side looks exotic in the eyes of the other. But as pretty as these exotic pairs may look, currency traders don't bet on them that much, and they are not traded as heavily as the majors or minors. And that's why transaction costs for trading the exotic pairs are actually higher. The spreads for these pairs can sometimes be twice or three times as large as those for the major or minor pairs.

So keeping this in mind, you might want to forget about trading the exotic currency pairs and just enjoy a cheap real-life flight to an exotic country—using the money that you made trading the minors and majors in the currency market.

Why Do Currencies Come in Pairs?

Because we wouldn't be able to trade them otherwise! A better question would be, "Are the pairs always quoted in the same way? Does the pattern ever change?"

You may have noticed that in each party, when you call up a currency pair, one currency is quoted first, and the other is quoted second. For example, in USD/JPY, Ms. USA comes first, followed by Mr. Japan. In EUR/USD, Mr. Europe comes first, followed by Ms. USA. This pattern is fixed and doesn't change.

This has nothing to do with whether or not the people in the currency's country are culturally expected to let ladies go first. In fact, in Japan, for example, it is exactly the opposite. In real life, men are expected to enter first to make sure everything is safe.

The first currency in the pair is called the *base currency*, and the second is called the *quote currency*. As the base and quote currencies come together, the currency pair shows how much of the quote currency is needed to purchase one unit of the base currency. We will talk more about this in the next chapter.

CHAPTER 6

How to Read Currency Pairs

Once you have picked an item to buy at a grocery store, the next thing you pay attention to is its price. The same thing happens when you attend a forex party and pick a currency pair. You want to know how much each pair is worth. In other words, their price shows their movements on the dance floor!

Every move that an international currency pair makes at a party is shown in numbers.

It doesn't take a genius to figure out that the number is the price of the pair. Don't worry, we are certainly not in the business of trading women. You are still learning how to trade currencies.

Okay, let's get down to business. Take a look at the following geeky statement announced by a currency analyst (me):

"EUR/USD is trading at 1.3125."

What does this tell us? It says that 1 euro can buy about 1.31 U.S. dollars. This means that we would have to pay 131 U.S. dollars to buy 100 euros.

Now, take a look at this:

"USD/JPY is trading at 88.34."

This is saying that 1 dollar can buy about 88 units of the Japanese currency.

Trick

How do you read the price of an apple in a grocery store?

You would probably say: "1 apple costs 1.50 dollars."

The simple logic behind this is filling in the brackets in the following sentence:

"One [object] is [price] [currency]."

The same thing happens when you buy currencies. The only difference is that in forex trading, you are not buying an object with your dollars (or whatever currency you have). You are buying another currency.

In order to read currency prices easily, you can remember this phrase, fill in the brackets, and pretend that you are a psychic who can read the hands of any currency pair. In the magical formula given earlier, just replace [object] with [first quoted currency].

One [object] is [price] [currency].
One [first currency] is [price] [second currency].

So when you see:

EUR/USD = 1.3125

it is exactly as if we were to write

Apple/USD = 1.50

Fill in the brackets:

One [apple] is [1.50] [dollars].
One [euro] is [1.3125] [dollars].
One euro is 1.3125 dollars.

That's it. The secret is out. Now you can easily impress your date by bringing up a currency chart on your mobile phone web browser, and showing him how to read the currency pairs.

Strong Dollar Versus Weak Dollar

You have probably heard about this when you accidentally switched your TV channel to economic news. So what does it mean exactly? If you were to travel to Japan with dollars in your bank account, what could your strong dollar buy you when you were there? What if the dollar is weak? (See Figure 6-1.)

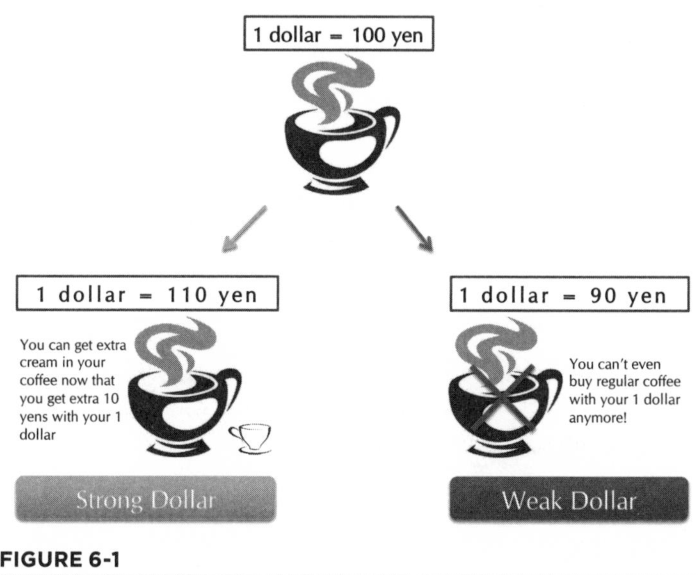

FIGURE 6-1

A strong dollar can be a blessing for U.S. travelers (if they decide to get out of their shell and visit the rest of the world, that is). You can buy more foreign goods for the same amount of money. When times are good, you can go to Italy and buy a Gucci purse with an extra wallet for the same price you would pay for the purse alone in the United States.

But when the dollar is weak, you can't really buy much with 1 dollar in France, for example. In fact, at present,

5 dollars are worth about 3.80 euros, which is not enough to buy a Big Mac in the Eurozone.

Clearly, there are some advantages of a strong dollar. But is a strong dollar always good? It depends on which angle you are looking at it from. For example, when the dollar is strengthening, U.S. firms find it harder to compete in foreign markets because they have to compete with lower-priced foreign goods. Also, we will get fewer tourists in the United States because foreign travelers will find it more expensive to travel here, which can affect the tourism industry.

In general, a strong or a weak currency can affect a country's economy, especially if the country is very dependent on exports or imports.

CHAPTER 7

How Pips Can Change Your Fortune

Making money in forex all begins with learning the answer to the simple question, "What is a pip?" and it continues with, "How can pips change your fortune?"

The simple answer is, a pip is the tiniest possible change in a currency pair at a forex party; it is usually the last decimal place in the pair's price. At your broker's forex party platform, a pip is the final digit of the largest numbers you are looking at (see Figure 7-1).

FIGURE 7-1

Now don't get fooled by their small size. A single pip may have minimal value, but when you're trading large amounts of money, its value can totally kick butts. If you add a large amount of leverage to your trade, that originally tiny pip can become humongous.

That is why, in the forex world, we usually calculate our profits and losses based on pips. It just makes the whole process much easier, because, like me, most of us hate calculating stuff. So on most trading platforms, you can find a "pip calculator" that magically calculates your trade's pip value in a matter of seconds. That's just how cool forex is.

But just for the heck of it (and also to better understand the whole pip thing), let's manually calculate a pip value and pips earned from a trade. Say you want to buy 10,000 worth of Canadian dollars. At the forex party that you're at, USD/CAD is quoted at 1.1111.

Challenge: Read this number out loud in a public place: one point one one one one. I bet you feel better now.

Let's get back to work.

USD/CAD = 1.1111

Now you want to see how much you would have to pay in U.S. dollars to buy 10,000 Canadian dollars. Don't be scared. They are just numbers. Okay, let's do it together, my brilliant newbie traders. Bring out your calculator.

(1/1.1111) × $10,000 = 9,000.09

You will have to pay 9,000.09 U.S. dollars to get 10,000 Canadian dollars.

So you are at the forex party, enjoying your coffee and debating whether or not you want to enter the game, and before you know it, the currency pair makes a move and you see a 1-pip increase to 1.1112. In the geeky forex world, this means that the U.S. dollar has appreciated relative to the Canadian dollar.

Hah. Now you have to pay only 8,999.28 U.S. dollars to buy 10,000 Canadian dollars! You now can pay 81 cents less!! Yay!

But, wait a minute; 81 cents doesn't sound like a big difference. Did you check how much your position was leveraged? Was it 50 times? Now that's what I'm talking about.

With 50 times leverage, that single pip equals 40 dollars and 50 cents:

$$0.81 \times 50 = 40.50$$

And the naughty currency pairs can easily move something like 100 pips a day. That means that a $10,000 position with 50:1 leverage can see gains or losses of $4,000 during the course of the trading day. Cool stuff, huh?

To conclude, pips are the most basic unit of measure in forex trading. And since you already know that learning the basics step by step is very important in forex trading, you need to understand how a pip value relates to your positions in every forex party that you attend.

CHAPTER 8

What Makes Currency Pairs Move?

Nope, it's not music. I mean, we wish the currency pairs at the forex parties would jump up and down to the rhythm of the latest Lady Gaga song playing on a particular radio station that everyone knew about. It would make traders' lives much easier. All you would need would be to know the song by heart to be able to predict what moves the pairs were going to make next.

The currency pairs at the forex party sure like to move it, move it, but they listen to totally different stuff.

They usually like to listen to smart and geeky stuff such as information on economic growth, interest rates, political stability, technical factors, and market psychology. All these things come together like a puppet master and make the pair move on the dance floor.

Therefore, forex traders need to analyze the movements from different perspectives to be able to figure out what movements the currencies are going to make next.

And just for the record, being geeky is considered super awesome these days.

11 Reasons Why Forex Traders Lose Money

Leaving aside the new traders who experience beginners' luck, many new forex traders lose money. When you go to a party, you sure want to do it in style, and you would prefer not to appear as a loser.

Here are some "loser" factors at a forex party:

1. You don't treat forex trading as an investment.
2. You think trading forex is a get-rich-quick solution.
3. You don't understand the risks of forex trading.
4. You follow only your heart and your intuition.
5. You only listen to the news.
6. You only do technical analysis.
7. You follow only the market sentiment.
8. You combine only two or three of the factors just given.
9. You get emotional about your losses, and you get into another wrong trade just to prove that you are not a loser.
10. You get overly excited about your wins, think you are the Nostradamus of forex, and place a foolish trade.
11. *You are not educated in trading forex.*

One of the main arguments against forex is that it's "too risky." Well, that is true, but so are all the other investment and trading instruments. While trading currencies off a platform can be very easy, you need to learn and be educated on how to read the market, how to place safe trades, and how to manage your risk. That is why at InvestDiva.com we have created the easiest and most entertaining forex education videos that you can watch during your coffee breaks, and learn all about how to invest safely in the forex market.

Invest Diva Diamond Analysis

Forex trading should be treated as an investment. Your forex platform is not Las Vegas to gamble. The currency pairs may seem to be having a party, but in order to get to a forex party in style, you need to equip yourself with the most sophisticated piece of jewelry: your investment diamond. Diamonds traditionally are the symbol of clarity, ascension, and wisdom. In the modern world, a diamond in a ring is the ultimate gift, a physical symbol of the love two people share with each other. Have you ever looked at the sparkle of a diamond and thought about how it got its shine? The answer is time and pressure. Invest Diva brings a new meaning to the iconic symbol: you should treat forex trading as an investment, and analyze your trade from five points of an Invest Diva Diamond: technical, fundamental, sentiment, capital, and overall (see Figure 8-1).

This may take some time, but the outcome, just like a diamond, is wise and clear.

Fundamental Analysis

Fundamental analysis is the art of using all the gossip, stories, and events involving a country's economy and politics to make a decision concerning whether that country's currency is worth buying or not.

Most of the news that you hear on the radio and TV is trying to help you get a glimpse of the fundamentals. Fundamental analysis is a way of looking at the market by analyzing the economic, social, and political forces that affect the supply of and demand for a currency.

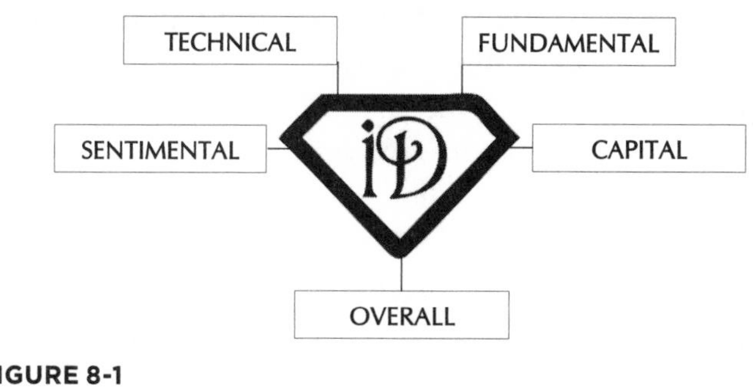

FIGURE 8-1

Forex traders buy and sell currencies with the hope of making a profit when the value of the currency changes in their favor, whether because of market news or because of events that take place around the world. Currencies, just like anything else that can be bought and sold, are subject to the laws of supply and demand. When people want a particular currency, the cost of that currency in terms of other currencies will go up.

This law also applies to real-life shopping, dating, and relationships. The more desirable a brand is, the higher the price. More demand makes it more expensive! (Think Gucci and Louis Vuitton.)

Similarly, when demand decreases or people do not want to hold a country's currency, the value of that currency will go down.

Forex traders have to analyze all the factors that affect supply and demand. In this case, a forex trader is just like someone who is deciding whom to marry. The demand for popular guys is much higher, right? Why is that? What does a woman look for in an ideal catch? If we put aside the chemistry and having things in common, a woman tends to analyze different aspects of a guy's "profile" before she makes a final decision.

She wants to know if he is financially stable. She wants to know if he is honest or, in other words, if he isn't going to put her in a "political turmoil." She wants to know whether or not he is productive, is going to be a good father, doesn't pick his nose in public, pays his bills on time, and has a bright future.

A Forex Diva analyzes different aspects of her prospect before she says yes—that is, before she puts in an order for a specific currency in the forex market.

In other words, when you are at a forex party, you have to look at different factors to determine which country's economy is a good catch, who is a keeper, and whose economy sucks. You have to understand the reasons why certain events like an increase in unemployment affect a country's economy and, ultimately, the level of demand for its currency, and how they do this.

Even if a country's current situation is reasonable, you also want to analyze where its economy is going in the future. The idea behind this is that if a country's current or future economic outlook is good, its currency should strengthen.

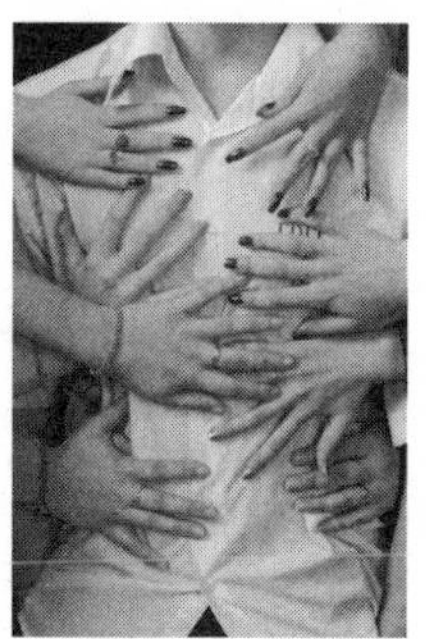

Just as when a man seems to be a good partner for now and a good father in the future, women won't leave him alone, the better shape a country's economy is in, the more foreign businesses and investors will invest in that country, which will ultimately lead to a higher currency value.

Popular Guy, Popular Currency: Are the Girls After the Guy or the Dollar?

Things That Make a Country's Currency *Unpopular*

- Rise in unemployment
- Fall in GDP (gross domestic product)
- Fall in exports
- Fall in interest rates
- Geopolitical tensions
- Natural disasters
- Threat of terrorism

Things That Make a Country's Currency *Popular*

- More jobs
- Rise in GDP
- Rise in exports
- Rise in interest rates
- Super-stable political system
- Discovery of gigantic oil or mineral resources

You will learn more about fundamental analysis in Chapter 16.

Technical Analysis

Technical analysis is the art of using history to predict the future.

At all forex parties, all the currency pairs have been making history with their "dancing" moves. A technical analyst looks at how a currency has been performing and determines its potential future price movements.

Here is the difference between fundamental and technical analysis via an example that's perfect for all the shopping lovers.

Let's say you are trying to find the perfect shop where you can buy everything you need for your new home. If you are a fundamental analyst, you ask all your friends about the different products of different shops that you have in mind. After you have gained all this information, you will decide which store to shop at and what to buy.

By contrast, if you are a technical analyst, you skip all the gossip; instead, you sit on a bench in the middle of a shopping mall and watch the people going in and out. You analyze their shopping bags, their facial expressions before and after shopping, and so on. Your final decision will be based on the patterns of activity of the people going into each store. To take it to another level, you repeat this during different periods of time to see which store is a better target in different seasons and how a store's products and prices change after or during specific calendar points.

Your grandma had a point when she told you, "History repeats itself." She would have made a good technical analyst, because this is basically what technical analysis is all about!

There are lots of fabulous tools and gadgets that can help you understand the historical movements and patterns. By learning how each indicator works, you can have greater accuracy in predicting future price actions.

Technical analysis looks for patterns similar to those that have formed in the past and will come up with trading ideas based on the belief that prices will make the same movements as they did before.

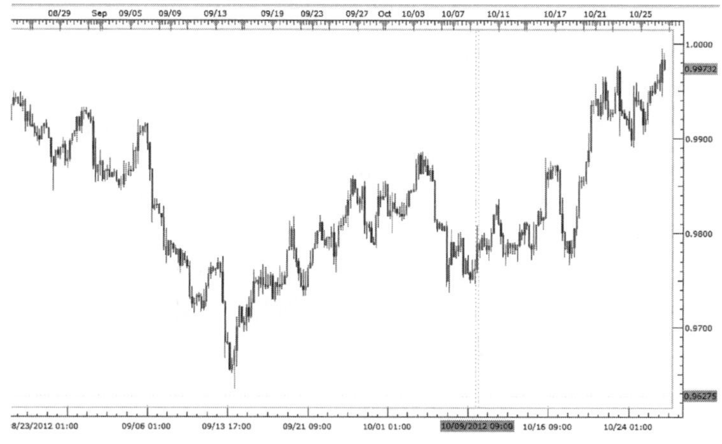

FIGURE 8-3

Let's take a look at a currency pair's historical dancing movement printed on a chart (see Figure 8-3).

Charts are the best way to see all the moves a pair has made at a glance. You can literally see the prices jump up and down over whatever period of time you like.

I almost forgot to mention that currency pairs can sometimes be very trendy as well. Often they follow the latest direction (trend), which help analysts to come up with trend-trading strategies.

You will learn about all these cool things in detail in Part 2.

Market Sentiment

Market sentiment is the emotions and attitudes of traders at the forex party concerning a specific currency pair. Sentiment analysis is the study of the love-hate relationship between the currency pairs and traders, who in the geeky (or maybe animal loving?) forex world are described as "bulls" and "bears."

If traders expect upward price movement by a specific currency pair, the sentiment is said to be bullish. On the contrary, if the market sentiment is bearish, most traders expect downward price movement.

Most traders have their own opinion, feeling, or intuition about the markets; that's why the prices don't simply reflect all the information that's out there.

Each trader expresses her thoughts and opinions through the positions she takes in the market (bullish or bearish). This helps create the overall sentiment of the market.

Just as in technical analysis, there are indicators that help in having an understanding of the market sentiment, such as the Elliott Waves, and the SSI (Speculative Sentiment Index). We will talk more about this in Chapter 17.

Capital Analysis

Depending on your capital and the amount of money you have in your account, your trading strategy should differ. Every time you get into and out of a trade, you pay a fee to your broker, which is called the *spread*, or the difference between the bid and ask prices. Furthermore, you have the option of using leverage of anywhere from 2 to 50 times in the United States.

Before you make a decision on a trade, you need to calculate your capital, the spread your broker is quoting, and the amount of leverage that makes sense given the trade and the amount of capital you have to avoid unacceptable losses.

Overall Analysis

Finally, you need to make a general evaluation of all these factors. Are at least 90 percent of the points just discussed signaling a successful trade? And most important, do you feel comfortable with this trade, or is there something deep down in your gut that is preventing you from taking the final step and placing the order?

I call this last element "women's intuition." We've all heard the term, and there is in fact research evidence (according to Ronald E. Riggio, who has a PhD in cutting-edge leadership) suggesting that women have some sort of psychic ability to discern other people's feelings and what they are thinking. Many fellow forex trading heroines, such as Jody Samuels from J. P. Morgan, also admit that they sometimes follow their heart and their gut feeling as to whether the market is going up or down.

Your intuition or instincts can be either a starting point for your analysis or a final determination of what position to take.

For example, you open up the chart of EUR/USD (the Mr. Euro and Ms. USA forex party room), and at first you feel that the market is bearish. Then you look for fundamental, technical, and sentiment support to back up your feeling.

Another scenario is that after you have done all your study and analysis, you are sweating and are still not sure that the trade is going to work. That is when you can use your intuition to confirm (or negate) your trading decision. The best advice here is, if you are not sure, then don't do it! And certainly don't simply hope that the market will move in your favor. As Martin J. Pring wisely points out: "Hope is not a good thing to have in forex trading."

Do Not *Ever* Trade Based Only on Your Intuition!

While you may be able to use your intuition and follow your heart in trading, you need to make sure that you are not confusing these feelings with fear and greed. You *always* have to back up your intuition with the other types of analysis that you are going to learn throughout this book and in the Invest Diva's online education course.

There is a *big* difference between intuitive trading and emotional trading, and you should be very careful not to confuse them. If you are making a trading decision and you find that your heart is racing as if you are about to go on a first date with the man of your dreams, you are probably making an emotional rather than an intuitive decision.

Forex Words to Remember

Figure 8-4 provides a list of words that are commonly used in the forex world and throughout this book. You may want to come back to this page at every stage of your forex learning and trading process. Don't let a word go by without knowing exactly what it means!

FIGURE 8-4

Forex Term	Meaning
Long	Being in a *buy* position.
Short	Being in a *sell* position.
Bullish market	Prices are rising.
Bearish market	Prices are falling.
Bid	The price at which a trader is willing to *buy* the base currency.
Ask	The price the broker is willing to accept from the trader.
Spread	The difference between the bid and the ask prices. This is how most brokers make money.
Range	The difference between the highest and lowest prices in a given trading period.
Resistance	An estimated price level that a currency pair has trouble breaking above. You can *sell* at this price.
Support	A price level that a currency pair has trouble falling below. You can *buy* at this price.

CHAPTER 9

Are You Ready to Hit the Forex Party?

To recap the previous chapter, *technical analysis* is the study of price movements on the charts, while *fundamental analysis* takes a look at how the country's economy is doing.

Market sentiment analysis determines whether the market is bullish or bearish on the current or future fundamental outlook, and you make the final decision on whether or not you should enter the market based on your *capital* and your *overall* analysis.

All of these form your *Invest Diva Diamond*, which you can wear proudly to a forex party. Well, first you need to start with a *fake forex party*, aka trading in a demo account. Don't worry, you don't have to dress up or put on makeup to attend this party. You don't even have to leave your home. All you need is the Invest Diva Diamond and this book by your side. Attending a number of fake parties is absolutely crucial as you proceed with this book.

Just reading about all the different types of analysis and memorizing them one by one won't help you. As you may have already noticed, this book is not a novel. (Um, sarcasm right at your face.) You are now required to get off your bed (or wherever you are reading this book), go to your computer (or iPad, or smartphone, or any other gadget that hosts free forex demo accounts), type "Free Forex Demo Account" into your search engine, and download whichever looks reliable to you. At this point reliable demo accounts would be the ones that aren't viruses and wouldn't ask for your credit card number right away. To get more information about reliable demo accounts, you can also visit the Invest Diva Community page online to find out what other Forex Divas have experienced with different demo accounts.

Remember, you don't have to—in fact, you should not—stick to the first demo account you open for the rest of your life. Free demo accounts are the largest advertising expense for most brokers, and once you open a demo account, they will try *very hard* to get you to open a live account with them right away. A smart Forex Diva won't fall for these marketing strategies. So my recommendation for you is to try many brokers' demo accounts throughout the course of this book. They are all free, and you will have no risk of losing money. In Chapter 20, I have dedicated a full chapter to guide you in choosing a forex broker for your real account. But for now, it's time to study.

Did you open a demo account yet?

We are waiting.

Finished? Cool. Now you are qualified to proceed with this book.

It's time to attend a fake forex party wearing your Invest Diva Diamond! We are going to make sure that each point of your diamond is clear enough to help you shine like a star when you attend the real forex party.

Preparty Warm-Up

1. Based on what you have learned in this book so far, what is a forex party?
2. What are the five essential points of your Invest Diva Diamond?
3. What is a fake forex party?

If you gave the following answers, you are ready to go!

1. A forex party is a metaphor we use in this book to visualize a forex trading platform.
2. The five essential points of the Invest Diva Diamond are:
   a. Technical analysis
   b. Fundamental analysis
   c. Sentiment analysis
   d. Capital analysis
   e. Overall analysis
3. A fake forex party is a free demo forex platform that you can download from the Internet. It has all the functions of a real account, but the money isn't real.

Now that you have opened your demo account, you are probably looking at a giant platform filled with numbers, charts, and different currencies. Such a crowded party!

But we want to start slowly. There's no need to complicate things.

Step 1. Go back to Chapter 5 and quickly take a look at the currency pairs that can be invited to your party (majors, minors, exotics).

Step 2. Close your eyes and pick the currency pair that you think is the coolest.

Step 3. Open your eyes.

Step 4. Go back to the demo trading platform and click on the chart that represents the currency pair that you picked.

Now on your monitor you should see something like Figure 9-1.

As you may have noticed, I picked EUR/USD as my favorite currency pair for today. That's right, this is the EUR/USD dance floor! This currency pair can jump up and down and change colors.

Charts are useful because they show you where the pair was dancing during any given month, week, day, hour, or even

FIGURE 9-1

FIGURE 9-2: EUR/USD Hourly Chart

minute! You just need to set the chart for the specific time frame on which you want to check out the movements, then look at the horizontal axis for the time and the vertical axis for the price.

In Figure 9-2, you can see the hourly candle chart of EUR/USD for January 16, 17, and 18. At any given hour in these three days, the approximate price of the euro against the dollar can be discovered from the chart. I have a reason for saying "approximate price." We will get into this in more detail in the coming pages, but for now, let me congratulate you for finishing the Basic Forex Stuff. See you in the next part!

PART 2

Technical Stuff

I can sense that you are getting cold feet just from hearing the word *technical*. It's not that unusual to have doubts about becoming a forex trader and committing to finishing your essential education before you start trading.

But don't step back yet!

Technical analysis can be easy. If you have no investment or math background, this book and the Forex Coffee Break with Invest Diva education course (check out the QR code on the right) is the place for you to start learning. You can get engaged with technical analysis and even have a few laughs while you are sipping your coffee. There may be times when you feel like giving up, but you can always get cheered up by coming to the Invest Diva community and talking to the wonderful members. Our method is to bring the technicals to life, make them visual, and connect them to your daily experiences.

Obviously you have been enjoying the Basic Forex Beans, and that is why you decided to take the next step until you got scared by the title. But remember, when we are first involved, we tend to focus on the things we have in common (our similarities), and even our differences can seem exciting. As intimate relationships progress, differences come more to the fore and can lead to conflicts or even feelings of alienation. This is normal, but many people are confused by this dynamic, and it is a big source of affairs. Many people have the notion that there is a "perfect match" for them and that the happiness and success of marriage depends on finding this match. . . .

Oops . . . I think I lost track of what I originally was saying and started giving you prewedding tips. But you get the point, right?

CHAPTER 10

The Evolution of Charts

A chart is where the whole forex party happens. It's the place where the market data and the prices are connected to help us make informed decisions about when to buy or sell. Since the charts were born, they have been undergoing many optimizations to make them more user-friendly. Here is a look at the evolution of the charts.

Line Charts

Ancient traders (from the past decades) did their technical analysis mostly on line charts, which look pretty boring compared to modern charts. Line charts are also called first-generation charts, and they can be compared to first-generation telephones, which didn't have many functions, were good only for making phone calls, and didn't even show the caller's ID.

Line charts display only the closing prices of the market. That means that for any given time period, you can know only where the pair was dancing at the *end* of that time period; you won't know their adventures and their movements on the dance floor *during* that time period.

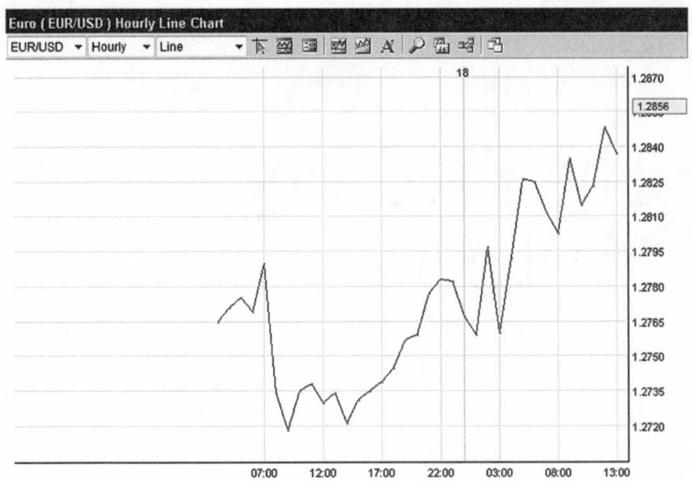

FIGURE 10-1: At the End of Every Hour, the Pair Was Dancing on the Dots (Close Prices)

A line is drawn from one closing price to the next closing price, and you can see the general movement of a currency pair over a period of time (see Figure 10-1).

In the hourly line chart of euro-dollar shown in Figure 10-1, at the end of every hour, the pair was dancing on the dot, which is the closing price; in other words, every dot shows the price of the pair at the end of the hour.

Line charts are good for a simple and general overview of the market, but when it comes to technical analysis, they wouldn't give us enough room for exploration. I wonder what happens when human beings are curious to know something? . . .

Bar Charts

The nosy and geeky traders were dying of curiosity and wanted to be able to see how the currency pair had been moving during a specific time period, especially for longer periods such as hourly, 4-hour, daily, or monthly. They could, of course, set their charts to 1 minute to see the most recent movements, but if they did that, they would miss out on the

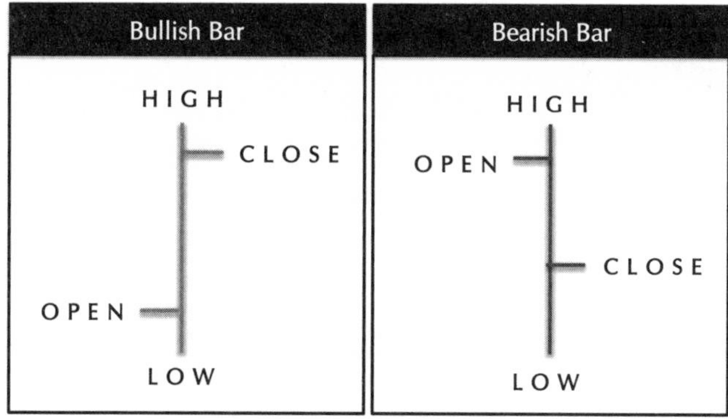

FIGURE 10-2

general view of the market. If only there were a way to know what prices the pair had covered during a specific period of time.

This led to the invention of the second-generation charts, the bar charts. Bar charts are more informative than line charts because they display not only the closing prices, but the opening, high, and low prices as well.

In other words, by keeping an eye on a bar chart, you can know, for a given time period, where on the forex dance floor (aka platform) the pair started dancing, where it dipped, where it jumped, and where it ended the round. Now this might not be useful at all if you were just watching a couple dancing the Argentine tango, but in forex trading, it can reveal many useful secrets. Figure 10-2 shows what a bar looks like (not to be confused with a chocolate bar, a legal bar exam, or a retail establishment that serves alcoholic beverages).

Open. The little horizontal line to the left is aligned with the open price for a given time period.

High. The top of the vertical line shows the highest price during that time period.

Low. The bottom of the vertical line is the lowest price during that time period.

Close. The little horizontal line to the right is the last price or the closing point for the time period.

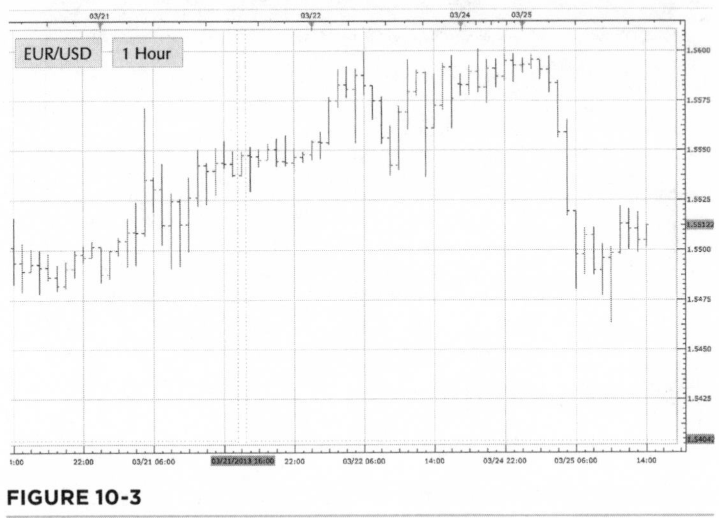

FIGURE 10-3

Figure 10-3 shows how bars are shown in action on the forex dance floor.

In the hourly bar chart in Figure 10-3, it takes one hour to form one bar. Each bar displays the open, high, low, and close prices for that hour.

Candlestick Charts

Bar charts were popular for a while, but just as our phones need upgrades all the time to give us cuter colors and better shapes, the charts needed to be upgraded, too. And just as most upgrades and improvements to phones are done by the Japanese, here, too, the artistic touches to the bars are believed to have been provided by the Japanese, but not recently and not by a Japanese forex trader. The candlestick chart was actually developed by a Japanese rice trader in the sixteenth century. We don't mind the outdated development and will go on to read more about the candles because we all like pretty, colorful, and romantic stuff.

Many of us girls have grown up with candles around us, and many of us probably experimented with candle making in middle school. Sometime later in life, we discovered that

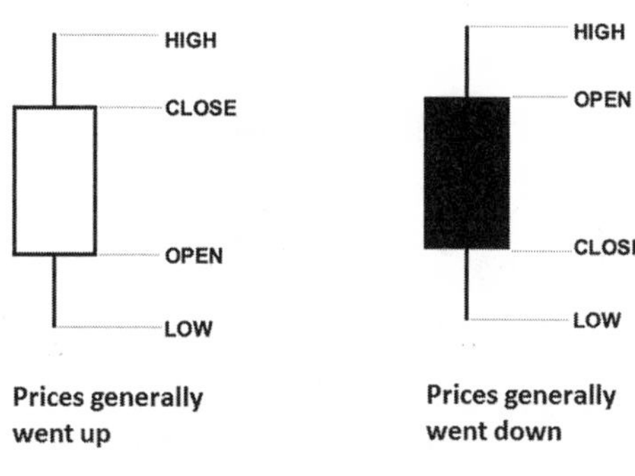

FIGURE 10-4

making our own candles—of all shapes and sizes—gave us more satisfaction than buying them at T.J.Maxx or Walmart. And now here we are, bringing candles into forex trading. So let's get down to business and learn how to make candles.

The idea behind candlesticks in forex trading is simply filling the area between the open and close prices with "wax." The distance between the open and close prices can be considered the wick inside the candle, and the extra wick that comes out of the top and bottom of the candle shows the high and low prices in the specific time period during which the candle was made (see Figure 10-4). In the forex world, the wicks coming out of the top and bottom of the candle are called the upper and lower shadows.

The next exciting step in our candle making is adding colors. (We would love it if we could add fragrance, too, but computers with smelling abilities have not yet been invented.)

On the forex trading dance floor, only two colors at a time are allowed for the candlesticks, one for the rising candles and one for the falling candles. You can choose black and white, pink and yellow, green and red, or whatever you want. You can do this by clicking on the "settings" button on your trading platform.

What Do Different Colored Candlesticks Mean?

We basically use two different colors to distinguish candles that are bearish from candles that are bullish. In other

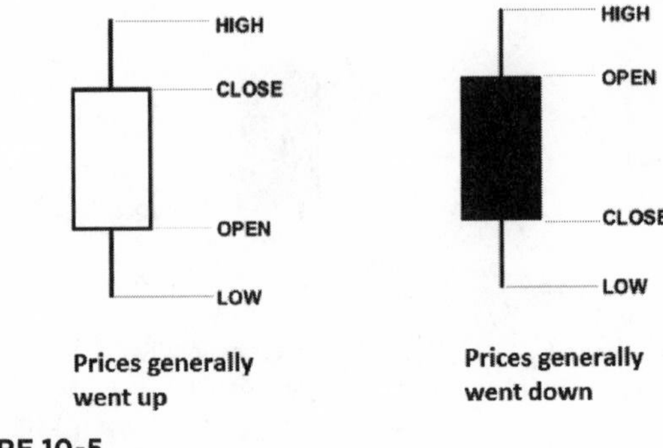

FIGURE 10-5

words, we can see whether prices went up or went down between the start and ending of a specific period of time.

Traditional forex traders (mostly geeky guys) use white candles to show that the market opened at a lower price than the close price in a specific time period (bullish candle). They use black to show the opposite, that in a specific time period, the prices generally went down (bearish candles).

But since we are smart, pretty, and creative ladies, we can color our candles with any two delightful colors that our hearts desire. On your demo forex trading platform, just look for the candlestick settings and change the colors. If you can't find it, simply contact your broker's support team for help. Today, I'm actually feeling nerdy, and thinking to stick to the traders tradition: white for bullish candles and black for bearish (see Figure 10-5).

Just by taking a glance at a white candle, we immediately know that in the specific period of time during which this candle was completed, prices generally went up. The opposite is revealed by a black candle.

One quick point is that forex traders usually use a lighter color for bullish candles and a darker color for bearish. Green and red are the colors most commonly used by stock traders, because in stock trading the positive price movements happen only when the prices go up (bullish), so they use green (the winner's color) for these candles. When the stock markets go down, most people lose money, so stock traders use

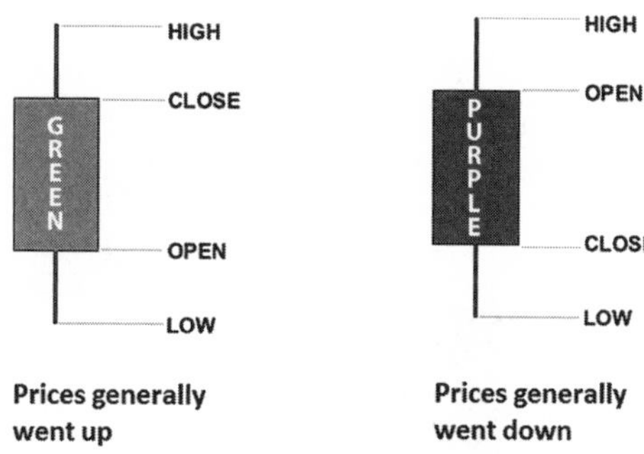

FIGURE 10-6: The Meaning of Candle Colors: Green and Purple

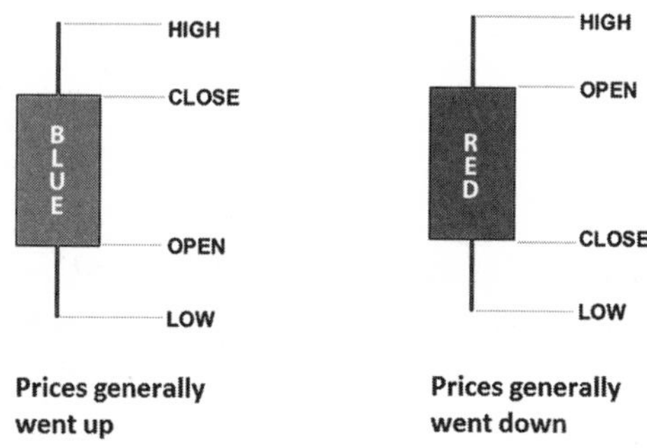

FIGURE 10-7: The Meaning of Candle Colors: Blue and Red

the red color for bearish candles. But as we said before, in the forex market, bears and bulls can both be winners depending on their position in the market, so we can use whatever colors we feel like! But it is better to be consistent with our personalized candlestick colors so that our eyes get used to them and we don't get confused.

Figures 10-6 and 10-7 show some other candle color possibilities.

How Long Does It Take to Make Candles?

Here is the good news: we don't actually need to get up and buy wax, wicks, and colors to make candles for forex trading. The platform that you downloaded (and that I hope is open on your computer right now as you read this) does all the work for you.

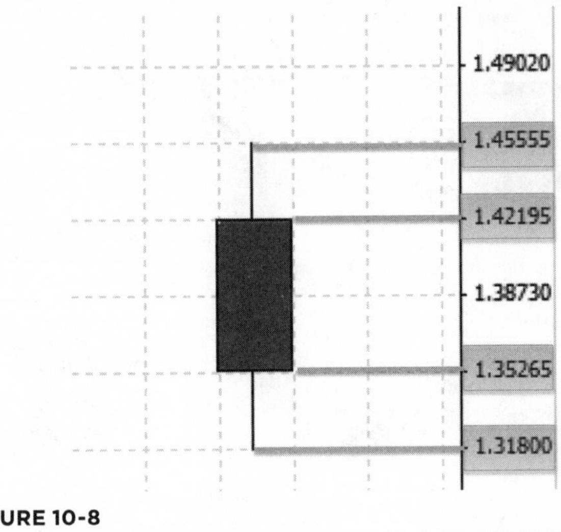

FIGURE 10-8

You can play around with the time tab on your platform, checking out candlestick charts with candles that were made in 1 minute, 5 minutes, an hour, a day, or even a month. The longer it takes for a candle to form, the less information you will have about the price movements over shorter periods, but the chart will give you a better idea of the general movement of the market. A candlestick chart that is set to 1 minute shows almost immediate price actions in the market and is perfect for day traders, while a monthly chart is mostly used to analyze the general and long-term direction of the market.

Now let's take a look at one bearish candlestick picked from the EUR/USD monthly chart and see what secrets it reveals about the pair's movements during one month (see Figure 10-8).

Okay, Now Answer These Questions

1. What was the price of 1 euro on the first trading day of the month?
2. What was the highest price of 1 euro during the month?
3. What was the lowest price of 1 euro during the month?
4. How much was 1 euro on the last trading day of the month?

Answers

1. EUR/USD opened at 1.42195 on the first day of the month. That means that you had to pay $1.42195 to buy 1 euro.
2. 1.45555 was the most expensive the euro got during the month.
3. 1.31800 was the lowest price for the euro against the dollar during the month.
4. The pair closed at 1.35265 on the last day of the month.

EXERCISE

On your demo trading platform, set the currency pair to EUR/USD on the candlestick chart, then play around with the time period and check out where the currency pair has been in different periods. First check the 1-minute chart. Then check the 5-minute chart. Then look at the 15-minute chart, the hourly chart, the 4-hour chart, the weekly chart, and the monthly chart. Which one gives you the most insight into the most recent price actions? Which one gives you a longer-term view?

Bonus for Pros: ProSticks

The evolution of charts didn't end with candlesticks, just as the evolution of cell phones didn't end with the Motorola Razr.

Some curious but lazy traders also wanted to know what other traders had been doing so that they could make better decisions on their own trades. They wanted to be able to see the volume of trades in a specific period of time. They wanted to know when and at what price the longer-term investors took advantage of high or low prices, or at what price the short-term traders were comfortable with both buying and selling.

Imagine knowing all the daily gossip about a currency pair just by looking at one chart!

In the 1980s, a genius called Peter Steidlmayer and the Chicago Board of Trade developed a system called Market Profile that integrated time and volume on a daily basis. While it looked ugly and was not user-friendly, it did help traders study the *underlying nature and strength of the market.*

In this book, we are not going to learn about how Market Profile works because it will just give us a headache. Instead, we are going to talk about the revolutionary *ProSticks* (Stick for Pros).

ProSticks not only visualized Market Profile, but also let the bars and candles into the game as well.

Now you're happy you learned about the bars and the candles, aren't you?

In a ProStick, the open, high, low, and closing prices are displayed exactly as they are in a bar chart. A ProStick's body looks very much like that of a candlestick, with a white stem signaling an up day and a darker color signaling a down day (see Figure 10-9).

ATTENTION

In ProSticks, unlike candlesticks, the top of the colored body does *not* represent the open or close price. Similarly, the bottom of the colored body does *not* represent the open or close price.

The close and open prices in ProSticks are displayed as they are displayed in bar charts.

The body of a ProStick is mainly used for two things: (1) its color, which shows whether the prices went up or down, and (2) the *active range*.

The active range basically shows where the short-term traders or day traders took advantage of the prices, thinking that nobody would notice. But the ProStick users will catch them off guard!

But it doesn't end here. In addition to this nasty little secret and all the other gossip about currency pairs, including open, close, high, and low, ProSticks' charts also provide

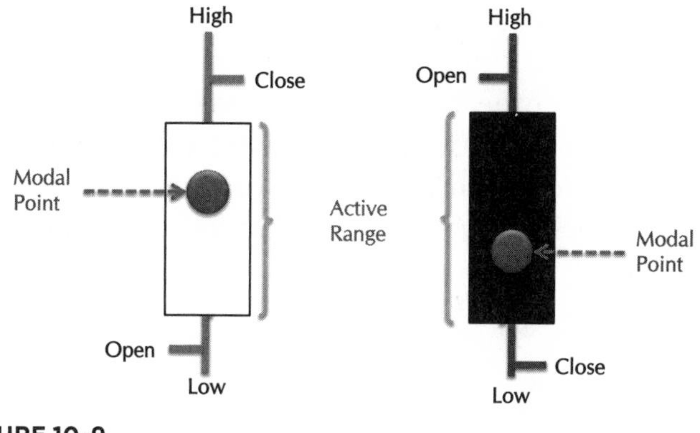

FIGURE 10-9

one other piece of information that is perfect for all the ladies out there who hate to be manipulated.

They give the most heavily transacted price for a specific time period. This is called the *modal point*, and it is shown as a dot in ProSticks.

The modal point in the forex market helps weed out manipulation of financial markets. These manipulations are usually caused by large inflows by a major player during a short period of time, like during the open and the close, when the price can be influenced very easily. The major players are basically like the celebrity tabloids that create false gossip and take your attention away from the real world, which in a forex trader's life is the market sentiment. That's why false breaks are less likely to happen with ProSticks than with the previous-generation charts. (You will learn about false breaks in the next chapter.)

To sum it up, ProSticks is an enhancement or complement to the previous-generation charts. It can be compared to the iPhone and BlackBerry, which are the most convenient cell phones in the history of phones. (Okay, maybe not BlackBerry.)

With ProSticks, you can now identify within a second exactly where most of the trading for any time period took place, spot false breaks accurately, and avoid being manipulated by the heavy hitters.

That being said, many forex platforms don't include the Prosticks in their chart collection. That is why we are going to display most of the charts in this book in the candlesticks form. One thing you can do after mastering the candle-based technical analysis is to simply reconfirm your analysis with the free ProSticks charts online before you make a final trading decision.

CHAPTER 11

Time to Draw Some Lines on the Dance Floor

So our currency pair is dancing on the dance floor (the chart). One of the ways to forecast its next move (or moves) is to find patterns in its previous moves. Since we have all the history of its movements right in front of us in our chart, the easiest way to find the patterns is by drawing lines and interpreting them. It's that easy.

Now the question is, what's trending on the dance floor?

I'm going to turn to my good friend Twitter to find out. Let me see—at the time I'm writing this, the trends are on #ILovePeopleThat, #TheBestFeelingIsWhen, #MentionAn Addiction . . . wait a minute. This doesn't sound quite right. Is Twitter the right place to look for trends in the forex world? I guess not in general. Unless I search for forex-related topics such as #forex, $EURUSD, or #InvestDiva.

In the forex world, the most well-known expression is, "The trend is your friend." A trend on the forex dance floor (chart) is basically the direction in which the currency pair has been moving for a while. The idea behind it is that the pair will probably continue to trade in that direction until it hits an "obstacle." These obstacles are called *support* and *resistance*.

Of course, depending on the time frame of your chart, you may see different trends for different periods of time. For

FIGURE 11-1: Hourly Chart Showing a Downtrend

example, you may see a downward trend in the 1-hour chart of EUR/USD on April 15, 2011, as shown in Figure 11-1.

But if at that very moment you switch to the daily chart of EUR/USD, you will see that the pair is on an overall uptrend, with the downtrend being a temporary minor trend (see Figure 11-2).

On an hourly basis, the pair is moving downward, but in a longer-term daily time frame, the pair is seen to be in an uptrend.

So as you can see, trends can be long term, short term, upward, downward, and even sideways. As the first step in determining the trend, many traders check out a long-term time frame like the daily chart of each currency pair, look for the strongest trend in its direction, then eventually move to shorter-term time frames. However, some other traders do the opposite and move from a shorter time frame to a longer one (zoom out).

Trading in the direction of the trend on the daily chart is like riding a bicycle with the wind at your back. You don't want to go against the wind, do you? By trading with a trend, you will have the momentum of the market behind you.

FIGURE 11-2: Daily Chart Showing an Uptrend

The Art of Drawing Trend Lines

You never thought you would find a place for your artistic skills in forex trading, did you?

Drawing trend lines is an art. And just as with any other type of art, everyone has his own unique opinion on them! There is no perfect way to draw trend lines, but if you have an artistic eye, you usually won't miss a strong trend.

To draw a trend line, once you have casually identified a trend with your naked eyes, you simply have to click on the "trend-line instrument" on your trading platform and connect two or more major valleys (bottoms) or two or more major peaks (tops), as shown in Figure 11-3.

For newbies, identifying valleys and peaks may be easier on line charts, but with just a little bit of practice, you will be able to see any mountain, hill, or lake on next-generation charts crystal clear.

Remember

1. To draw an *uptrend*, connect the valleys (higher lows).
2. To draw a *downtrend*, connect the peaks (lower highs).
3. You can identify *no trends* when you connect either the peaks or the valleys, and the lines turn out to be horizontal or sideways.

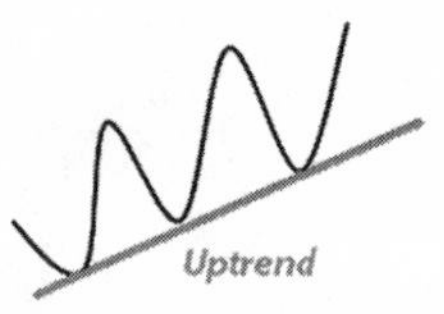

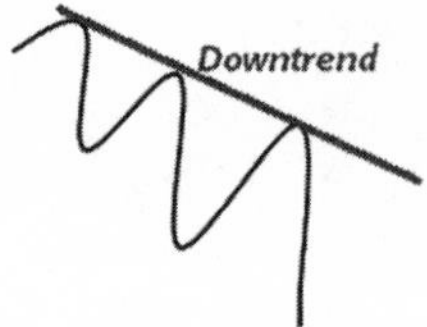

FIGURE 11-3

> Do not ever let a trend line cross through prices or draw trend lines by forcing them to fit the market!

Now you may ask, "What if the prices break the trend line after I draw it?"

The answer is simple: draw another one! You can have several trend lines on a single chart.

Let the art touch the chart. Look at all the fine lines in Figure 11-4!

Once you get comfortable with the waves, you can easily surf the trend lines under any circumstances and nail the next price action by identifying support and resistance. We will get into that in a little bit.

Support and Resistance Levels

Have you ever tried to tango like a pro? First, you need to find a partner. Next, you need to select a dance floor. Then, you need to feel the beat. And finally, you need to watch out not to get out of line.

This was a human tango. How do currency pairs dance on the dance floor? The procedure is pretty similar. We put currencies in pairs and watch them moving on the chart (dance floor) as they listen to the beat (market news) and are on the watch for the market sentiment so that they won't get out of line. These "lines" are called *support* and *resistance*.

Support and resistance are thought of as limitations on the currency pair's ability to dance freely on the dance

FIGURE 11-4

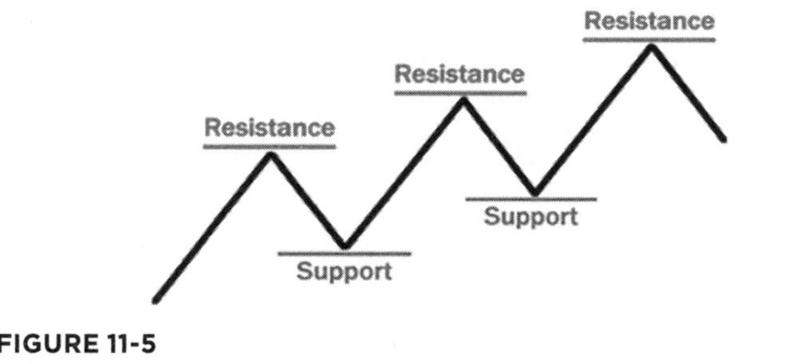

FIGURE 11-5

floor. All we need to do is to identify the support and resistance and use them in our analysis. If we can figure out where the pair is likely to stop moving further, we can make a better investment decision.

Support and resistance are two of the most discussed concepts in technical analysis. They can come in various forms, from very basic ones to more advanced and exciting ones. Let's start with the basics (see Figure 11-5).

As you can see, every time the pair tries to dance in a specific direction, it is stopped at the support or resistance level. It is actually the trading superpowers who determine the movements; after that, the little traders like you and me try to discover the barriers and patterns.

Experienced traders (aka trading grandpas) will be able to tell many stories about how certain price levels tend to prevent traders from pushing the price of a currency pair in a certain direction.

Resistance is a barrier that prevents prices from going *higher*. That is because the superpowers are waiting to sell the pair at that level.

Support is a barrier that prevents prices from going *lower*. That is because the superpowers are waiting to buy the pair at that level.

Channels

Channels are another way of visualizing support and resistance through an artistic combination of trend lines. A channel is actually the space between the support and resistance levels, which can be two parallel trend lines. In other words, you can also use trend lines as support and resistance.

You can create your very own forex trading channel (no, it is *not* a TV channel or a YouTube channel) by drawing a trend line parallel to an existing trend line, as shown in Figure 11-6.

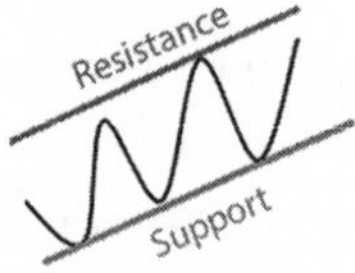

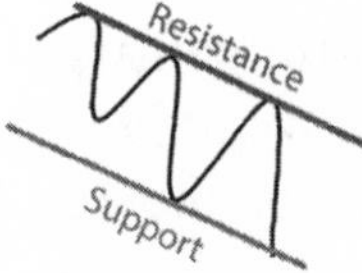

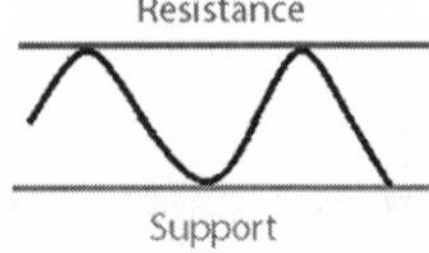

FIGURE 11-6: Trading Within Channels

As you can see in Figure 11-6, we drew a channel just by adding a *parallel* line to the uptrend or downtrend charts that you saw in Figure 11-3.

Sticking to our universal trading law of "buy low and sell high," you can go long a pair—for example, you can buy the euro against the dollar when EUR/USD's price is near the bottom of the channel, and sell it when the price gets close to the top of the channel.

Which Line Is Your True Friend?

Remember how we said that the trend is your friend? So which trend line in a channel is your true friend? Here is the answer:

The support line is your friend in an uptrend; you want to buy around the support level.
The resistance line is your friend in a downtrend; you want to sell around the resistance level.

Just like trend lines, channels also come in different variations with cool names: flat, ascending, or descending. I think the names are pretty self-explanatory, so we won't go into them more deeply.

> **IMPORTANT NOTE**
> Do not ever force the two lines of the channel to become parallel! If the prices are getting in the way, then you just can't use the channel as a technical tool. Just let it go. Seriously.

Testing and Teasing

The support and resistance levels are lines we draw at the level where we think the end of a trend is going to be. The end of an uptrend is the resistance. The end of a downtrend is the support. However, sometimes the naughty currency pairs merely *test* (tease) the support or resistance line to see if they can get past that level and continue riding on the trend. You may get all excited when you see this and think that the market is continuing to ride on the trend, but then the pair goes back to the other side of the level, and Mr. and Ms. Whatever-Currency-Pair put their hands behind their ears and stick out their tongues, pointing and laughing at you and making you realize that it was a mere tease.

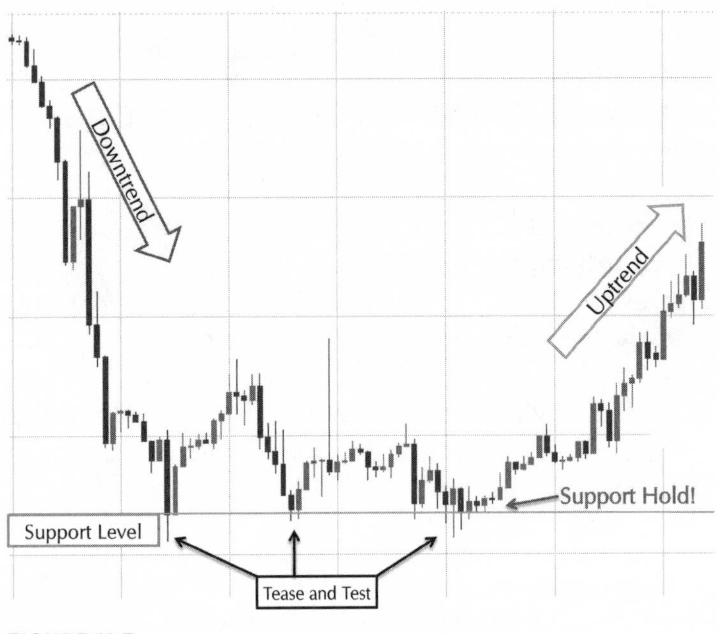

FIGURE 11-7

This is called *testing a support or resistance level.* In candlestick charts, these tests are mostly done by the shadows (the wicks) of the candles, as in Figure 11-7. They keep attempting to break the level, but the prices close inside it. When this happens, we say that the support or resistance held, and it indicates that the market trend has changed.

As you can see in Figure 11-7, the lower shadows of the candles are breaking the support level, but the prices ultimately close above the support level. The support level supported the falling prices.

Metaphorical Example

Let's say you have been watching Ms. USA and Mr. Japan dancing the tango on the dance floor. They keep moving back and forth, moving up and down, going in circles, going in zigzags, and so on. Then you notice that there are certain lines on the dance floor that they haven't crossed on the dance floor. Every time the two of them get close to those lines, they pull

FIGURE 11-8: Dancing Couple "Testing" the Barrier Line

back immediately. So you start to think that maybe those lines indicate a forbidden area that they are not supposed to dance on. As you are talking about this with your gal pal, you both draw an imaginary line and bet that it separates the dance floor from the forbidden area. Sometimes the two of them get really close to that line, and maybe they even extend their legs over it (see Figure 11-8)! But after a teasing pause with their legs extended, they go back inside.

The Breakout

As my friend Fan Yang, CMT, the chief technical strategist at FXTimes, puts it, any obstacle in life will eventually break, and so do support and resistance. In fact, sometimes the currency pairs not only completely break the barriers, but go all the way out of line (see Figure 11-9). That is when you know that the trend is here to stay, and that the door has opened for further rides on the previous trend. If the pair breaks the line, it may indicate the continuation of a trend; the pair

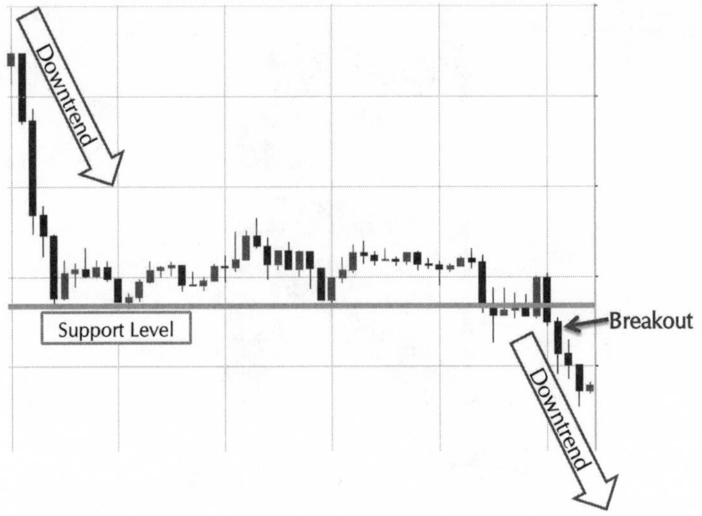

FIGURE 11-9: Candles Testing and Breaking the Support Level

was just so comfy riding on the trend that even the strongest obstacles couldn't stop it! This is called a *breakout*.

> The support and resistance levels usually are not specific prices, but more like zones.

What's Behind the Breakout?

As much as the currency pairs want to behave, dance beautifully on the dance floor, and make it easier for traders to anticipate their next movements (yeah, right!), they often act in a chaotic manner. This is because there are so many different things that can change the beat of the market. Just imagine that you and your partner are trying to practice dancing on a dance floor, but the music keeps changing. Just when you start getting comfortable dancing the tango, the DJ changes the beat to salsa. I bet you would become rebellious and break all kinds of barriers.

In the currency market, sometimes the fundamental news about the economy of the country of one of the currencies

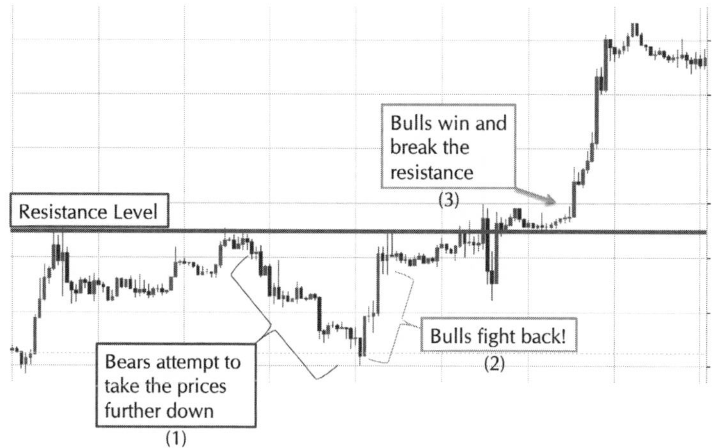

FIGURE 11-10: After a Long Battle, the Bulls Finally Win and the Pair Breaks the Resistance

drives prices insane, and the currency falls down, breaking all the support levels. Sometimes important news out of either country can shake things up.

Other times, the superpower traders move the market with their gigantic trades. They get into a head-to-head battle and drag the poor pair around with no clear direction. The buyers (or the bulls) push the prices higher, while the sellers (the bears) lower them. The battle goes on until one side wins and forces the pair to cross the support or resistance level (see Figure 11-10).

False Breaks

When is a break not a real break? When it's a false break!

Sometimes the currency pair gets naughtier than just testing a support or resistance level with its shadows as we saw in Figure 11-7. Look at the example in Figure 11-11.

After testing the support level a couple of times, the prices actually closed below it, getting the traders all excited. The pair was probably secretly laughing when it heard the traders behind the computer shouting: "It broke the level! It

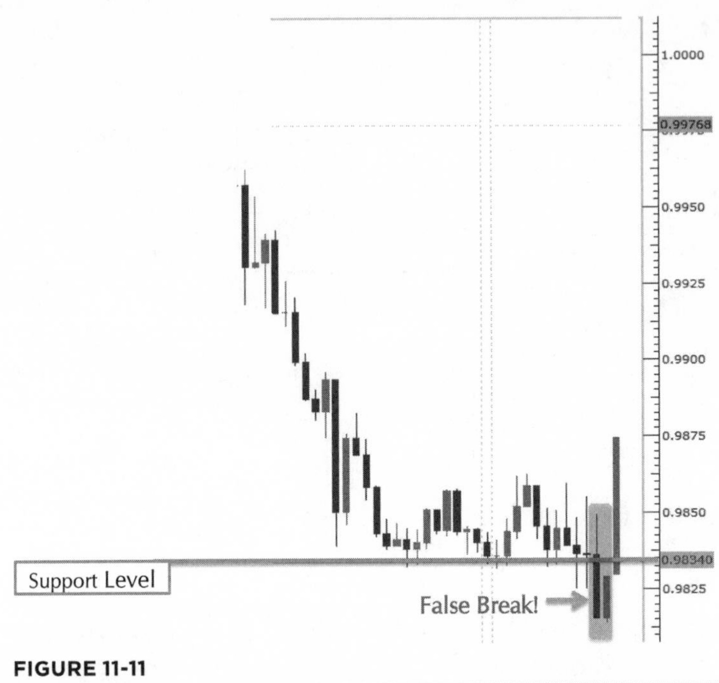

FIGURE 11-11

broke the level!" After having fun below the support level for just a little bit, the two of them moved back to where they had been before. And guess what? Sometimes a false break is actually a signal that an actual breakout in the opposite direction may come along soon! Those naughty pairs!

Look what happened after the false break in Figure 11-11 (see Figure 11-12).

After the false support break, the pair found a way to break the resistance. And this time the two of them were not kidding. The market went all the way up to a previous key resistance level after that, and broke it.

Tips and Tricks About the Lines

1. Three makes a trend. You need at least two tops or bottoms to draw a trend line or a support or resistance level, but it takes three to confirm it.

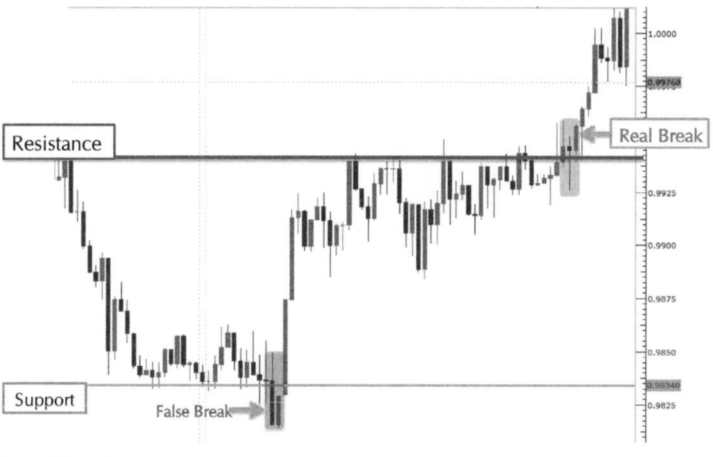

FIGURE 11-12

2. Trend lines, support or resistance levels, and channels become stronger the more times they are tested.
3. A previous support level can become a new resistance level, and vice versa. When prices break through a level, that level can potentially change its role, but remain a key level.

CHAPTER 12

Forex Dance Patterns

As naughty as the currency pairs may be, they often give us signals before they break out. The forex dance floor (chart) records each and every move they make. Just as you would memorize a dance pattern (see Figure 12-1), memorizing the possible forex patterns and analyzing the currency pair's movements on the chart can help you get a better idea of the market, which will eventually lead to a better investment decision.

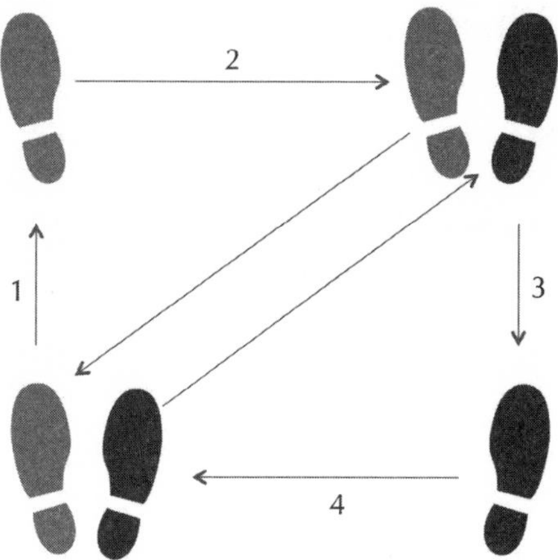

FIGURE 12-1: Real Life Dance Patterns—Forex Pairs Have Patterns Too!

Will the currency pair's price continue dropping, or will its trend shift? One way to figure this out is to study the patterns.

Identifying these patterns on the charts (the forex dance floor) makes it easier for us to make short-term or long-term forecasts.

Our ancestors (trading grandpas) have already created cool and catchy names for different patterns. So the road has already been paved for us. Now all we have to do is to get comfortable with the patterns and use them in our analysis.

Here are a few steps that you need to take in order to become comfortable with chart pattern analysis:

1. Memorize the patterns.
2. Memorize the interpretation of the patterns.
3. Practice identifying the patterns in different charts over and over again.
4. Follow up with the patterns that you identified, and see whether the interpretation came true.
5. Hang a copy of the Chart Patterns Cheat Sheet provided to you at the end of this chapter on your fridge, and review it every day.

As we said previously, you can't rely on only one method of forex analysis, let alone one method of technical analysis. Identifying chart patterns and recognizing what they forecast can become biased even at the best of times. We should always use other types of analysis and tools of technical analysis to confirm a pattern. In other words, we should always use the Invest Diva Diamond analysis.

Reversal Patterns

Reversal patterns are chart patterns that, when confirmed, indicate that the trend of a currency pair will reverse. Here is a list of some of the coolest and most trusted ones:

1. Double top or double bottom
2. Triple top or triple bottom
3. Head and shoulders top or bottom
4. Saucer top or saucer bottom

Depending on the direction of the trend (up or down), each of these patterns can indicate either a top or a bottom, but they are basically the same thing and have the same shape.

Doubles

Figure 12-2 is a picture of a double. They are hugging. What does this have to do with forex chart patterns? A lot! It helps you visualize the pattern and remember it more easily.

But it is important to remember that on a forex chart, a double top and a double bottom never happen at the same time. You can find either the shape of a double top (heads) or that of a double bottom (tushies). The two have exactly opposite interpretations.

Double Top

A double top is the formation of a pattern that looks like the letter M or the heads of twin babies hugging. After a period of an uptrend, the pattern is formed by two consecutive peaks that are almost equal to each other, with a "valley" in between. This usually means that the pair has finished moving up and that now we could be expecting its price to go down.

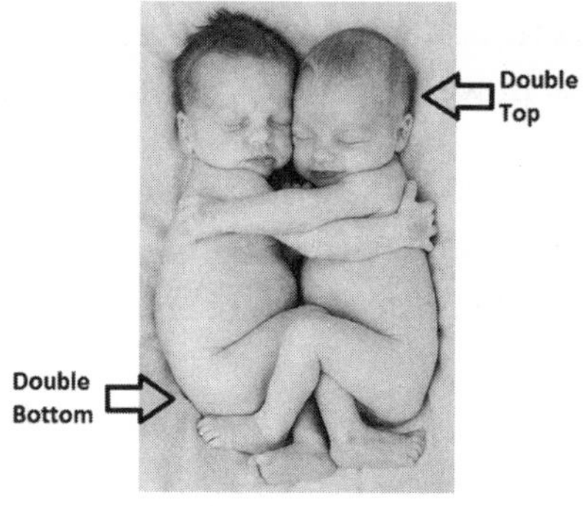

FIGURE 12-2

FIGURE 12-3: Double Top Formed on EUR/USD Hourly Chart

Identifying Tops

The "tops" are peaks that are formed when the price hits a certain level that can't be broken.

The story behind the chart in Figure 12-3 is that the pair was moving up strongly until it hit an obstacle, the 1.2625 level. This formed the first top. Since the pair was very stubborn, it decided to go back, gain energy, and try that level one more time. This formed the second top. It's a shame, but the pair couldn't make it. So the two currencies got upset and said to each other: "Since we are not able to continue up even with such a powerful uptrend, let's just turn around, switch directions, and show those traders who they are dealing with!"

And that was the beginning of a new downtrend.

Now, this scenario happens a lot! So just by knowing this behavior of currency pairs, you can predict the beginning of a new downtrend once you have identified a double top.

But wait a minute. I know what you are thinking. We should never rely on only one signal before making a trading decision. We should pay close attention to whether or not the pattern has been confirmed by a subsequent break of support (the neckline). Once we see that, we can place a bearish entry order below the neckline (sell order) and hope that the price will stick to the pattern and go down.

An example of my short-term bearish forecast using a double top technical strategy was reported on the Forex Diva Report of September 5, 2012 (see Figure 12-4), helping me to keep face in front of you guys. Look!

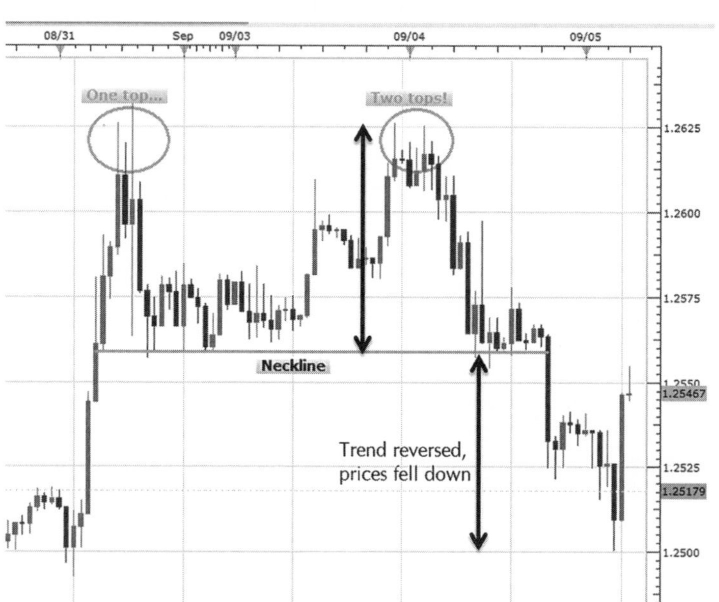

FIGURE 12-4: Uptrend Reversal After Formation of Double Top Chart Pattern

I set my stop order carefully to avoid risk in case the market moved against me. In addition, experience shows that the distance between the peak and the neckline is almost the same as that between the neckline and the lower end of the pattern. So I simply set my buy order at 1.2500 and went to a charity event with some friends. When I came back, the money was mine!

What happens next? After a double top pattern is completed, the previous support level that was broken will often act as a resistance level. You see, everything we've been learning is coming together.

A Story of a Long-Term Double Top Formation

Once upon a time, a currency pair was in an uptrend from point A to point B (see Figure 12-5). It then hit a resistance level and subsequently drifted downward for about a month. Then it peaked once more at point C, but it plummeted right afterwards and formed a double top pattern. A wise trader waited for a confirmation to signal that the trend had indeed reversed. The confirmation would have been issued by a break of the support level seen at point A.

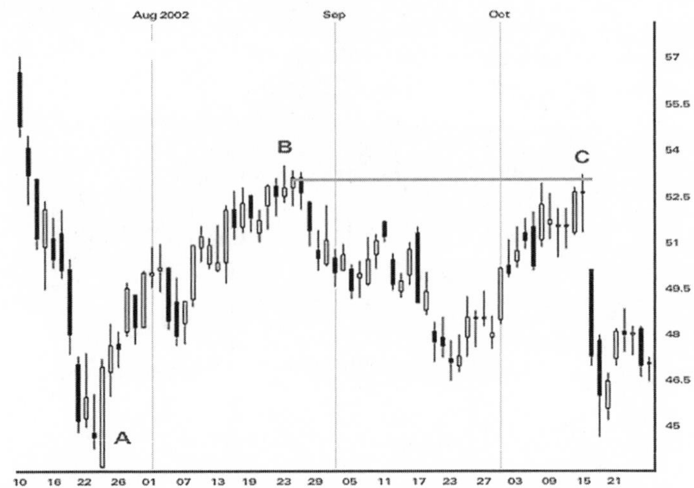

FIGURE 12-5: Long-Term Double Top Example

However, the ending of this story was lost in the database, and whether the reversal was confirmed or not remains a mystery.

Note: It is normal for both peaks to form at the same price level, but it is also possible for the second peak to slightly exceed the first or to top out just a little below it.

Double Bottom

A double bottom pattern is the mirror image of the double top pattern. It looks like the letter "W" or the tushies of

FIGURE 12-6: Double Bottom Formed on USD/CHF 4-Hour Chart

twin babies hugging. It happens when the pair is in a strong downtrend, followed by two consecutive valleys that are approximately equal to each other, with a peak in between.

Identifying Double Bottoms

The "bottoms" are valleys that are formed when the price hits a certain level that can't be broken.

Figure 12-6 shows the Dollar-Swissy pair on a 4-hour candlestick chart. The story behind this chart is that the pair had been falling rapidly until it hit a support level, the level of the low of the first bottom. Since the pair was very stubborn, it decided to go back, gain energy, and try that level one more time (the second bottom). It's a shame, but it couldn't make it. So the U.S. dollar and the Swiss franc got upset and said to each other: "Now that we are not able to continue down even with such a powerful downtrend, let's just turn around and switch directions and show those traders who they are dealing with!"

And that was the beginning of a new uptrend.

Take a look at Figure 12-7. Tada! Just as with the double top pattern, we should pay close attention to whether or not the pattern has been confirmed by a subsequent break of

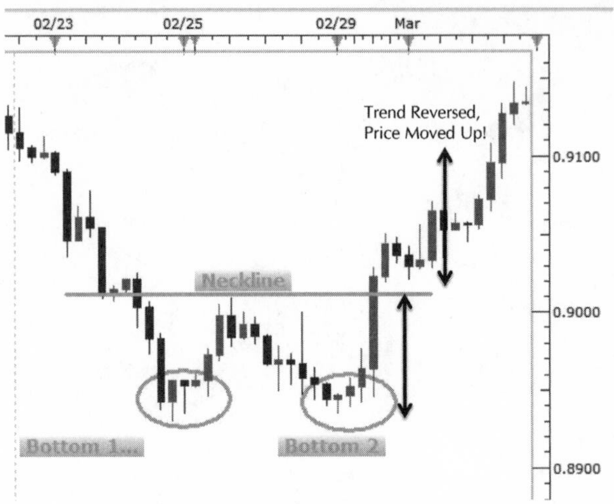

FIGURE 12-7: Downtrend Reversal After Formation of a Double Bottom Chart Pattern

resistance (the neckline). After seeing that, along with other points of the Invest Diva Diamond analysis, we could place a bullish entry order (buy order) above the neckline and enjoy the ride up. Just to be safe, we usually set our limit order the same distance as that between the bottom and the neckline.

Figure 12-8 shows another example.

In this example, the price is in a downtrend from point A to point B. It then hit a support level, subsequently rallied back, and was in a trading range for about two months. At point C, the price then retested the low set by point B and rebounded nicely off of it. Afterward, the price rallied strongly as the double bottom began to form. A confirmation, however, would be needed to signal that the trend has indeed reversed, and this may be issued by a break of resistance at a previous high, point A.

Also Good to Know

Doubles are typically accompanied by high volume on the first top (or bottom), very light volume on the second, and very heavy volume on the breakout.

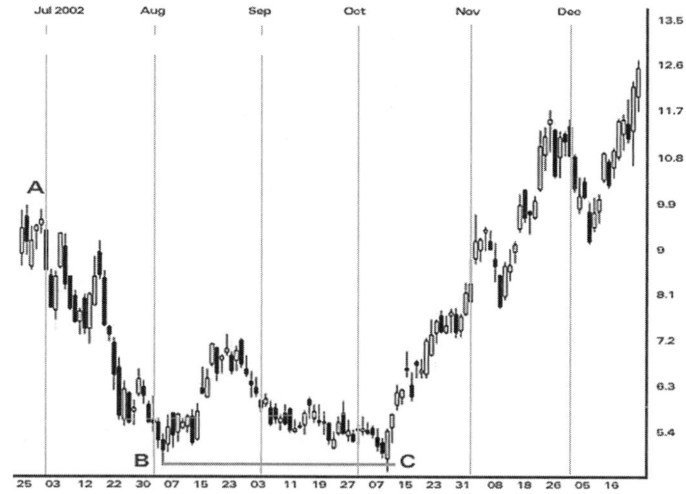

FIGURE 12-8: Double Bottom Pattern Example on Chart

Triples

A triple top and a triple bottom are both reversal patterns, but they have exactly opposite interpretations. They resemble the head or tushies of a triplet as seen in Figure 12-9. A triple top pattern reverses an uptrend, whereas a triple bottom pattern reverses a downtrend. Just like the doubles, in trading, a triple top and a triple bottom don't happen at the same time. You can have either a triple top or a triple bottom pattern formation on a chart.

A triple top is a reversal pattern made up of three similar highs; it usually follows an uptrending market as seen in Figure 12-10.

Confirming a Triple Top

1. The peaks follow an uptrend.
2. The pattern is formed in a relatively short period of time.
3. There is a break below the common support level (neckline) after the triple top.

Certain things happen after a triple top formation:

1. *A key support level is born.* The lowest point of the triple top marks a key support level.

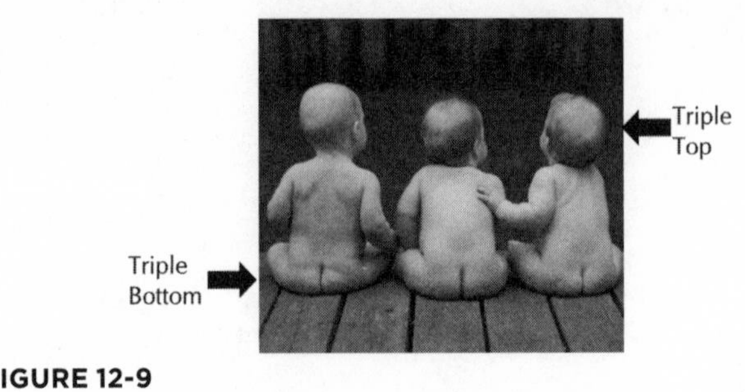

FIGURE 12-9

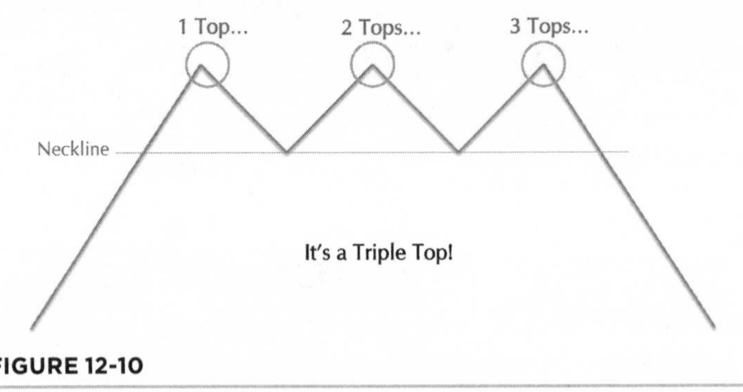

FIGURE 12-10

2. *Support becomes resistance.* After the rebellious pair breaks the key support level, the broken support becomes a potential new resistance level.

A Story of a Triple Top

Once upon a time, the price of the Aussie-Dollar pair was on an uptrend (see Figure 12-11). It went up until it got to point A, and then wasn't able to go any further. It seemed as if it had hit a resistance level. It then traded in a range for about an hour and completed five candlesticks before starting an upward movement to point B. Failing to pierce through resistance even at points B and C, with not enough demand from the traders and a decrease in volume, the tired pair's price had no choice but to fall. It fell all the way to and through the support of the triple top pattern, which is also called the neckline. This was the end of a glamorous uptrend for the pair. The bears had won the battle, and the price was now in a downtrend.

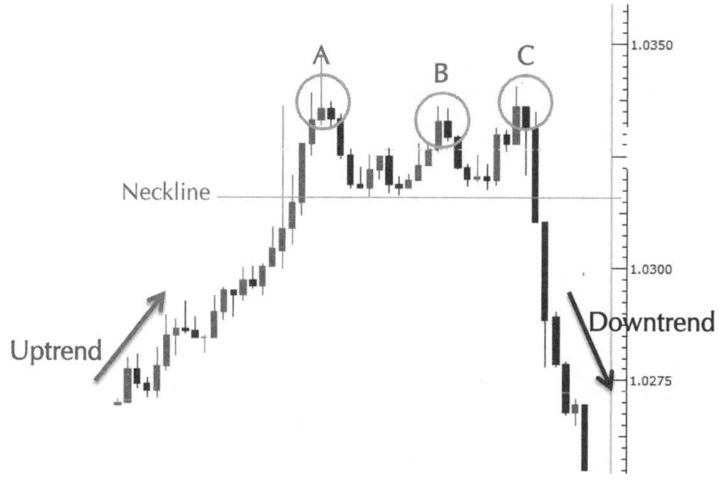

FIGURE 12-11: Triple Top Pattern Formation on AUD/USD 15-Minute Chart

And what happened to the broken support level? Is it ever going to get back on its feet again after this? Well, there is still hope for this level. As they always say, what doesn't kill you makes you stronger. The broken support level has now, in fact, turned into a powerful resistance level. Subsequent rallies in the future will test this new resistance level on their way up, and this level is now happy because it has been honored with the title "key level."

Homework

What, you thought I would be kind enough to tell you the stories of all the top and bottom patterns? That's wishful thinking, for sure. It is now your turn to open up your demo trading platform, go through the different charts in different periods of time, and look for a triple bottom. It could be something in the past, or it could be something that's just in the process of forming now. Then write the story of the triple bottom in your own words in your forex notebook and share it on the Invest Diva's Forex Community later.

Good to Know

Double or triple patterns can sometimes extend to quadruple tops or bottoms or other complex formations, but the laws of confirmation are basically the same as those of doubles and triples.

Head and Shoulders

The pair may have been partying too much, and it may be time for the two of them to take a shower. But we are not advertising a brand of shampoo here. This is simply another cool name for yet another reversal pattern in technical analysis.

A head and shoulders pattern is very similar to a triple, but the three peaks kind of look like a head and two shoulders! It is basically formed by a peak (shoulder), followed by a higher peak (head), and then by another lower peak (second shoulder). We are going to call this pattern the H&S dude.

The H&S dude sometimes shows his ugly head after an uptrend (head and shoulders top; see Figure 12-12). Other times, he peeks upside down after a strong downtrend (head and shoulders bottom; see Figure 12-13).

The neckline of the H&S dude is the support level for a head and shoulders top and the resistance for a head and shoulders bottom.

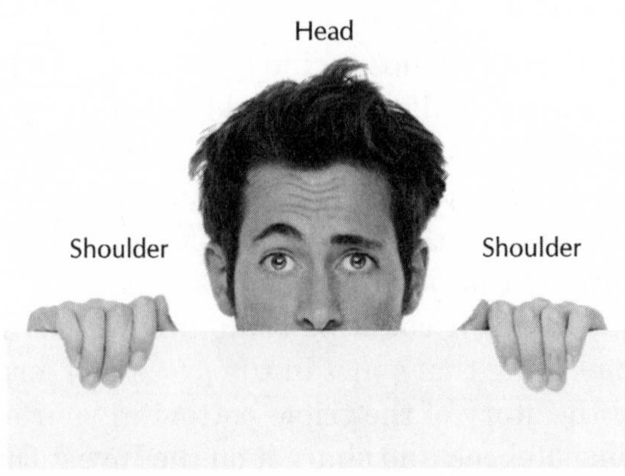

FIGURE 12-12: H&S Dude

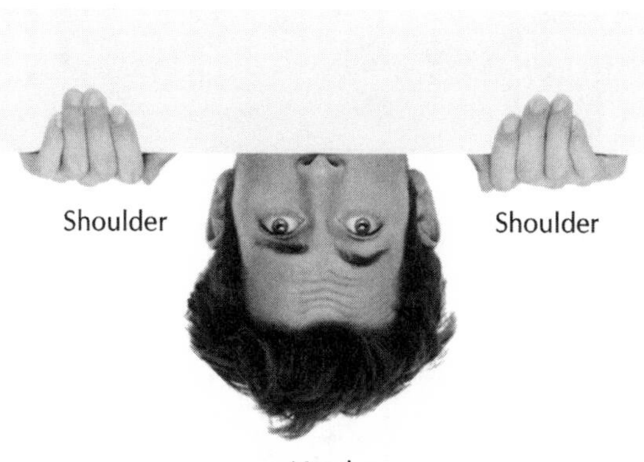

FIGURE 12-13: H&S Dude Upside Down

Figure 12-14 shows a head and shoulders top pattern in action.

The support level or neckline is determined by connecting the lows after each peak, and once this level is broken, the head and shoulders pattern is confirmed. This indicates a new willingness by investors to sell at lower prices. The slope of the neckline can be either up, down, or flat. In a head and shoulders top pattern, when the slope is down, it typically produces an even more reliable signal.

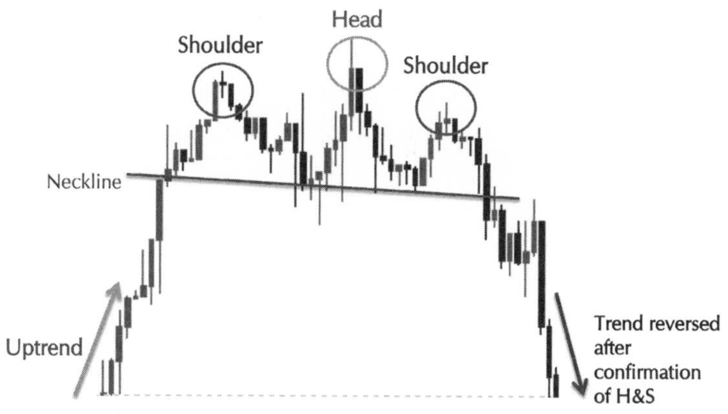

FIGURE 12-14: Head and Shoulders Top Reversal Pattern on USD/CHF Hourly Chart

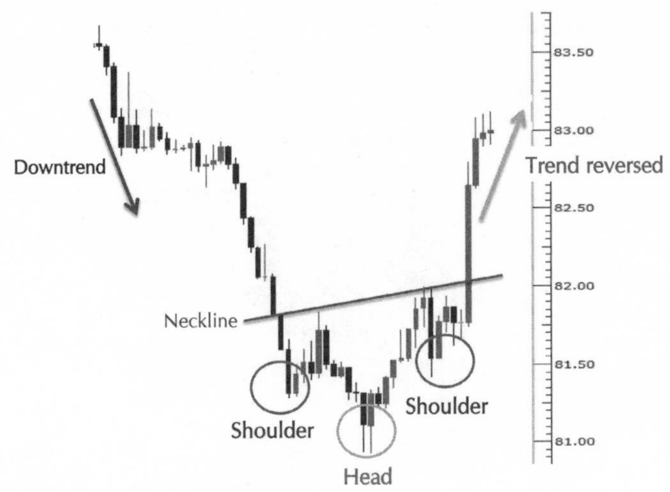

FIGURE 12-15: Head and Shoulders Bottom Reversal Pattern Formed on USD/JPY 4-Hour Chart

A head and shoulders bottom behaves similarly (see Figure 12-15).

The resistance level or neckline is determined by connecting the highs of each valley. Once this level is broken, the head and shoulders bottom pattern is confirmed. This indicates a new willingness of investors to buy at higher prices. When the neckline's slope is up, it produces a more reliable signal.

Good to Know

Volume can serve as an important indicator for the head and shoulders pattern. Volume levels should be higher during the rise of the left shoulder than during the subsequent rise of the head. This decrease in volume along with new highs of the head can serve as a warning sign that a trend reversal could be on the horizon. A second warning sign may come with increasing volume levels on the decline from the peak of the head. Final signs of a reversal may come when the volume level increases further during the decline of the right shoulder.

Just as with other patterns, once the neckline of our poor H&S dude is broken, it changes roles. It becomes resistance if it was acting as a support, and it turns into support if it was acting as a resistance.

Saucers

Saucers, or rounded tops and bottoms, are another form of reversal pattern that is used in long-term technical analysis. A saucer top (see Figure 12-16) is considered a bearish signal, indicating a possible reversal of the current uptrend to a new downtrend.

A saucer bottom (see Figure 12-17) is considered a bullish signal, indicating a possible reversal of the current downtrend to a new uptrend.

Saucers typically occur over a period of three weeks, but they can even be observed over several years.

Important Characteristics of a Saucer Top

1. It represents a long consolidation period that turns from a bullish bias to a bearish bias.

FIGURE 12-16: A Saucer Top Pattern

FIGURE 12-17: A Saucer Bottom Pattern

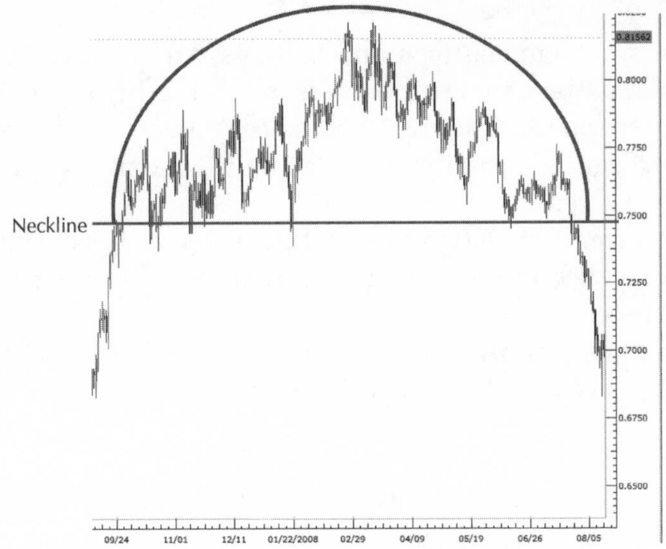

FIGURE 12-18: Rounding Top or Saucer Top Pattern Formed on NZD/USD Daily Chart

2. Volume usually follows the inverse of the price pattern. As the price begins to go up, volume tends to decrease. Once the top of the price pattern starts its downtrend turn, volume tends to increase.
3. It is not confirmed until there is a breakout to the downside below the resistance level, which is the beginning of the upward movement at the start of the pattern (see Figure 12-18).

Important Characteristics of a Saucer Bottom

1. It represents a long consolidation period that turns from a bearish bias to a bullish bias.
2. Volume levels usually follow the shape of the rounding bottom: high at the beginning of the decline, low at the end of the decline, and strengthening during the rise.
3. It is not confirmed until there is a breakout to the upside above the resistance level, which is the beginning of the decline at the start of the pattern (see Figure 12-19).

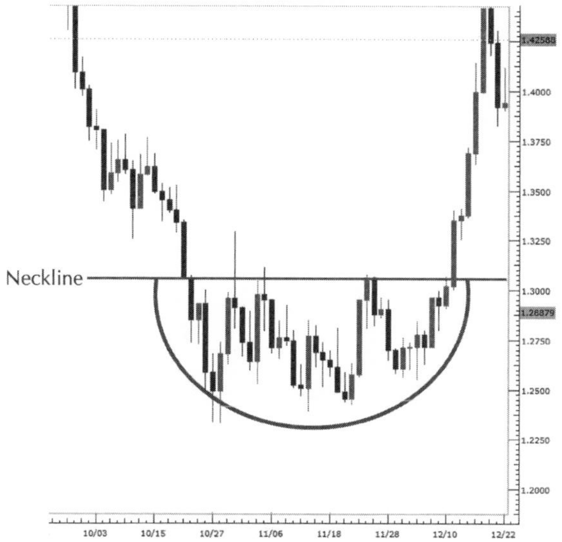

FIGURE 12-19: Rounding Bottom Pattern Formed on EUR/USD Daily Chart

How to Set a Profit Target

In case you have forgotten, we are learning about all these patterns in order to be able to make a trade at a better and more profitable price. The most important question in the mind of every awesome trader is, "When do I enter the market? When should I buy, and what is the best price to sell at?"

For all the reversal patterns we have learned (doubles, triples, head and shoulders, and saucers), the steps in ordering a trade are as shown in Figure 12-20.

Once the technical pattern is confirmed, you need to check in with the four remaining points of the Invest Diva Diamond before you place an order. If everything looks fine, you can continue with the rest of the steps (see Figure 12-21).

Of course, the price sometimes keeps moving even after it reaches the target price. But as we are smart and risk-averse traders, we don't take greedy and nonessential risks.

As you may have noticed as you went through the steps, trading currencies needs a lot of patience and time. You need

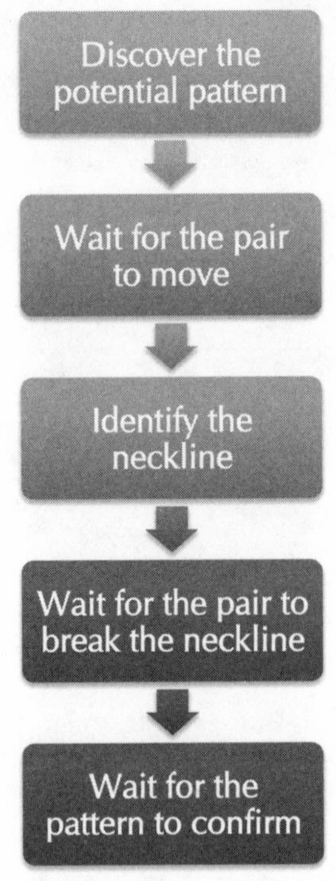

FIGURE 12-20

to give the market time to move and the currency pairs time to dance! That is why trading forex is perfect for someone who is busy doing a lot of other things at the same time, which is true of many women. Once you have confirmed all the points of the Invest Diva Diamond about a specific market movement, all you have to do is wait and let the markets do their job. You can wait for the markets to move while doing stuff like, but not limited to:

1. Waiting for your nail polish to dry
2. Waiting for your lasagna to finish baking
3. Working in the office
4. Pumping milk for your baby
5. Working out in the gym
6. Chatting on the phone
7. Watching TV

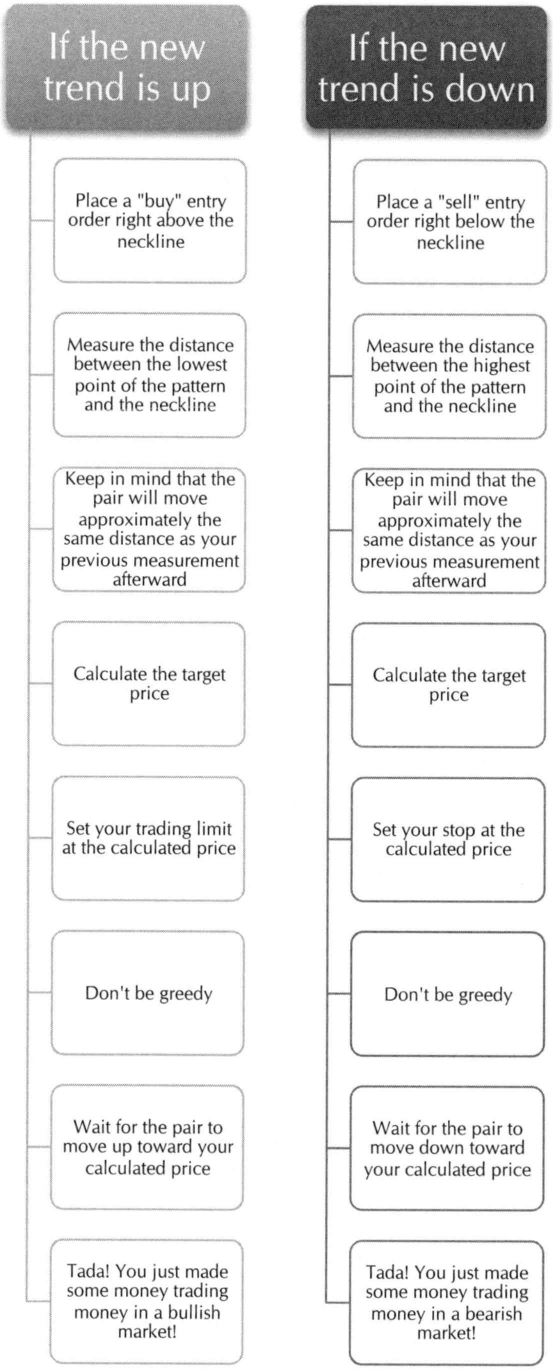

If the new trend is up

- Place a "buy" entry order right above the neckline
- Measure the distance between the lowest point of the pattern and the neckline
- Keep in mind that the pair will move approximately the same distance as your previous measurement afterward
- Calculate the target price
- Set your trading limit at the calculated price
- Don't be greedy
- Wait for the pair to move up toward your calculated price
- Tada! You just made some money trading money in a bullish market!

If the new trend is down

- Place a "sell" entry order right below the neckline
- Measure the distance between the highest point of the pattern and the neckline
- Keep in mind that the pair will move approximately the same distance as your previous measurement afterward
- Calculate the target price
- Set your stop at the calculated price
- Don't be greedy
- Wait for the pair to move down toward your calculated price
- Tada! You just made some money trading money in a bearish market!

FIGURE 12-21

8. Going on a date
9. Sleeping
10. Going on vacation
11. And so on

Have the prices hit your stop or limit target yet? Congratulations! You just made some money while you were doing other things. Now you can reward yourself by going shopping for that cute dress you just saw on your way home.

Continuation or Reversal Patterns

Continuation patterns indicate a pause in a trend. It's as if the pair takes a rest for a while before it resumes dancing in the previous direction. It is also called *consolidation*. Many patterns that are known to indicate continuation often turn out to be reversal patterns, so they can be very tricky. That is why we have to be very careful before we put in an order based on a continuation pattern and refrain from jumping to conclusions too quickly.

The best-known continuation patterns are:

1. Triangles
2. Rectangles
3. Wedges

Triangles

Triangles can be considered to be the celebrity of all chart patterns because they appear a lot on many dance floors, but unfortunately, they are the least reliable. Still, we need to add them to our analysis tools but be cautious about them because they happen a lot.

There are different types of triangles: symmetrical triangles, ascending triangles, and descending triangles (see Figure 12-22).

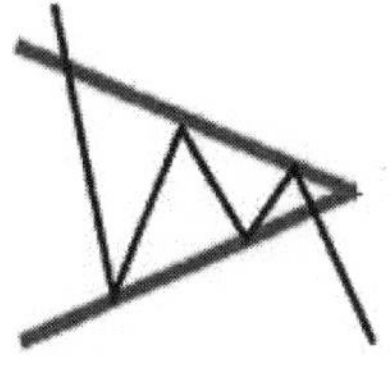
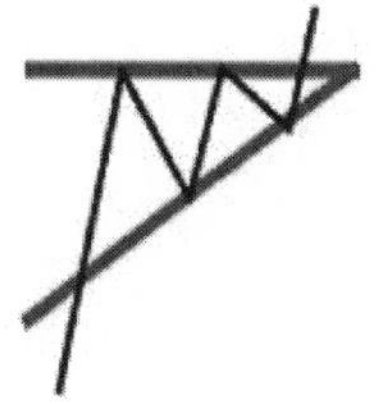
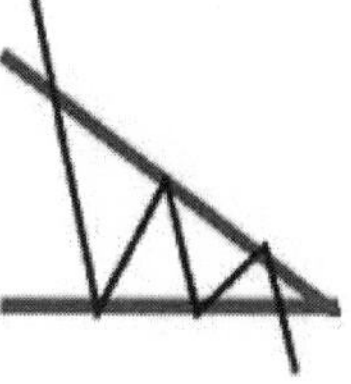

Symmetrical Triangle   Ascending Triangle   Descending Triangle

FIGURE 12-22

Symmetrical Triangles

A symmetrical triangle looks like a slice of pizza, as you can see in figure 12-23, and is often a continuation pattern that forms during a trend. The pattern contains at least two lower highs and two higher lows—a series of two or more zigzags in which each succeeding peak is lower than the one before it, and the bottom of each succeeding reaction is higher than the one before it (see Figure 12-24). When these points are connected in a trend line, the lines get closer to each other as the pair moves forward with time. The two lines finally reach each other and kiss. This is how a brand new symmetrical triangle is born.

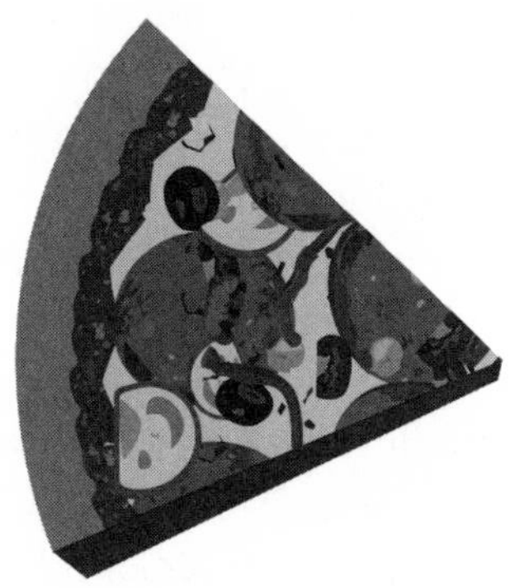

FIGURE 12-23

The reason this happens is that neither the buyers nor the sellers are able to push the pair in their direction. After one side gives up, we can expect a breakout. Symmetrical triangles can be the opening of an important reversal too, but

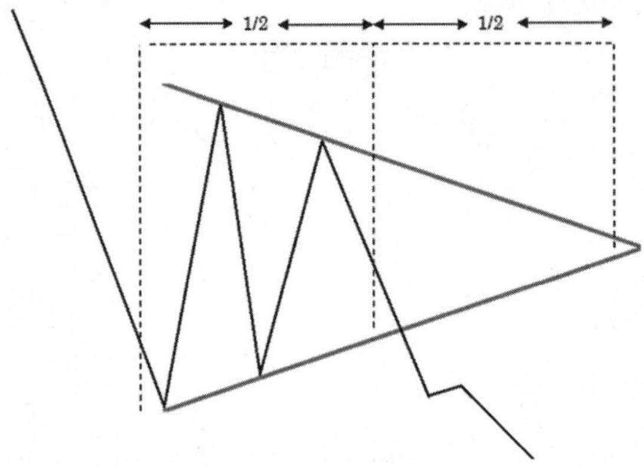

FIGURE 12-24: Symmetrical Triangle Breakout

more often than not the pair continues in its old direction after the formation of the triangle is completed.

As the lines of the triangle get closer to each other, we get more excited, waiting for an explosion of the price action. We want to make sure which direction the price is going to shoot in, so that we can take advantage of it and make a smart entry.

So how do we do this?

One thing we can do is wait for a breakout (while being cautious of a false breakout), then ride in the new direction and place an order. Triangles seem to work best when the pair breaks out somewhere between half and three-fourths of the distance between the widest zigzag of the price movement and the apex of the triangle (see Figure 12-24).

It is widely believed by certain young anonymous female traders that when the pair breaks out through the halfway, it is dancing to the song "Meet Me Halfway."

Figure 12-25 shows an example of a symmetrical triangle continuation pattern in action.

A Story of a Pair Dancing in a Symmetrical Triangle

Once upon a time, a certain currency pair was dancing on a downtrend when it drifted into a symmetrical triangle at point A (see Figure 12-26) and its dancing range began to contract.

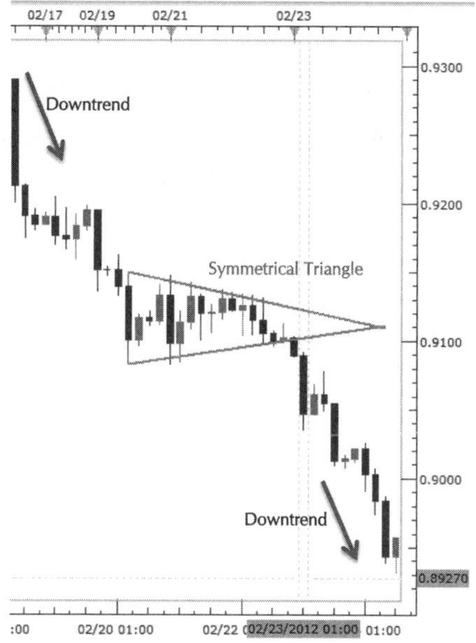

FIGURE 12-25: Symmetrical Triangle Continuation Pattern Formed on Dollar-Swissy 4-Hour Chart, February 2012

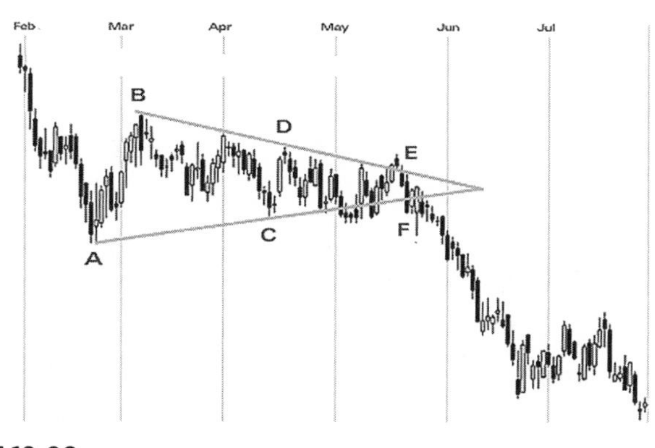

FIGURE 12-26

Trend lines were formed over the next two months (A–C and B–D), and the pair was trapped in between them. One day the pair broke through the resistance trend line at point E, pushing for a trend reversal, but it failed right away. It was a false breakout. Some traders who got too excited too soon and didn't wait for the day's close for the breakout confirmation got fooled and lost money. The following day, after point E, the pair's price opened below the trend line. This was a confirmation that the previous day's signal had been a false breakout. Now many patient and wise traders who hadn't placed an order the previous day were making fun of the ones who had done so. Subsequently, the pair broke through the triangle at point F with strong volume accompanying the sell-off, which helped confirm the symmetrical triangle as a trend continuation pattern. The pair continued dancing on a downtrend, and the traders who were familiar with this pattern made some dough.

Right-angled triangles, aka ascending or descending triangles, are a special form of the symmetrical type in that one of the two trend lines is formed horizontal to the vertical axis. These triangles are much cooler than the symmetrical triangles, because a symmetrical triangle doesn't give an indication of the direction in which the pair is likely to break, but the right-angled triangle does. The new trend direction can be easily identified by looking at the triangle's level of support or resistance and by following the zigzag movement of the pair as it gets squeezed.

Ascending Triangle

The *ascending triangle* looks like a floating piece of cake (see Figure 12-27) is a bullish formation that usually forms during an uptrend. In most cases, the formation is a continuation pattern with some instances of reversals at the end of a downtrend. Figure 12-28 shows an ascending triangle in action.

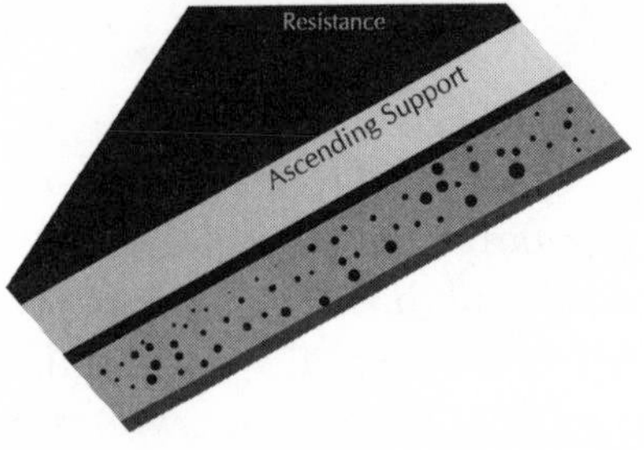

FIGURE 12-27

FIGURE 12-28: Ascending Triangle Continuation Pattern Formed During an Uptrend on Aussie-Dollar 4-Hour Chart

Two or more highs that are almost equal to one another form a horizontal line on the top (resistance). Two or more lows, each one higher than the previous one, form an ascending trend line (ascending support) that converges on the horizontal line as it rises. As the pattern develops, fewer traders participate in the market, and the volume levels usually lessen, or even become flat. This is a quiet period before the storm!

When the upside breakout happens, the reenergized bulls and bears usually attack the market, causing an expansion of volume to confirm the breakout and the continuation of the current uptrend (or a reversal of the prevailing downtrend).

And as in most cases, once the resistance is broken, it transforms into a support level for future price movements. When the horizontal resistance line of the ascending triangle is broken, it turns into support. Sometimes the price will retest this support level before the upside move resumes.

Unlike symmetrical triangles, where a breakout is needed to determine the bias of the market, an ascending triangle pattern has a more definitive bullish bias because of the higher reaction lows as the formation extends to the right. It is these higher lows that indicate increased buying pressure and give the pattern its bullish bias.

Descending Triangle

The descending triangle looks like a piece of cake waiting to be eaten as seen in Figure 12-29 and is the reverse of the ascending triangle. It is a bearish formation that usually forms during a downtrend (see Figure 12-30).

The steps needed to identify, confirm, and take advantage of this pattern are basically the same as those for the other triangles, so without further ado, I welcome you to the next fake forex party.

> **FAKE FOREX PARTY TIME**
>
> Open your demo trading platform and go through different currency pairs in different time frames. Find a potential or developed triangle pattern. Draw your trend lines carefully and determine what type of triangle it is. Leave the chart with the trend lines open and see whether the prices eventually break through the lines. Depending on your time frame settings, this may take anywhere from one hour to more than five months. Confirm that this is not a false breakout, and then place a fake order with virtual money based on the new trend.

Was this triangle a continuation pattern or a reversal pattern? Share your story at Invest Diva's Forex Community.

Rectangles

Does it feel like you are back in kindergarten reviewing all angled shapes? This is just the beginning! The rectangle is the *king of consolidation*. As the currency pair tries to dance freely in the forex party, circumstances try to confine it

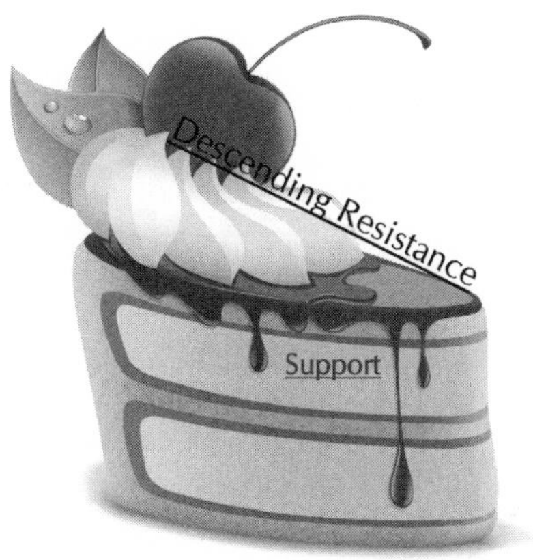

FIGURE 12-29

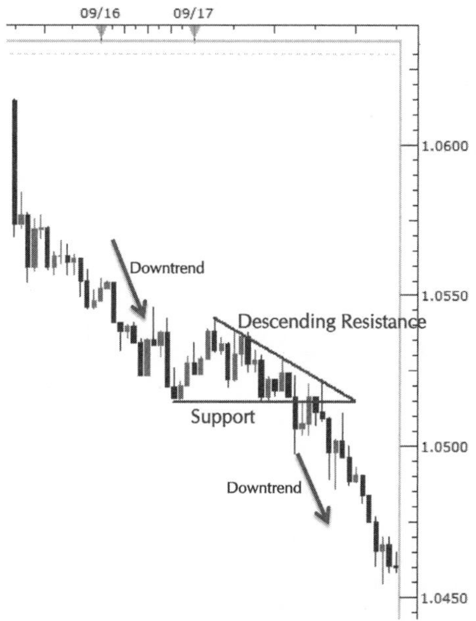

FIGURE 12-30: Descending Triangle Formed During a Downtrend on Aussie-Dollar 30-Minute Chart, August 2012

inside a box. It could be the indecisive superpower buyers and sellers as they take turns throwing punches and pushing the poor currency pair up and down like a puppet. Or maybe the world's political powers are just taking a rest on their economic decisions.

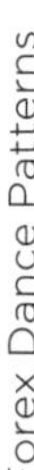

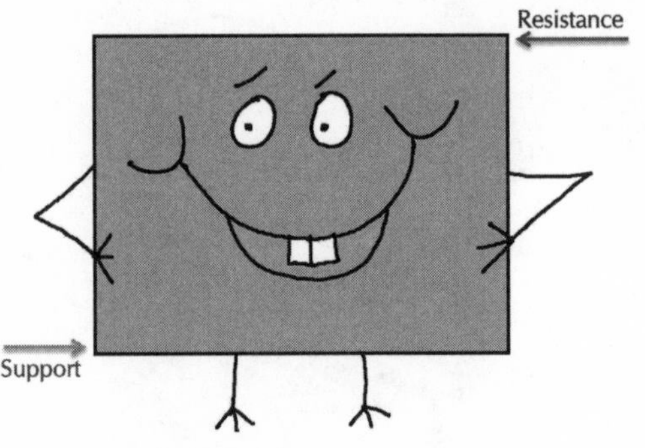

FIGURE 12-31

You can identify this pattern by two highs that are about equal and two lows that are approximately equal, forming two horizontal lines that represent the top and bottom edges of a rectangle (see Figure 12-31)!

A rectangle is a neutral formation in terms of the direction in which it will break out. The pair will test the support and resistance levels over and over again until it is able to break one of the levels. That is why, as always, we should wait for a confirmation before opening a position after a rectangle breakout.

Figure 12-32 shows a rectangle pattern formation on a Dollar-Yen (USD/JPY) 4-hour chart.

USD/JPY was in a downtrend when it got stuck in a box. After three weeks, it was finally able to break the box (and think outside the box!). In this case, it broke the resistance and moved up.

Here is what happened: the pair was bouncing in a narrow range between the support and resistance levels. It even tested below the support level, but it soon erased its rebellious action. Finally it was able to break above the resistance level at 78.764. However, this action still wasn't confirmed. The confirmation came six candles later, when a 4-hour candle opened above the resistance level on August 15, at 1 p.m. EST. Now it was safe to open a short-term buy entry, given that you have also checked the other four points of the Invest Diva Diamond!

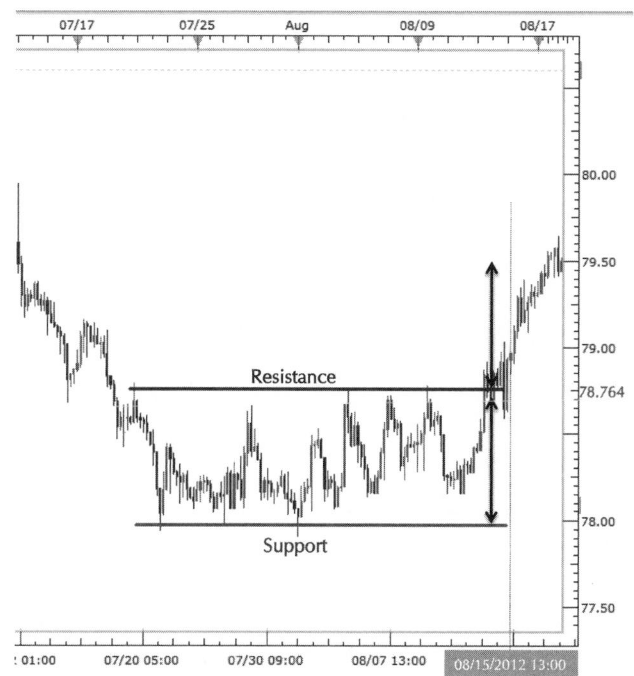

FIGURE 12-32: Rectangle Pattern Formed on Dollar-Yen 4-Hour Chart

Why short term? First of all, because this chart is set on a 4-hour time frame. Second, because we know that once the pair breaks a level, it tends to make a move that is about the size of the pattern. It may move further, but would you rather make some profit and be happy about it, or lose all your money? In my case, the former applies. Never be greedy in forex trading.

When a Rectangle Is a Continuation Signal

As mentioned before, a rectangle can be either a reversal pattern or a continuation pattern (see Figure 12-33). You can tell the two apart by keeping an eye on the resistance and support levels. Which one are the candles more likely to break?

Wedges

Now doesn't the shoe in Figure 12-34 look cute? In our forex party, the pairs sometimes move in a pattern that looks like the wedge of this shoe. All of us shoe lovers should have no

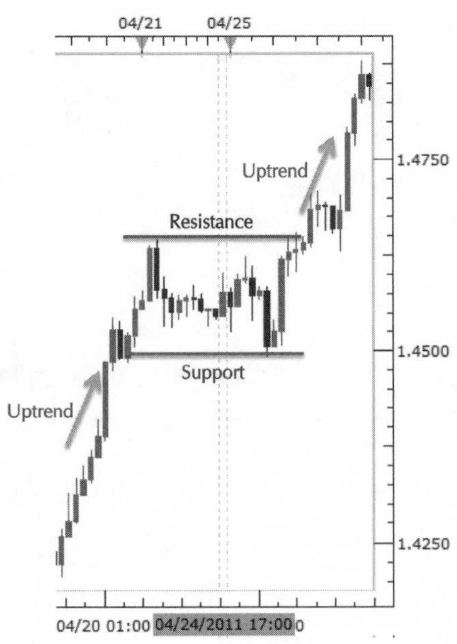

FIGURE 12-33: Rectangle as a Continuation Pattern on EUR/USD 4-Hour Chart

FIGURE 12-34

problem identifying this pattern, and this is yet another privilege of being a woman trader.

Just like triangles and rectangles, wedges signal a pause in the current trend. The trend can either reverse or continue after the formation of a wedge.

A wedge is very similar to a triangle in that you can draw two converging lines from a series of peaks and valleys. The difference is that a triangle has one *rising* and one *falling* line, but in a wedge, both lines are moving in the *same* direction. Both lines are either moving up or moving down.

Falling Wedge

In a falling wedge, both lines are falling, but one of them is steeper than the other, therefore, they are not parallel (see Figure 12-35).

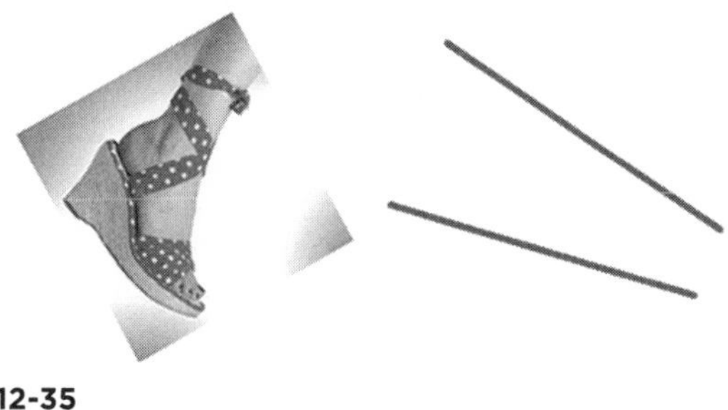

FIGURE 12-35

Falling Wedge Pattern

As we said before, a wedge can serve as either a reversal or a continuation pattern. This is how to distinguish the two: *a falling wedge is a temporary interruption of an uptrend, but it is a reversal signal for a downtrend.*

In other words, if the falling wedge is formed during an uptrend, chances are that the uptrend will continue after the completion of the wedge (see Figure 12-36). If the wedge is formed during a downtrend, we can expect a reversal (see Figure 12-37). Put another way, after the falling wedge pattern is completed, the pair usually breaks out to the upside, regardless of the previous trend.

How to Make Some Pips off a Falling Wedge

As always, this pattern is not confirmed until the resistance level is broken. Whether the falling wedge is a continuation pattern interrupting an uptrend or a reversal pattern during a downtrend, the pattern is considered bullish. Why? Because as you can see in the figures, every time the pair comes out of a falling wedge, it is likely to go up! Figures 12-38 and 12-39 show falling wedges in action.

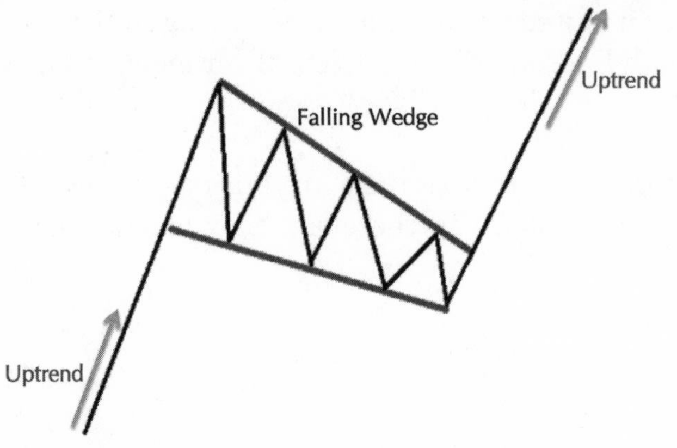

FIGURE 12-36: Falling Wedge During an Uptrend

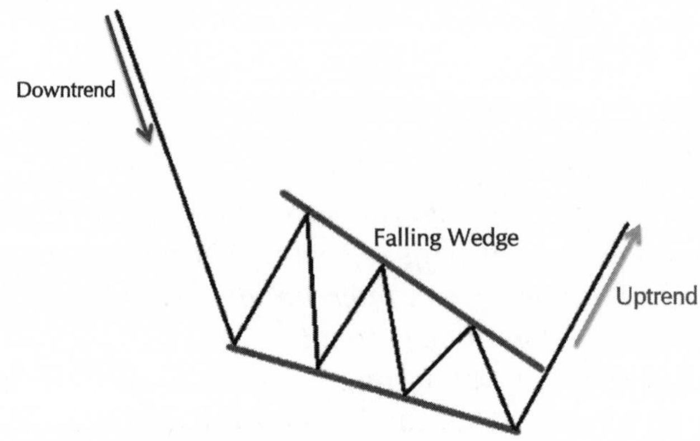

FIGURE 12-37: Falling Wedge During a Downtrend Is Followed by an Uptrend

Here is how a Forex Diva would make money off a falling wedge, after checking with other forms of the Invest Diva Diamond:

1. She places an entry order to buy the currency pair above the upper line of the falling wedge.
2. She sets a limit to close the position at the price to which the pair has moved up the same amount as the height of the beginning of the formation.
3. She refrains from being greedy.
4. She enjoys her newly earned pips.

FIGURE 12-38: Falling Wedge Reversed a Downtrend on Pound-Dollar Daily Chart

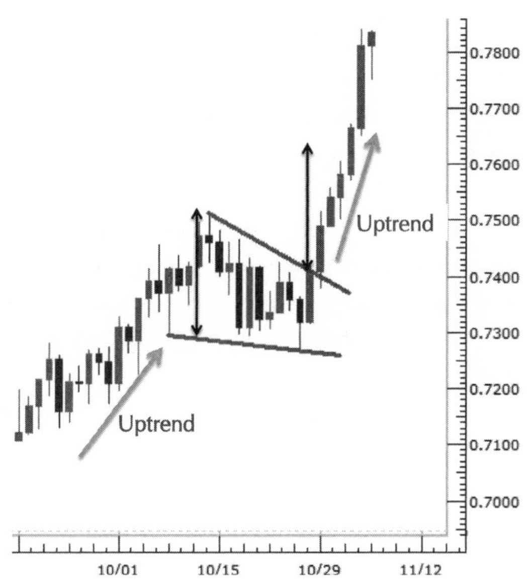

FIGURE 12-39: Falling Wedge Interrupted the Uptrend Briefly on Kiwi-Dollar Daily Chart

Rising Wedge

Just as its name suggests, a rising wedge is the opposite of a falling wedge. In a rising wedge, both lines are rising, but one of them is steeper than the other, as shown in Figure 12-40.

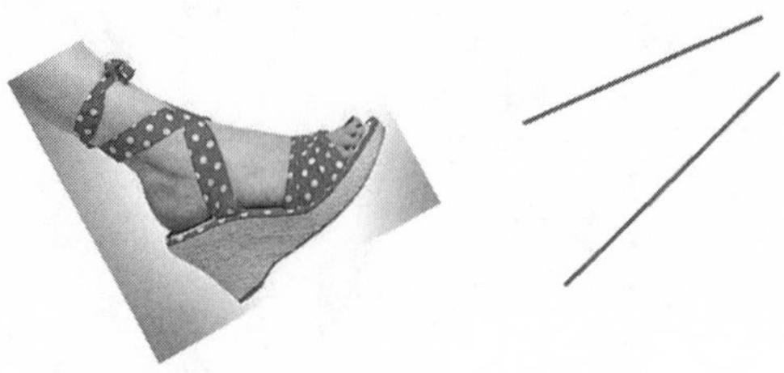

FIGURE 12-40: Rising Wedge Pattern

A rising wedge can serve as either a reversal or a continuation pattern, and it usually causes a sharp bearish market.

> A rising wedge is a temporary interruption of a downtrend. It is a reversal signal when it forms during an uptrend.

Let's think of a wedge as a "squeezing factory." The happy pair is dancing upward when it starts getting squeezed in a wedge. The puppet masters of the forex party are deciding where to take the pair next, and therefore trading volume drops toward the end of the wedge. After the pair is squeezed enough that it can't take it anymore, it suddenly and sharply breaks out—to the downside. This is called a *rising wedge breakdown* (see Figure 12-41).

If the pair is dancing in a downtrend before entering the "squeezing factory," the wedge is nothing but an interruption in the pair's downward movement, as shown in Figure 12-42.

Wedges can take anywhere between two and eight weeks to complete. So they sometimes occur on weekly charts, but they are too brief to appear on monthly charts. The best time frames for trading a wedge are daily or 4-hour charts.

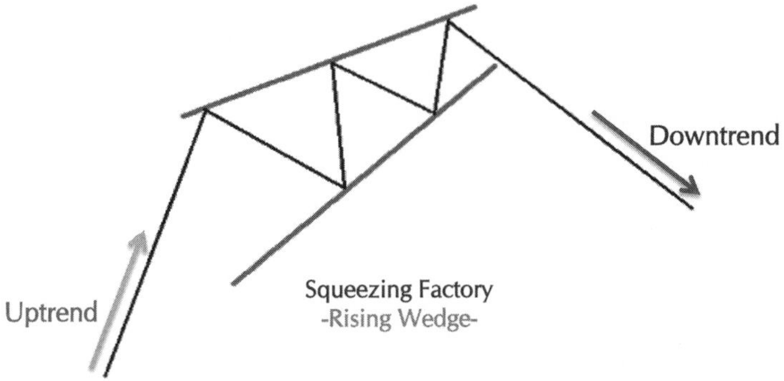

FIGURE 12-41: The Upward-Moving Pair Gets Squeezed in a Rising Wedge, then It "Breaks Down"

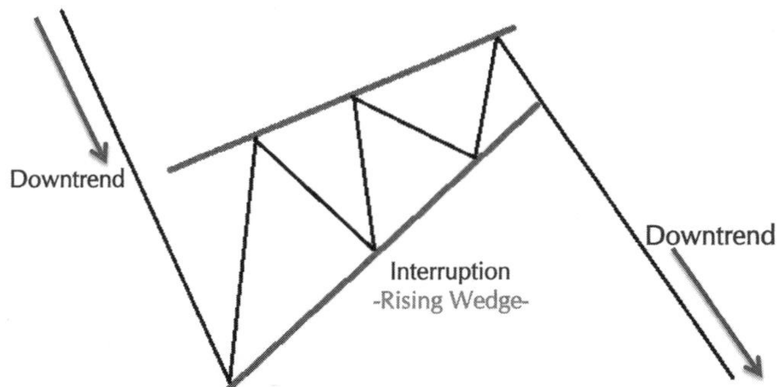

FIGURE 12-42: The Downtrend Is Interrupted by a Rising Wedge Formation

How to Make Some Pips off a Rising Wedge

1. Confirm the pattern.
2. Wait for the confirmation of a break in the support level (the lower line of the wedge).
3. Be aware of false breaks.
4. Place an entry order to sell the pair right below the lower line of the wedge.
5. Close the position at the price where the pair has moved down the same amount as the height of the beginning of the formation.
6. Enjoy the pips.

Summary of the Wedges

Simply put, a falling wedge often leads to an uptrend, which means that it is a bullish chart pattern. A rising wedge may lead to a downtrend, which means that it is a bearish chart pattern. That's it!

Printable Chart Patterns Cheat Sheet

BEARISH REVERSAL PATTERNS

Chart Pattern	Looks Like	In Reality
Double top	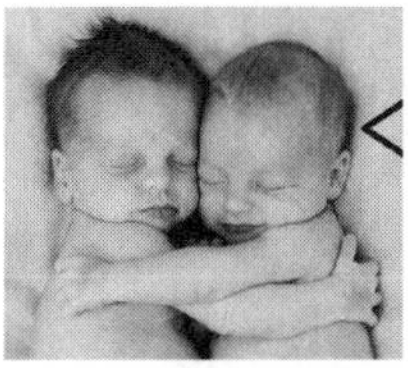	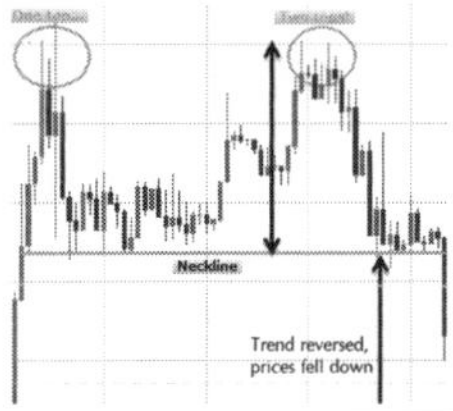
Triple top	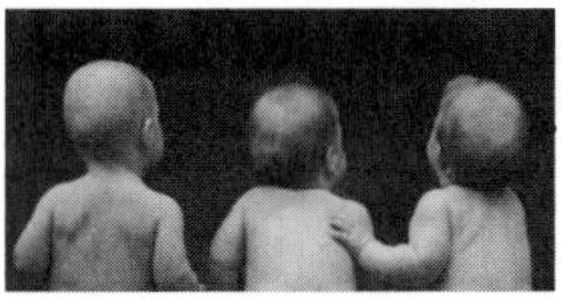	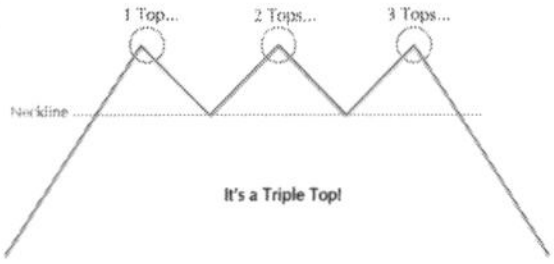
Head and shoulders top	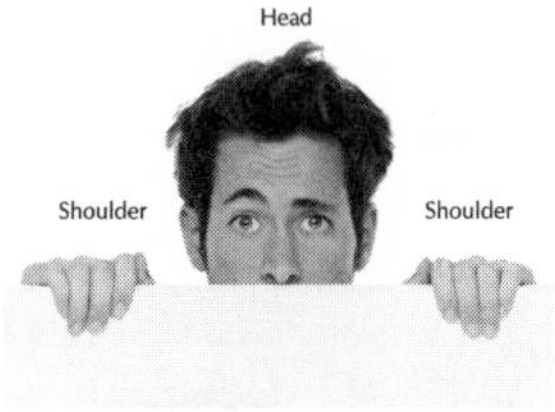	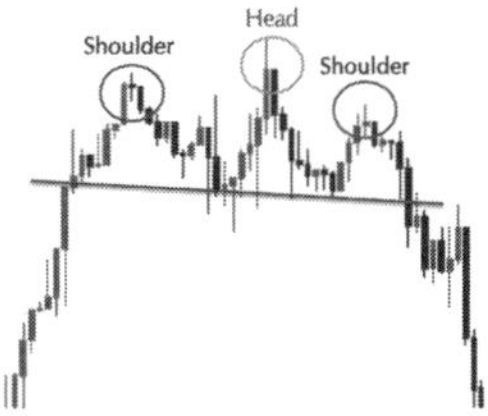
Saucer top		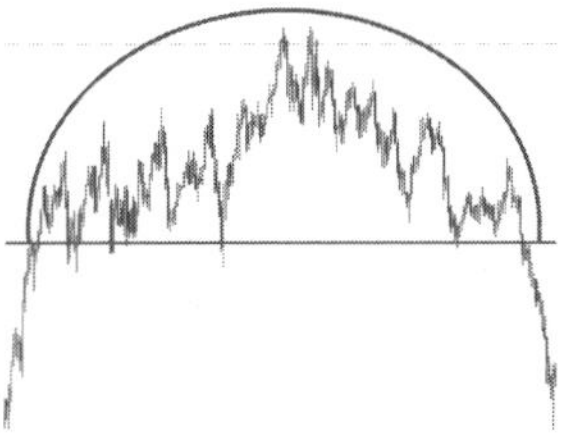
Rising wedge during uptrend		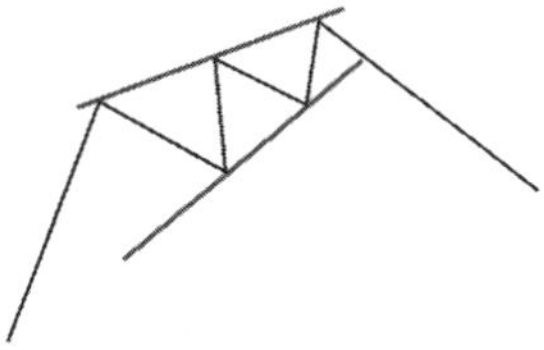

The next market move is *down*.

BULLISH REVERSAL

Chart Pattern	Looks Like	In Reality
Double bottom	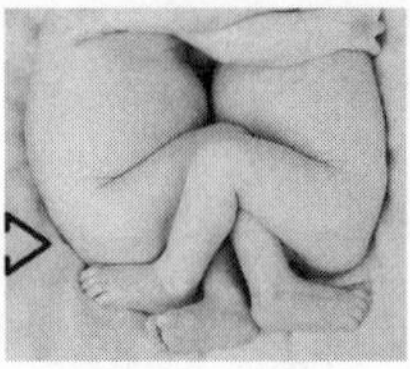	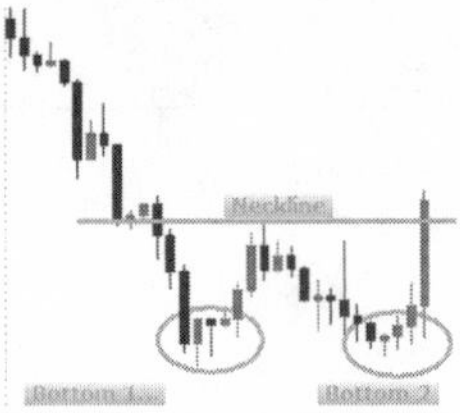
Triple bottom		
Head and shoulders bottom	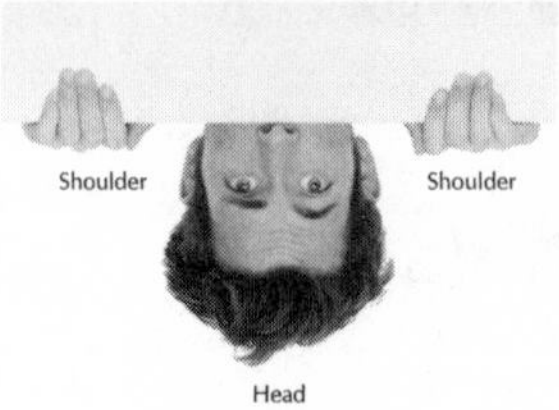	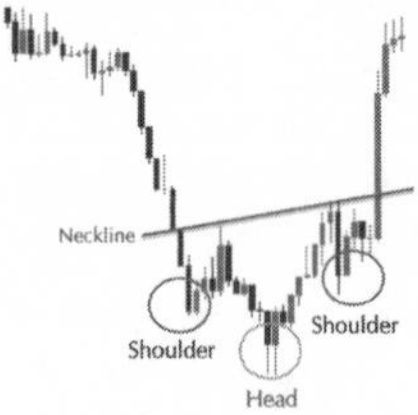
Saucer bottom		
Falling wedge during downtrend		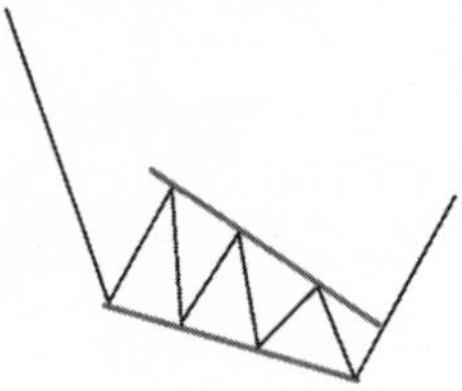

The next market move is *up*.

CONTINUATION PATTERNS

Chart Pattern	Looks Like	In Reality
Symmetrical triangle		
Ascending triangle	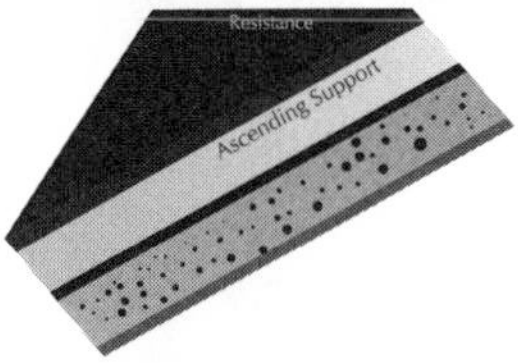	
Descending triangle	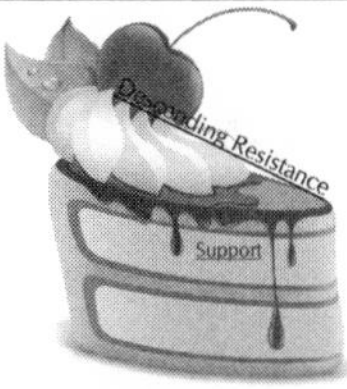	
Rectangle		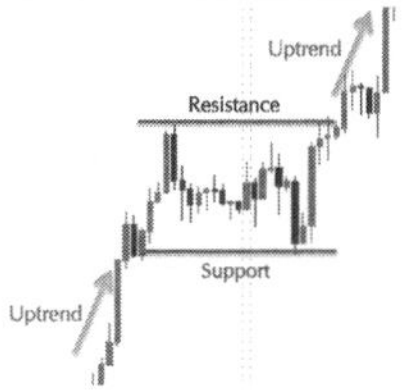
Falling wedge during uptrend		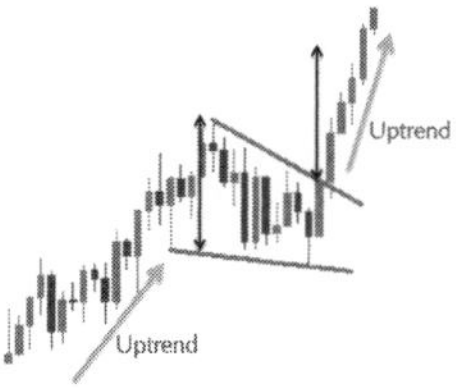
Rising wedge during downtrend	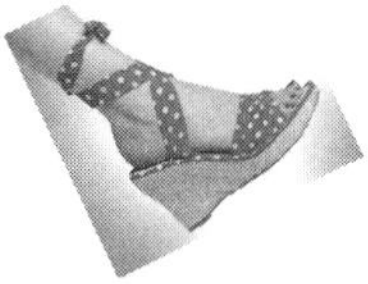	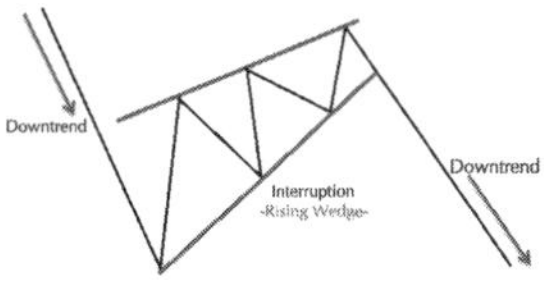

CHAPTER 13

Romantic Candle Patterns

Adding a little bit of romance to your life is always good, and candles are known for creating a romantic atmosphere. Many people use candles not only for romance, but also for celebrations, for spiritual purposes, or just for relaxing. If you are a candle lover, then you know you are on the right track in your decision to learn and trade forex, because all the forex parties are filled with candles!

We talked about the formation of candles briefly in Chapter 10. Just like the real candles that you have in your home, forex candles come in all different sizes and shapes, but this is not just for the sake of romance. Each shape and color has a deep meaning behind it as well. What is more romantic than gazing at candles, analyzing their shapes and patterns, and understanding what they are trying to tell us?

As you can see, forex takes the deepness and beauty of candles to a whole new level.

Long Candles and Short Candles

Forex parties are filled with candles with bodies and shadows (that is, wicks) of different sizes.

Candles of different sizes indicate different trading pressures. As we said before, we can set our trading platforms to build candles in different time frames. The color of the candle tells us whether the price of the currency pair is generally going up or going down in that specific time frame. The height of the candle shows us how intensely the pair was forced to move by the forex puppet master.

The longer the candle, the higher the trading pressure. In Chapter 10, we set the color of bullish candles to white and that of bearish candles to black.

Question: What does a long white candle have to tell us?

Answer: The white color indicates that the price generally went up during the given time frame. The length of the candle means that the price went up big time!

Basic Candle Shapes and Their Names

Since the forex candlesticks come in many different shapes, these shapes have been categorized, and each shape has a different name. Also, since the trading candlesticks were invented by the Japanese, many of the names are Japanese! So get ready to learn some Asian vocabulary as you get a deeper understanding of the candles.

Marubozu (Translation: Completely Bald/Shaved)

Figure 13-1 shows what happens to a pretty lady when she is marubozu, and Figure 13-2 shows what happens to a candlestick when it is marubozu.

If the candle is completely "shaved," with no shadows coming from either the top or the bottom of it, it is called marubozu.

Spirit

Marubozu candles have very powerful spirits. In fact, they are the most powerful candlesticks known to the trading

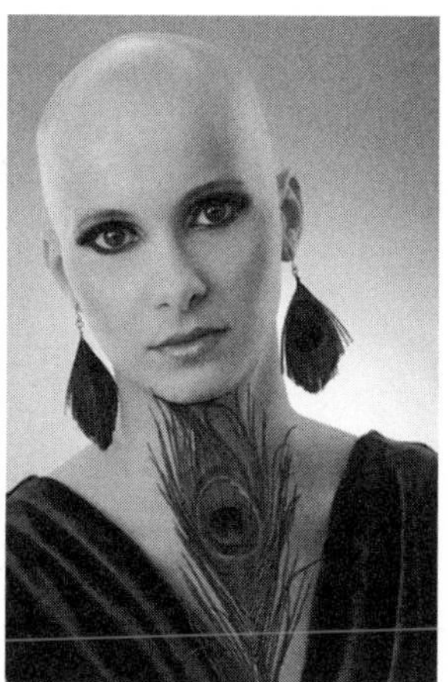

FIGURE 13-1

FIGURE 13-2

community. They have no upper or lower shadows, which means that the pair didn't even bother to test a price outside of the open and close prices. The price just went straight up (if it is a bullish marubozu) or straight down (if it's a bearish marubozu).

Spinning Tops

This one has an English name! And as the name suggests, these candlesticks have very short bodies but long shadows (see Figure 13-3).

Spirit

Spinning tops have very indecisive spirits. During the specific time frame in which a spinning top is formed, the pair

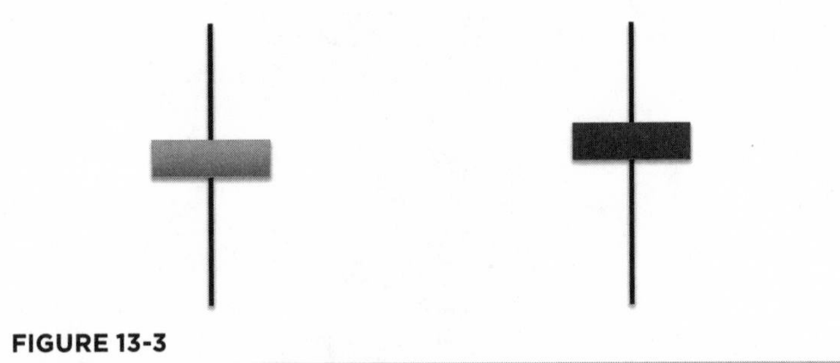

FIGURE 13-3

was mostly testing different prices and didn't really move that much. This can also mean that the forex puppet master (which includes the traders and the markets) was kind of indecisive on which way to move the pair.

You kind of want to yell: "Make a decision already!"

But who would listen?

Doji (Translation: Same [Time])

Another Japanese word to add to your dictionary! Doji candles (see Figure 13-4) have *equal (same)* open and close prices. That is why their bodies are nothing but a line. You can't even distinguish their color!

Depending on the length of the shadows of a doji candle, it can be put into different categories such as the "long-legged doji," the "dragon fly doji," and the "gravestone doji."

Spirit

A doji by itself is neither bullish nor bearish. But when it comes after other candles, it can have very powerful interpretations. We will get into that later.

Candle Arrangements

While candle arrangements in real life create a mood-setting tone for parties or for your table, candle arrangements in a forex party can give you a deeper understanding of the tone of the forex market.

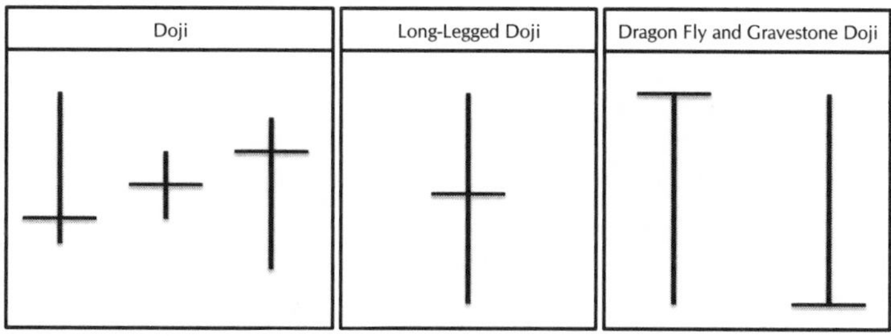

FIGURE 13-4

When candles of different shapes are arranged in a certain way on the chart, they can indicate the next movement of the currency pair. They can be either bullish reversal or bearish reversal indications. Together with chart patterns, candlestick patterns can give us more accurate signals of the next price action. Let's take a look at some famous bullish and bearish reversal patterns.

Bullish Reversal Candle Patterns

Here is a list of some of the most famous bullish reversal candle patterns:

- Morning star
- Bullish engulfing
- Hammer
- Bullish harami

Morning Star

A morning star is a bullish candlestick reversal pattern made up of three candlesticks: a long bearish candle, then a doji candle (or a spinning top), followed by a bright long bullish candle (see Figure 13-5). If you look closely, the combination of the doji candle and the bullish candle looks like Venus and Jupiter early in the morning. It also resembles the transition from the dark night (the darker bearish candle) to a bright

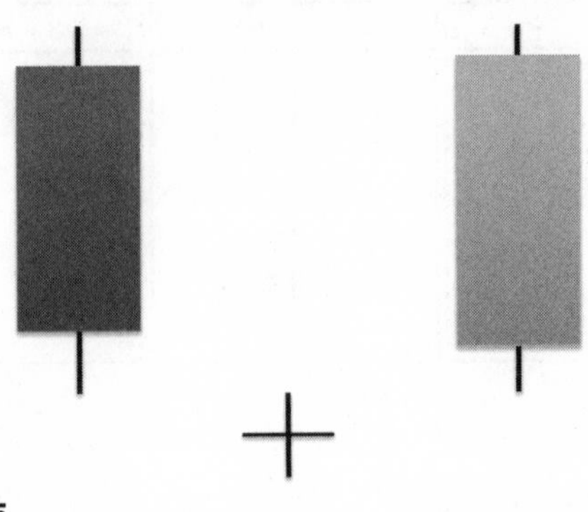

FIGURE 13-5

day (the brightly colored bullish candle) through the morning star (the doji candle).

The morning star forms after a downtrend and signals a reversal to an uptrend.

The first candle is a relatively long bearish candle that forms in the same direction as the prevailing downtrend. The middle candle can be either a doji or a spinning top, signaling indecisiveness in the market. The last candle is a relatively long bullish candle. This signals that the indecisiveness of the previous period has been resolved and that a reversal to the upside is under way.

Bullish Engulfing

A bullish engulfing candle pattern is made up of two candles. The first candle is short and bearish, and the second one is long and bullish—long enough to be able to completely cover, swallow, or "engulf" the entire previous candle (see Figure 13-6)!

The shadows of the candles are fairly short, if they have any at all. Bullish engulfing patterns form during a decline or a downtrend, or where there is potential resistance. They signal that the market trend may reverse into an uptrend (see Figure 13-7).

Don't forget to wait for confirmation of the bullish engulfing pattern before you jump into making a trade! As with most patterns, price action prior to and immediately after

FIGURE 13-6

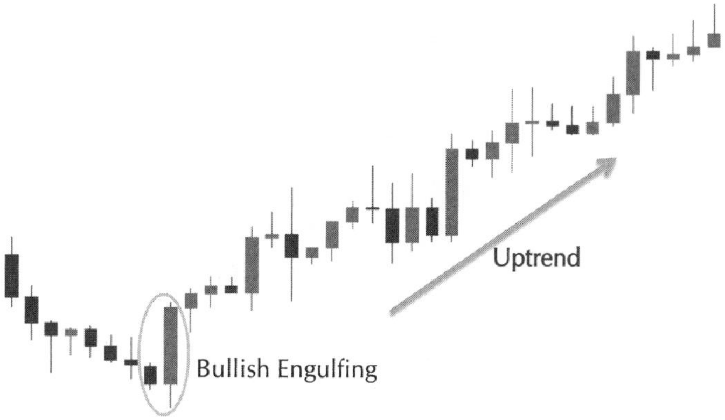

Uptrend

Bullish Engulfing

FIGURE 13-7

the bullish engulfing pattern needs to be analyzed for a confirmation of the uptrend.

Hammer

A hammer (see Figure 13-8) is a bullish reversal pattern that happens during a downtrend. It kind of looks like a hammer that is trying to hammer out a bottom on the chart (see Figure 13-9), and it signals that the price will start rising soon.

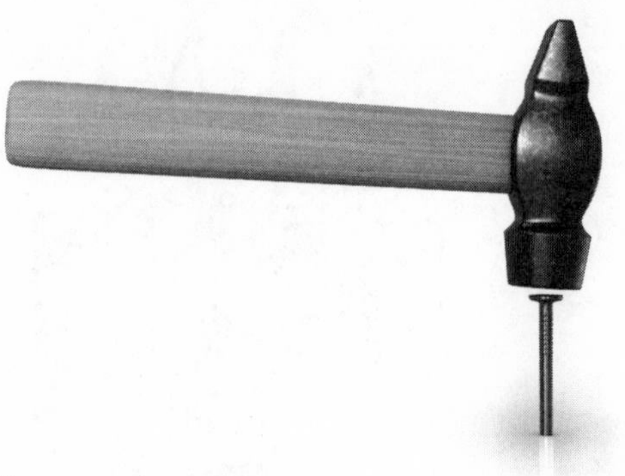

FIGURE 13-8

FIGURE 13-9

The long lower shadow indicates that the forex puppet masters tried testing lower prices, but didn't succeed. So the price closed near the open, and that is why the body of the hammer is so short.

Bullish Harami

Here is another Japanese word for you! You are going to love this one, though you may not be able to use it during your trip to Japan. *Harami* is an ancient Japanese word that means "the belly of a pregnant woman."

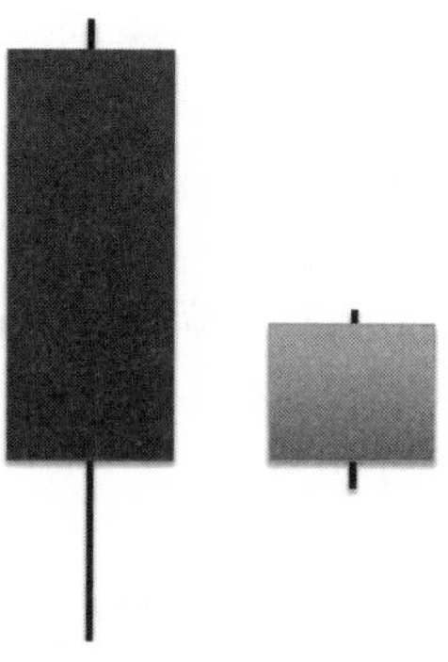

FIGURE 13-10

FIGURE 13-11

Now let's take a look at a bullish harami candle pattern (see Figure 13-10).

It could be named harami because the two candles arranged next to each other resemble the belly of a pregnant woman (see Figure 13-11).

To be honest with you, this could be just the reverse of a bullish engulfing pattern, but it's good to have different ways of visualizing different patterns, as this will ultimately help us remember the patterns and identify them more easily.

So basically, a bullish harami pattern consists of a long bearish candle (the close price is lower than the open price) followed by a short bullish candle (the close price is slightly higher than the open price).

Because the bullish harami indicates that the falling trend may be reversing, it signals that this may be a good time to open a "buy" position—that is, after you have confirmed the pattern and also consulted other points of the Invest Diva Diamond analysis.

Fake Forex Party Time

On your free demo account, set your chart to the "Candlestick" pattern and set the time frame to "daily." Go through different currency pairs and look for bullish reversal patterns. After you find one, try to confirm that it is in fact a bullish reversal indication by analyzing the chart pattern.

Do you see a double bottom, a head and shoulders bottom, or any other bullish reversal chart pattern at the place where you discovered your bullish reversal candle pattern?

If yes, place a "buy" position, wait a couple of days, and see where the markets go. Was your analysis correct? Was the pattern that you identified confirmed? If yes, how many (fake) pips did you earn?

Bearish Reversal Candle Patterns

Here is a list of some of the most famous bearish reversal candle arrangements.

- Evening star
- Shooting star
- Hanging man
- Bearish engulfing
- Bearish harami

A bearish reversal pattern happens during an uptrend and indicates that the trend may reverse and the price may start falling.

Evening Star

As the name suggests, the evening star projects an opposite signal from that of the morning star. It is a bearish candle reversal pattern made up of three candles (see Figure 13-12). It twinkles after an uptrend, and it signals that the price may fall.

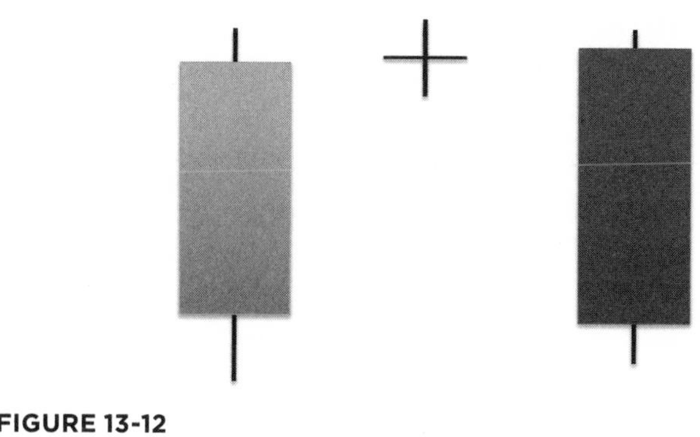

FIGURE 13-12

Shooting Star

Interestingly enough, shooting stars on a forex dance floor are not bright! Their small, bearish bodies are filled with a darker color to indicate that the price fell a little bit during their formation time frames. But they do leave a long trail (shadow) on the peak of an uptrend, which make us feel that they look like shooting stars (see Figure 13-13).

FIGURE 13-13

A shooting star indicates that a reversal in the pattern may be due, and that we could expect the price of the currency pair to fall.

Hanging Man

Oops, it seems like somebody made a mistake! Hopefully, as our beloved Lady Gaga put it, this man is "hanging on a moment of truth" (see Figure 13-14). It could be the last method to get your guy and his dirty clothes clean.

FIGURE 13-14

The hanging man looks a lot like the shooting star. It happens during an uptrend, and it is a bearish reversal signal. However, its long shadow is on its bottom (see Figure 13-15).

FIGURE 13-15

Bearish Engulfing

The bearish engulfing pattern is the opposite of the bullish pattern. It happens during an uptrend. A small bullish candle is followed by a big bearish one, and the big bearish candle is big enough to eat up the small one (see Figure 13-16).

FIGURE 13-16

Bearish Harami

Quiz: Do you remember what *harami* means in Japanese?

If you answered "the belly of a pregnant lady," you deserve a California-style salmon harami roll for dinner tonight. The bearish harami is the opposite of the bullish one. It is a bearish reversal signal during an uptrend, and it looks like Figure 13-17.

That's all you need to know about the romantic (and sometimes wild) candle patterns. Just keep your eyes open for the formation of these patterns while checking for other signals that you have learned so far or that you are going to learn from now on.

Fake Forex Party Time

On your free demo account, look for each of the candle patterns that you learned about in this chapter, whether it is

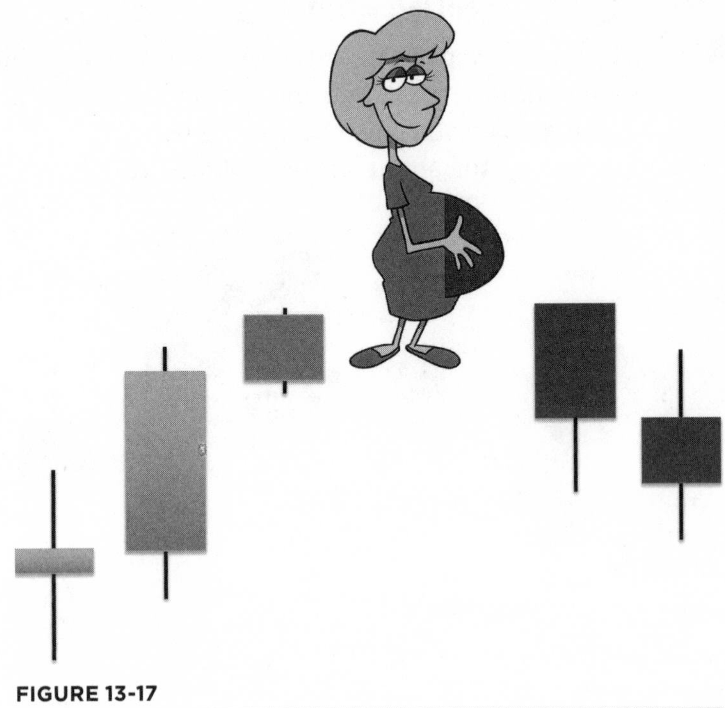

FIGURE 13-17

something that has formed in the past or something that is in the process of forming right now. If you are a Windows user, use the snipping tool to snip out a photo of the patterns as you find them. Copy all the patterns and paste them into a Word document with their names written beneath them. Print out the page and hang it from your fridge or above your mirror so that you can review the patterns every day.

CHAPTER 14

Forex Beauty Kit

Imagine trying to get dolled up for a party with none of the equipment you need to achieve the look you desire. No eyeliner, no brush, no powder. No matter how much mouth water you put on those lashes, they are not going to get any longer.

Just as for any other party, if you are going to attend a forex party, you need to gear up. There are plenty of cute and useful tools that you can easily fit into your forex purse. It takes a little practice to feel comfortable using all the equipment in your forex beauty kit, but hey, remember the first time you tried to use eyeliner!

In this chapter you will learn how to apply the most commonly used indicators to your analysis of the currency pair movements at a forex party. At the end, you will be invited to do the "Boyfriend Does My Forex Makeup" challenge.

Moving Averages (MA)

Moving averages help you identify trends and improve your buy/sell timing.

Let's face it, both in real life and in forex life, you always need to know what's trending! Sometimes the candles of all different sizes can make the forex party too crowded and prevent you from seeing the real beauty of the pair's movement. This is why we often reach out to our forex beauty kit and insert moving averages to smooth out their dancing movements.

Moving averages (MAs) show the average value of a currency pair's price over a set period. They appear on the forex party dance floor and help you identify the current trend more easily. Simply put, when the moving average is moving up, we would say that the pair is in an uptrend. When it is moving down, the pair is in a downtrend. It is that easy!

Depending on the length of the time frame you use to calculate your moving average, you can create short-term and long-term moving averages. If you want to see the short-term average movement of the pair, you use a shorter period (such as only 5 days). If you want to see a longer-term average movement, you will use a longer period, such as 200 days (duh!). Both short- and long-term moving averages have pros and cons (see Figure 14-1).

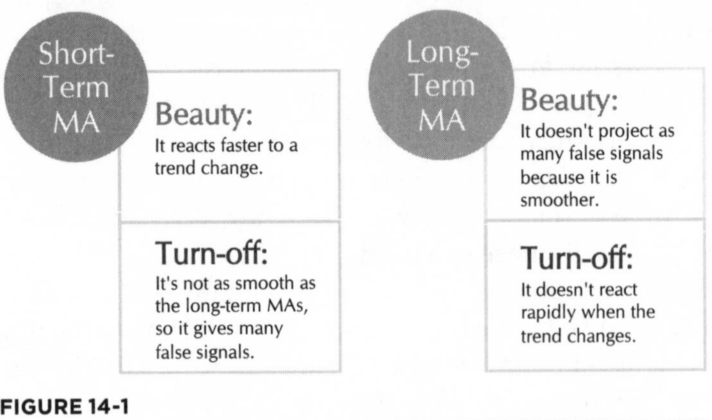

FIGURE 14-1

Eight Buy or Sell Signals from One Moving Average

You can use moving averages in different ways. One popular way is using the 200-day moving average to identify buy or sell signals. Depending on its position relative to the current market price, the 200-day MA can project buy or sell signals (false or real!). This is based on Joseph Granville's technique of technical analysis.

Buy Signals

1. The MA turns *up* or *horizontal* after being in a downtrend. The price *crosses above* the MA.
2. The MA is *rising*. The price *crosses below* the MA.
3. The MA is *rising*. The price is above the MA and gets close to it, but can't cross or touch it.
4. The MA turns *down* after being in an uptrend. The price *crosses below* the MA big time!

The four buy signals are shown in Figure 14-2.

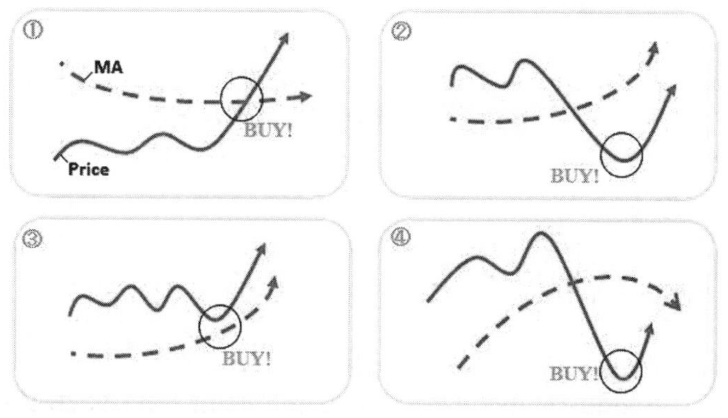

FIGURE 14-2

Sell Signals

1. The MA turns *down* or *horizontal* after being in an uptrend. The price *crosses below* the MA.
2. The MA is *falling*. The price *crosses above* the MA big time!
3. The MA is *falling*. The price is moving below the MA and gets slightly close to it, but can't cross or touch it.
4. The MA moves *up* after being in a downtrend. The price *crosses above* the MA and moves far away from it.

The four sell signals are shown in Figure 14-3.

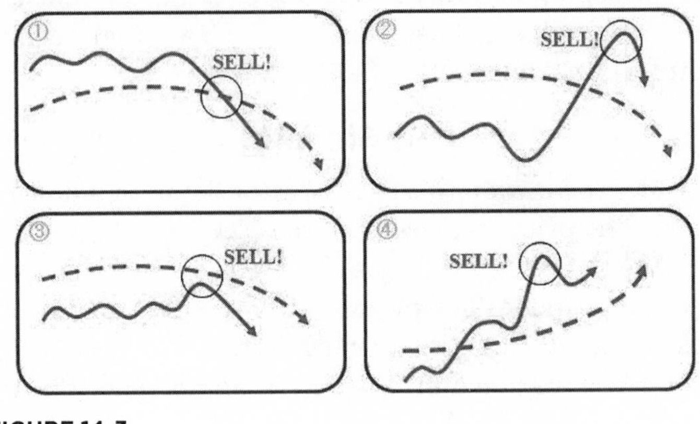

FIGURE 14-3

Two Is Better than One

How about using two moving averages to confirm the buy or sell signals? You'll have the best of both worlds! When you let two moving averages slither on your forex dance floor, they can't help but cross over each other. Sometimes the crossovers can be *golden*. But some other times—they're *deadly* (see Figure 14-4)!

- *Golden cross.* When a short-term moving average crosses *above* a long-term moving average, that means that the speed of the upward movement in a short period has become faster than the long-term speed. So this is a *buy* signal.
- *Dead cross.* Conversely, when a short-term moving average breaks *below* the long-term moving average, it indicates that the speed of the downward movement in a short period has increased. So this is a *sell* signal.

The dead cross is so called because it originates in security trading, where when the prices go down, you are screwed and you lose money. But as we said before, in forex trading

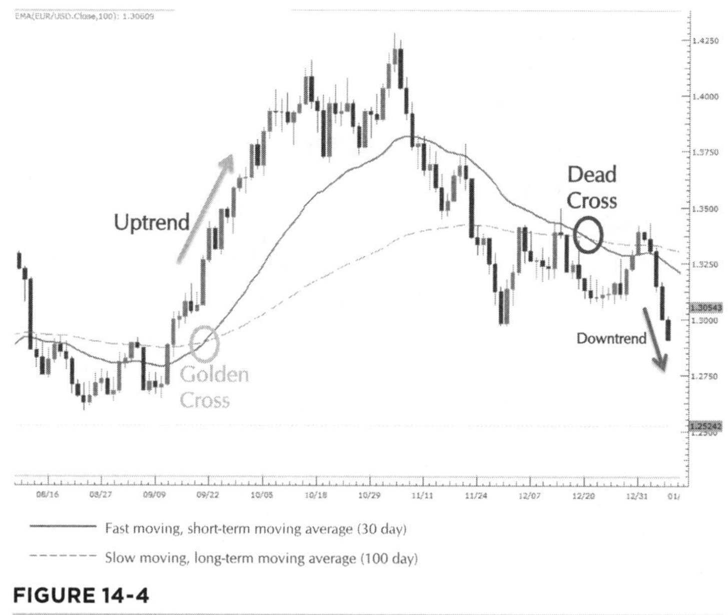

FIGURE 14-4

you can be a winner even in down markets depending on your position in the market.

Beware of False Signals!

You might have already gotten used to the idea that forex trading signals and indicators are often just full of $#?*. The forex trading party is just like any other party, and it often acts in an arbitrary fashion, ignoring all the laws and rules. That is why we should *never* rely on only one method of analysis and should *always* confirm our decisions with other tools and points of the Invest Diva Diamond.

Mr. Ichimoku (ICH)

This is another indicator that helps you identify buy and sell signals.

Yeah, here is another Japanese word you want to add to your dictionary. *Ichimoku* means "first sight."

This is love at first sight, babe! By applying Ichimoku to your forex chart, you will know a lot of secrets about the forex party right away!

Are you getting as excited as I am? I am excited just talking about Mr. Ichimoku.* And it is not only because I think Japanese guys are sexy.

Of course, love at first sight can be complicated. But once you get to know it, magic can happen.

Before we reveal the chart, let's prevent a major brain meltdown by first introducing the stuff you are going to see on your chart when you insert Mr. Ichimoku onto it (see Figure 14-5).

Name	Kumo	Kijun	Tenkan	Chiko
Meaning	Cloud	Base	Turn	Delayed
Image				

FIGURE 14-5

Now we are going to add all this stuff to the forex dance floor (see Figure 14-6). Don't panic; your eyes are going to get used to this, and after one day you will feel that a chart without Ichimoku is totally naked.

Am I going to bore you with an explanation of how all the lines are calculated? Nah. I don't feel like it right now. I'll just give you a basic introduction, and then I'll jump into the interpretation of Mr. Ichimoku.

Kijun line (base line, solid thick). This is the average of the highest high and the lowest low within the past 26 candles. We can also call it the "slow line" because it reflects a whole 26 periods.

*The full name of Mr. Ichimoku is actually *ichimoku kinko hyo*, which can be translated as "a glance at a chart in balance." A Japanese journalist invented this charting technique in 1936, and since then Ichimoku charts have become a popular trading tool in Japan.

FIGURE 14-6

Tenkan line (turn line, solid thin). This is the average of the highest high and the lowest low within the past 9 candles. We can also call it the "fast line" because it reflects a more recent average of prices.

Chiko (sometimes spelled *chikou) span* (delayed line, thick dashed). This shows the most recent candle's price, but it is drawn 26 periods behind.

Kumo (cloud). This is the area between two lines that plot the *future*! The first thin dotted line is calculated by averaging the tenkan line and the kijun line plotted 26 periods *ahead*. The second one is determined by averaging the highest high and the lowest low for the past 52 periods plotted 26 periods *ahead*. These two lines are called senkou spans. *Senkou* means "future."

One good thing about modern forex platforms is that you can choose different colors for each of the Ichimoku lines to make your party more colorful and to identify the lines easily. I usually like to use pink for Kijun line, black for tenkan line, blue for chiko line, and light green for the kumo. Try it out on your demo platform and enjoy!

Interpretation

Oh, Ichimoku, what you do to me! My head is in the Ichimoku cloud, dreaming about the future of the romantic candles dancing at a Euro-American forex party. I look back and see the blue chiko span following me. I look up, and I see the thick, pink kijun line and the thin black tenkan line dancing delightfully above me like danglers. I dream about the new set of earrings that I'm going to buy with my newly earned pips.

Wake up! You need to learn what each of these lines means before you think about buying new earrings with the money that you made at your forex party!

Figure 14-7 is a cheat sheet on how to trade using Ichimoku.

Buy Signal	Sell Signal
The candles are above the cloud.	The candles are below the cloud.
The chiko span crosses above the cloud.	The chiko span crosses below the cloud.
The tenkan line crosses above the Kijun line.	The tenkan line crosses below the Kijun line.

FIGURE 14-7

More Secrets Revealed

- As long as the five lines are parallel, the trend will continue in that direction.
- When the candles are inside the Ichimoku cloud, that means that the market is in the process of consolidating, and it is not a good time to buy or sell.
- The lower band of the prevailing cloud can be used as a layer of support (see Figure 14-8).
- The upper band of the prevailing cloud can be used as a layer of resistance.

Okay, enough advertising about Mr. Ichimoku. It certainly is very powerful in many ways, but just like any other method, you should not rely on it alone. You always have to check in with other analysis techniques before you make a final decision in your trading.

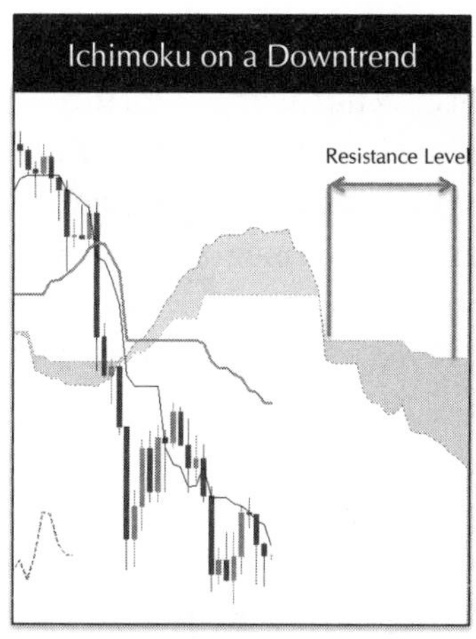

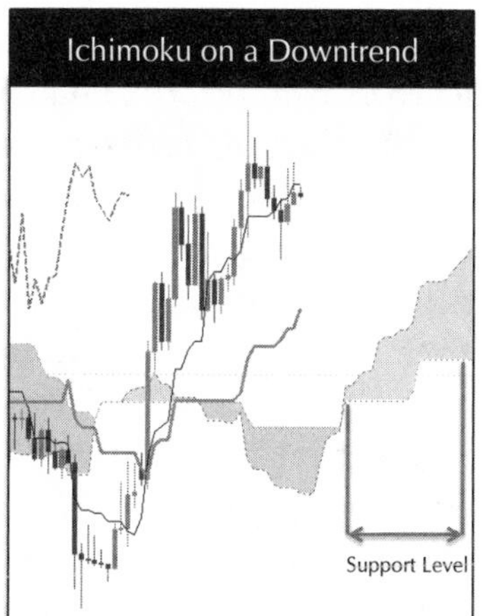

FIGURE 14-8

Fake Forex Party Time

On your demo trading platform, find the tab button that inserts Ichimoku. Identify the kumo (cloud), the chiko span, the kijun line, and the tenkan line by moving your mouse over each of them. Note that the colors of the lines are different from the way the lines are drawn in this book. In most trading platforms, you can change the color of the lines by going to Properties.

What is the position of the candles against the cloud? What is the direction of the kijun line and the tenkan line? Is the chiko span below or above the cloud? Is Ichimoku projecting a buy signal, a sell signal, or a wait-and-see signal?

MACD

This technique helps you identify where a trend starts and helps you confirm a buy or sell entry.

Let's start with pronunciation. You can call this indicator either Mac-D or M-A-C-D. Getting hungry yet? Just to clear things up, MACD is *not* an abbreviation for McDonald's. It actually stands for *m*oving *a*verage *c*onvergence-*d*ivergence.

MACD is one of the simplest and most famous momentum indicators in your forex beauty kit. “What is momentum?” you may ask. Momentum is the speed at which the price moves over a certain time period. Just like many other indicators in your forex beauty kit, MACD can also be used to identify buy or sell signals. As you can see, there are many ways you can confirm a buy or sell signal before you place a trade.

“So what is MACD?” you ask. Simply put, MACD is an indicator that shows the *difference* between a short-term moving average and a long-term moving average.

After clicking on the MACD button on your trading platform, you will see stuff similar to the things shown in Figure 14-9 underneath your forex dance floor.

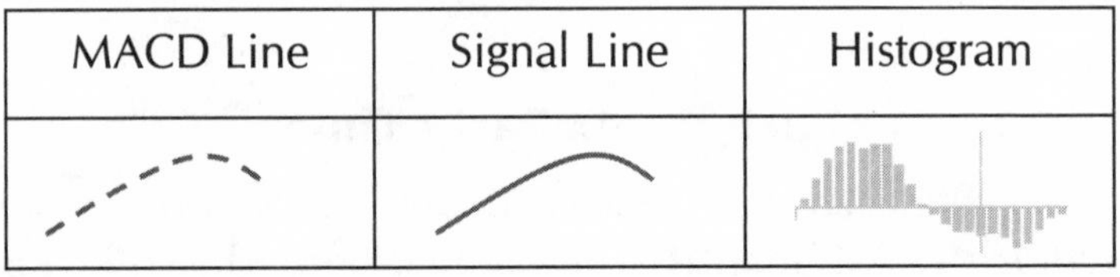

MACD Line	Signal Line	Histogram

FIGURE 14-9

Let’s first leave the histogram aside and focus on the MACD line and the signal line.

These two lines are two moving averages with different speeds, so the faster one (the MACD line) will obviously be quicker to react to price movements than the slower one (the signal line). Let’s say that the MACD line is an eligible bachelor, and the signal line is, well, me (see Figure 14-10).

The signal girl was minding her own business and walking in the opposite direction when the MACD guy crossed her over. This is how they met, and that is when the shopping begins!

Figure 14-11 shows a simple interpretation of MACD signals.

When a new trend occurs, the fast line will react first and eventually cross the slower line.

Note: The crossover MACD buy or sell signal works well in markets that are trending either up or down (see Figure

FIGURE 14-10

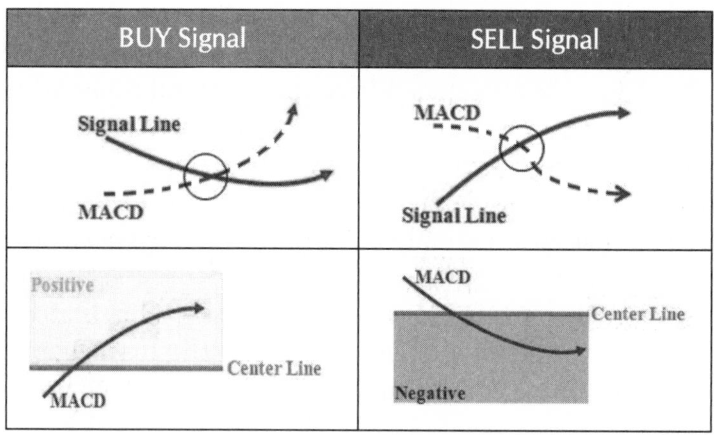

FIGURE 14-11

14-12). It will deliver mostly false signals when the trend is changing or flat.

MACD can also help you confirm a trend. When the MACD line is above the center line, whether its direction is up or down, the general daily trend is considered to be up. When the MACD line is below the center line, you can consider the general trend to be down. A change in the direction

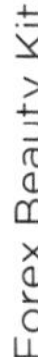

FIGURE 14-12

of the MACD line while it is still above the center line simply indicates that the market is having a temporary pullback and will eventually continue in its previous trend.

Now let's talk about the histogram with all those vertical bars. It looks as if it is very professional, has a lot to say, and only super-mega-smart financiers will understand it, but to be honest with you, the poor thing doesn't have that much to offer. The histogram simply plots the difference between the fast and slow moving averages.

As the two moving averages separate, the histogram gets bigger, while when they cross over, the histogram disappears. It's only there to make it easier for you to spot the crossovers!

Bollinger Bands (BOL)

Bollinger Bands help you identify extreme short-term prices.

Bollinger Bands (created by Mr. Bollinger in the 1980s) are two bands above and below the currency pair (see Figure 14-13), and they have a pretty cool mathematical explanation behind them that we are not going to bore you with.

Here are some things to know about Bollinger bands:

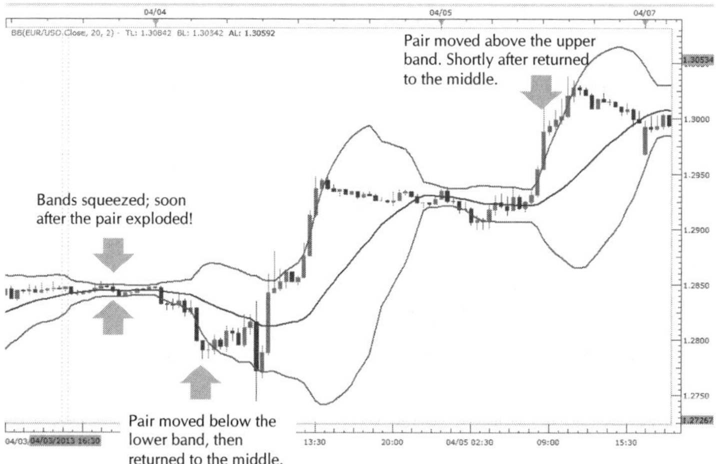

FIGURE 14-13

1. Under normal conditions, you will almost always find the pair within the bands; more specifically, it tends to return to the middle of the bands.
2. If the Bollinger bands start to squeeze, then there is a reasonable chance that the volatility will increase and a trading opportunity will soon appear.
3. When the pair moves above the upper band, it is thought to be overbought, and we can expect the price to fall (sell signal).
4. A move below the lower band suggests that the pair was oversold, giving a buy signal.

> When the pair reaches the lower band, it is a *buy* signal. When it reaches the upper band, it is a *sell* signal.

Mr. Fibonacci

This technique helps you understand potential support and resistance levels, helps you find a reasonable price at which

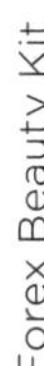

to buy or sell, and helps you with the timing for exiting your position.

From Japan to Italy! Mr. Fibonacci is an Italian dude. Don't get too excited, though. This doesn't mean that we are done with geeky stuff and are going to learn how to impress Italian guys. Although the stereotype is that Italian guys are very good at chatting up women, Mr. Fibonacci, whose real name is Leonardo Pisano Bigollo, was an ultra-geeky mathematician. In fact, his dad seemed to be so disappointed with him that he called him Bigollo, which means "good for nothing."

Little Mr. Fibo traveled with his daddy to exotic places like North Africa. He remained geeky throughout his travels, and he constantly studied numbers. When he got back, his souvenirs for his friends were, obviously, numbers. Fibo is actually the one who introduced the decimal system to the West, replacing those weird-looking Roman numerals. Didn't know that one, did you?

But things didn't end there. One day little Mr. Fibo was playing with his numbers. He started counting: 1, 2, 3, 4, 5 . . . He soon got bored with counting and started adding up the numbers. He added 1 and 2. The result was 3. Then he added 2 and 3. The result was 5. Then he added 3 and 5. The result was 8. He continued this game for hours and even ignored his mom when she shouted, "Fibo, lunch is ready!" (The accuracy of this part of the story remains under investigation.)

Later he showed his mom a whole new series of numbers: 1, 1, 2, 3, 5, 8, 13, 21, 34, 55, 89, 144, . . . This is how he investigated the growth of the rabbit population (see Figure 14-14).

Believe it or not, the beauty of this series of numbers doesn't end with rabbits and bunnies. After the first few numbers, if you divide any of the numbers by the succeeding number, you will get approximately 0.618. For example, 34 divided by 55 equals 0.618. If you calculate the ratio between alternate numbers, you will get 0.382. The ratio between every third succeeding number is 0.235.

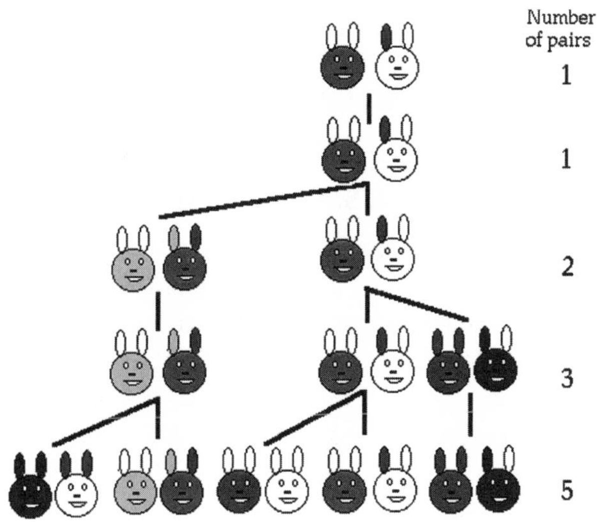

FIGURE 14-14

> Okay, please don't close this book yet! We're going to stop gibbering about numbers and get back to forex trading. You just need to know that Fibo's sequence of numbers is not important for forex analysis, but the ratios are. Also, the best news is that you don't have to do any math. Your forex beauty kit has special magical powers that create Fibonacci retracement levels at your command.

How to Trade with Mr. Fibo

1. Find a trend. The longer and stronger it is, the better.
2. Find the button labeled "Fibonacci Retracement" on your forex beauty kit.
3. If the trend is a downtrend, click on the highest point of the trend and drag your mouse to the lowest point of the trend.
4. If it's an uptrend, do the opposite. Click on the beginning of the trend (the lowest point) and drag your mouse to the highest point.

5. You will see Fibo's retracement levels magically appear. They are labeled 23.6%, 38.2%, 50%, and 61.8%. Yep, these are the famous ratios we talked about before.

The Story of Fibo and EUR/USD in an Uptrend

It's August 2010. You are at the EUR/USD daily forex party, where each candle takes one day to form. You notice that the pair has been moving upward for quite a while, since June 15, so you decide to use Mr. Fibo to identify support levels, as shown in Figure 14-15. The idea is that the pair will probably go back down (retrace) to one of the Fibo support levels, then will regain energy and shoot back up. That is when you want to place a buy order.

Of course, you want to buy at the cheapest price, so buying at the 61.8 percent or the 50 percent Fibo level would make sense. Since it's a strong uptrend, you wouldn't expect a sudden retracement back to 0 percent.

You draw the Fibo levels on the chart and go to sleep. You wake up two weeks later, and what you see is shown in Figure 14-16.

Hah! By September 2010, the pair has broken the 23.6 percent and 38.2 percent Fibo levels and is now holding at the 50 percent level! Do you want to wait a bit more and see

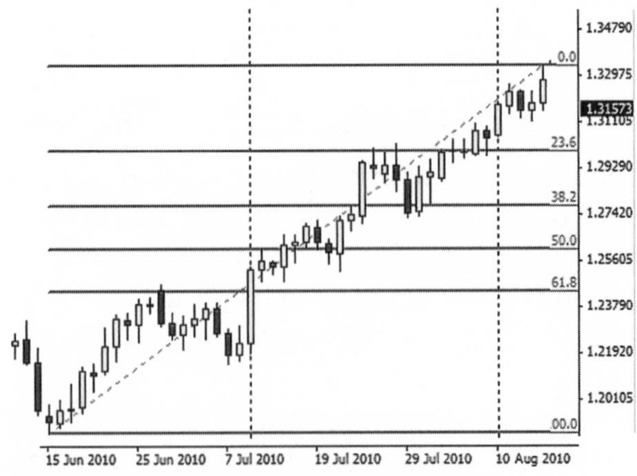

FIGURE 14-15: Fibo Levels in an Uptrend

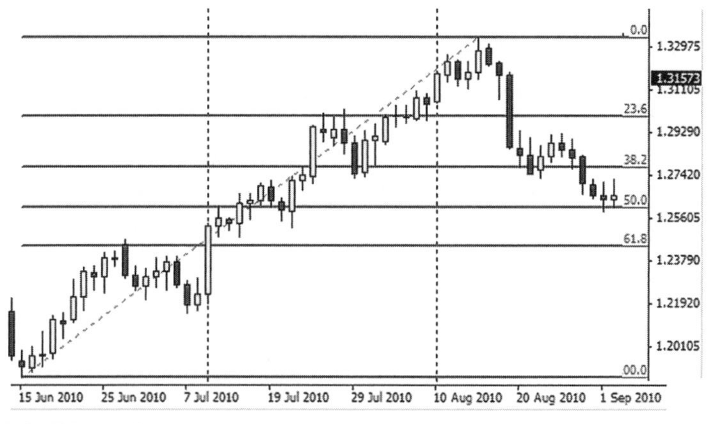

FIGURE 14-16

if the pair goes down to 61.8 percent, or do you want to place your buy order now? Well, it depends on what the other analysis tools are suggesting. You need to make sure that you always check in with all five points of Invest Diva Diamond before you make a decision.

Let's say you did your homework, checked with other analysis techniques, and decided that you want to make a buy order at the 50 percent Fibo retracement. You buy EUR/USD at the price of 1.26. The minute you place a buy order, you need to set your stop in order to prevent losses. One of the safe ways is to set your stop at the next Fibo level, which in this case would be 61.8 percent. Obviously, you always want to adjust your trades in accordance with the market environment and check in with other analysis methods as well.

Now you ask, at what price you should get out of the market and take profit? For that you need to set your limit, and please, don't be greedy. You can take profit at any of the upper Fibo levels to be safe. You can take a bit of risk and set the system to take profit right after the highest level of your Fibo retracement. In this example, let's say you buy the euro when it was 1.26 (Fibo's 50 percent level) and set your trading platform to take profit at 1.33 (Fibo's 0 level). You also adjust your leverage to make higher profit. Then you go to

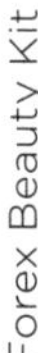

FIGURE 14-17

sleep again and wake up in mid-October! (However, sleeping for two weeks after placing an order is not recommended.)

Figure 14-17 shows what you see, Ms. Sleeping Head.

Where did the pair go? After holding around the 50 percent Fibo retracement level for about 15 days (including a break above the 38.2 percent level and going back down to 50 percent), the pair suddenly started to move back up and continued going up until October 26! The price went up all the way to 1.41. You had automatically left the market when it hit 1.33 at the end of September because of your original moderate settings. You obviously could have made more money if you hadn't set a limit at 1.33, but it's always better to be safe than sorry, right?*

Fibo on a Downtrend

Let's use a shorter time frame (4-hour) in the Pound-Dollar forex party for this example. The following are the steps I took to place a *sell* order on this downtrend using Mr. Fibo and other analysis tools.

*In this case, identifying a descending triangle right before the pair broke out of the 50 percent Fibo could have helped you readjust your limit order to take more profit. It is always important to check with different patterns and time frames to make the best decision.

FIGURE 14-18

1. I noticed that the GBP/USD pair had been on a downtrend for a number of periods, but showed a bullish signal in the most recent period (see Figure 14-18).
2. I clicked on the Fibo button on my trading platform.
3. I clicked on the swing high (the starting point of this downtrend) and dragged my mouse all the way to the swing low.
4. I confirmed with longer time periods (that is, the daily chart) and other points of the Invest Diva Diamond that the pair was generally in a downtrend.
5. I confirmed with other support and resistance indicators that the pair wouldn't rise higher than the 61.8 percent Fibo retracement.
6. Based on my analysis, I decided to place a *sell* order at the 50 percent Fibo level.
7. I clicked on the "New Order" button on my account (fake forex party!).
8. I set the order to "Pending Order."
9. I selected "Sell Limit" as the order type.

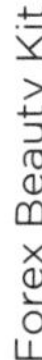

10. I entered the price at the 50 percent Fibo level, or 1.58770.
11. I set my "stop loss" one level higher, the 61.8 percent Fibo level, at the price of 1.59200.
12. I checked with other support levels to identify the best exit price and decided on the 0 percent Fibo level at 1.56620.
13. I set my "take profit" at that support level, or 1.56620.
14. I clicked on "Place Order."
15. I went to work.
16. I kept track of my account.
17. Two days later, I saw what is shown in Figure 14-19.

FIGURE 14-19

18. The pair held at the 50 percent Fibo level and my sell order was executed at 1.58770, then the pair bounced back down!
19. I got excited to see whether the pair would continue down to reach the 0 percent Fibo level, where I would be taking my profit.

20. The pair continued its downward movement and went past my exit order of 1.56620.
21. I made some pips!
22. The pair continued down (see Figure 14-20).
23. I got a little bit upset because I hadn't set my exit order lower, but I soon remembered the famous phrase, "Don't be greedy in forex trading." And felt all better.

FIGURE 14-20

Relative Strength Index (RSI)

The relative strength index (RSI) is yet another momentum indicator, or oscillator, that measures the relative internal strength of the currency pair against *itself*. Again, your trading platform will do all the calculations for you. Although it can be helpful to know the math behind the indicators, for now only knowing the interpretation is sufficient.

When you click on the RSI button, an oscillator will appear underneath your forex dance floor, scaled from 0 to 100. For a standard 14-day period, a reading over 70 indicates that the currency pair is overbought, while a reading below 30 indicates that it is oversold (see Figure 14-21). Therefore, when

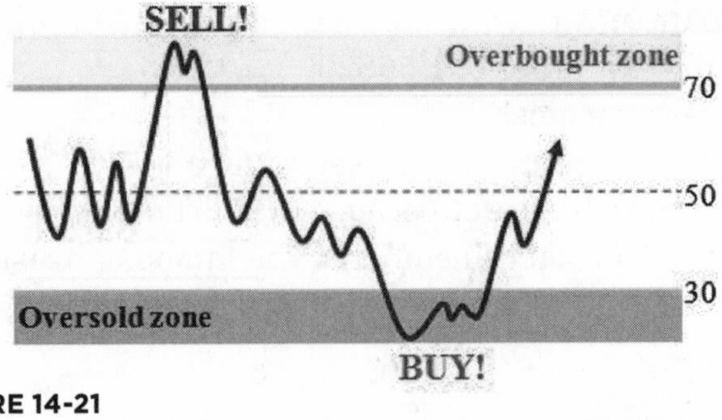

FIGURE 14-21

the RSI enters the overbought zone, it could be signaling that it is a good time to *sell* the currency pair. Conversely, when the RSI enters the oversold zone, it could be indicating a *buy* signal.

Longer time spans in the RSI calculation result in shallower swings, while shorter time spans result in deeper swings. Therefore, the 70/30 combination is inappropriate with a time span other than 14 days. (For example, for a 9-day RSI, an 80/20 combination gives a much better feel for the overbought/oversold extremes than the 70/30 combination.)

So be sure that your RSI is set to a 14-day period!

On your forex trading beauty kit, you usually can find many other forex beauty tools. When I go to a Sephora shop, I usually don't shop out the whole store to complete my beauty kit. The same applies to a forex beauty kit. You don't have to use every single one of the technical analysis tools to make a pretty trade.

However, if you find an interesting tool on your platform that we haven't covered in this book, make sure to visit the Invest Diva Forex Community at www.investdiva.com/forex-community and ask your burning question!

CHAPTER 15

Introducing Mr. Elliott

According to Mr. Elliott, the markets move because of investors' psychology, or crowd psychology. The most basic principle of this theory is that market movements are based on crowd behavior. The crowd's mood swings from optimism to pessimism, and these changes in sentiment create repetitive patterns. After staring at 75 years' worth of data on the charts and markets for days and nights, Mr. Elliott reached his aha moment.

Markets Trade in Repetitive Cycles

Elliott claims to have discovered that a trending market moves in what he calls a five-three wave pattern.

The first five waves are impulsive (moving either up or down).
The next three waves are corrective (generally moving in the opposite direction from the impulsive waves).

Figures 15-1 and 15-2 show how simple the Elliott wave pattern is. The first five waves are numbered from 1 to 5,

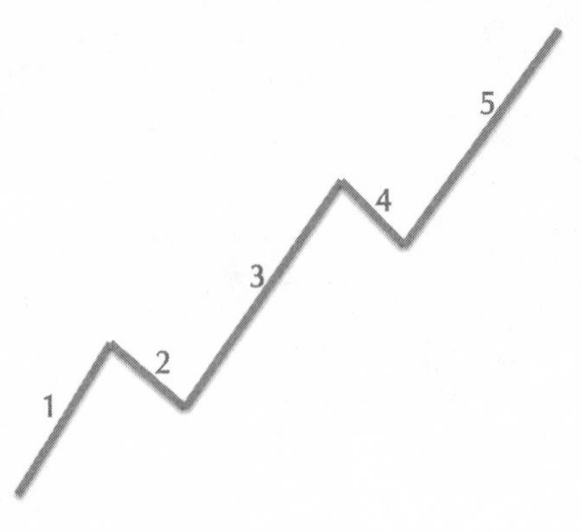

FIGURE 15-1

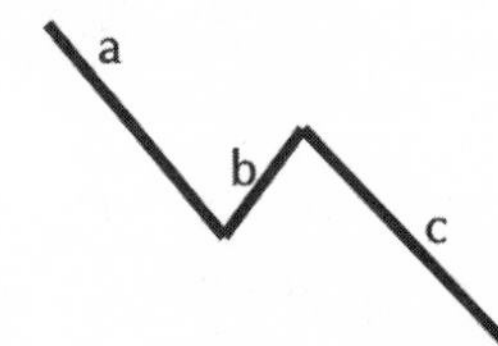

FIGURE 15-2

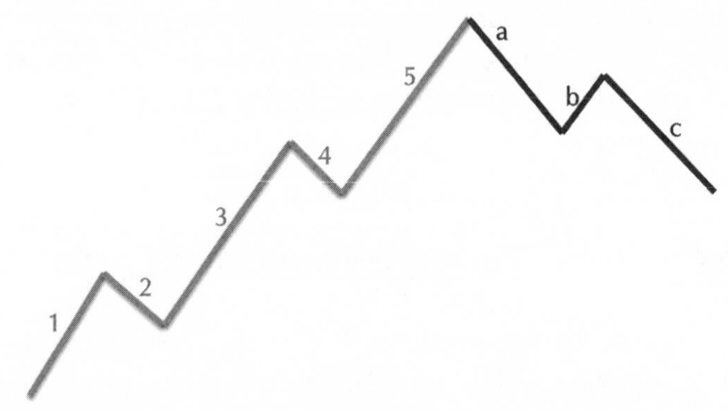

FIGURE 15-3: Elliott Wave in a Bull Market

as shown in Figure 15-1, and the corrective three waves are labeled a, b, and c in Figure 15-2.

Figure 15-3 shows how they come together.

So basically Mr. Elliott believes that every five impulsive waves are followed by three corrective ones. Just like

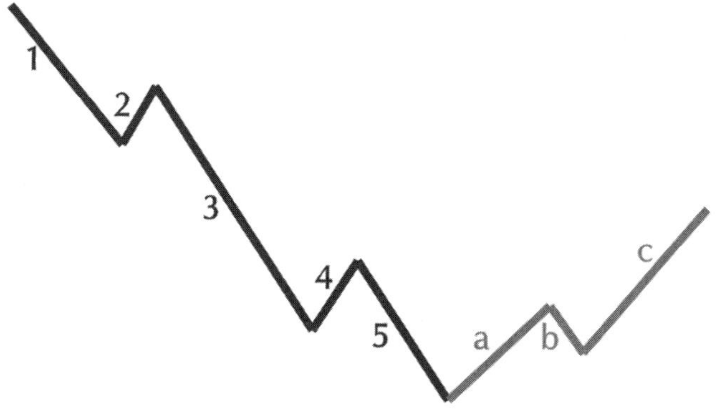

FIGURE 15-4: Elliott Wave in a Bear Market

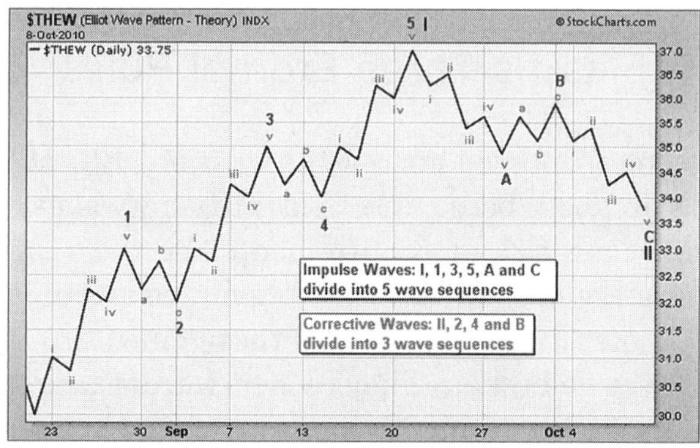

FIGURE 15-5: Elliott Wave Bull Market Subwaves

all patterns, this one works for both bull and bear markets. Figure 15-4 shows how the same five-three wave pattern can look in a bear market.

Now comes the natural question: "Do the Elliott waves always appear as neat and pretty as the images shown here do?" And the anticipated answer is: "No!"

Normally, each Elliott wave is made up of subwaves (see Figures 15-5 and 15-6).

Each of the waves 1, 3, and 5 can be made up of a smaller five-wave impulse pattern, while waves 2 and 4 can be made up of smaller abc corrective patterns. This pattern can repeat itself—well, *forever*!

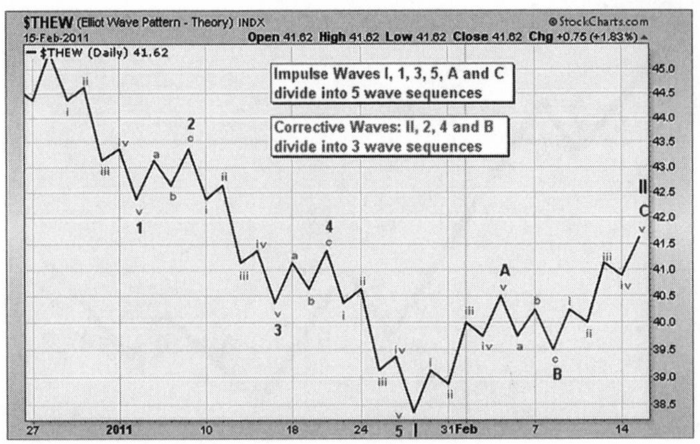

FIGURE 15-6: Elliott Wave Bear Market Subwaves

Elliott's Three Eternal Rules

When it comes to being successful with Mr. Elliott (aka Mr. Right), it's all about being able to identify his waves correctly. Unlike our long list of requirements for the real-life Mr. Right, there are only three rules when it comes to interpreting Mr. Elliott (Figure 15-7). But these rules are hard-core and can never be broken. They're even harder than the vows you take at your wedding. No joke.

Rule 1. Wave 2 can *never* go beyond the start of wave 1.
Rule 2. Wave 3 is *always* one of the longest impulse waves. (It can *never* be the shortest of the three impulse waves.)
Rule 3. Wave 4 can *never* cross into the same price as wave 1.

These three rules are shown in Figure 15-8.

Wave 2 cannot move below the low of wave 1. A break below this low would call for a recount.

Even though wave 3 is typically the longest of the three impulse waves, there is a specific rule that it cannot be the shortest. Wave 1 or wave 5 can be longer than wave 3, but both cannot be longer than wave 3. Elliott wave theory

FIGURE 15-7

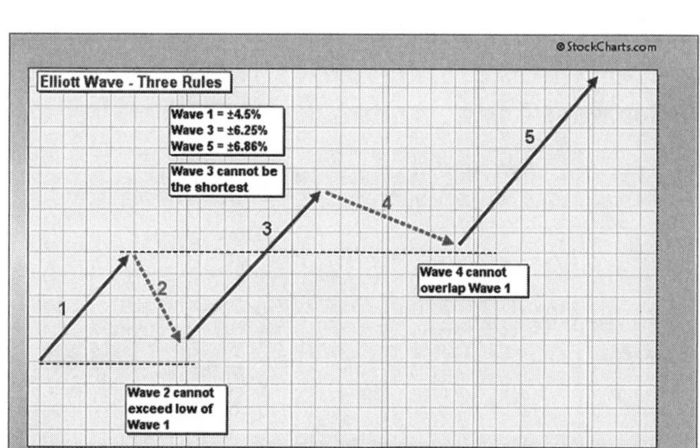

FIGURE 15-8

indicates that wave 3 must exceed the high of wave 1. Failure to exceed this high would call for a recount. *Impulse moves are all about making progress.* Failure to exceed the high of wave 2 would not be making progress.

The third, and final, rule is that wave 4 cannot overlap wave 1, which means that the low of wave 4 cannot go below the high of wave 1. Such a violation would be considered a red flag. It's time for a dramatic breakup and finding a new Mr. Right. In forex words, it's time for a recount.

Elliott's Three Guidelines

Mr. Elliott has also come up with many guidelines. Here we will introduce the three most important ones (see also Figure 15-9). Unlike the three eternal rules, these guidelines can be broken. It's like how you guide your husband to behave around the house, but he won't get into extreme trouble if he forgets to take the garbage out right at 9 p.m.

Guideline 1. When wave 3 is the longest impulse wave, wave 5 will be approximately equal to wave 1.

Guideline 2. The forms of wave 2 and wave 4 are alternative. If wave 2 is a sharp correction, wave 4 will be flat. If wave 2 is flat, wave 4 will be sharp.

Guideline 3. After a five-wave impulse advance, the correction waves a, b, and c usually end in the area of the prior wave 4 low.

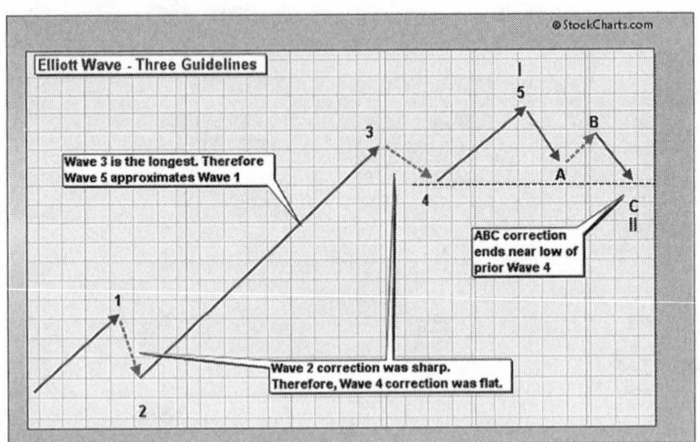

FIGURE 15-9

Fake Forex Party Time—Partying with Elliott

And the wave counting begins. As an Invest Diva learner, we always start checking any type of analysis on a demo account rather than a real live account. So, it's time for another fake forex party!

One thing we should keep in mind about Elliott waves is that they're the best method of analysis when they're used in certain situations. There are times, however, when the Elliott waves are not useful at all. The reason is that the Elliott waves are inherently contrarian, and if you are on a strong trend, you need to know that you are on wave 3 and you *shouldn't* be looking for a higher low. In other words, when you're riding on the Elliott waves, the trend isn't always your friend. Just like any other type of analysis, Elliott wave analysis should be used with other elements of the Invest Diva Diamond analysis, whether those elements are the technical patterns, momentum indicators, candles, or fundamentals.

Anyway, it's time to party again! I'm looking at the EUR/USD daily chart (see Figure 15-10), and I notice something interesting going on starting from April 2012. It seems the pair has been on a general downward move. Let's see if we can catch a number of downward Elliott impulse waves.

FIGURE 15-10: EUR/USD in a Downtrend. Can You Identify the Elliott Waves?

How do I start my count? Exactly the way I would start my analysis in the search for Mr. Right. I will go back to the three eternal Elliott rules and other guidelines to see which one of them I can apply here.

Rule 1. Wave 2 can never go beyond the start of wave 1.

This is shown in Figure 15-11. Looks good so far!

Rule 2. Wave 3 can *never* be the shortest of the impulse waves.

In Figure 15-12, wave 3 looks pretty long!

Rule 3. Wave 4 can *never* cross into the same price as wave 1.

Wave 4 is nowhere even close to wave 1 (see Figure 15-13)! Nice. It seems we've spotted an Elliott behavior in the market sentiment. So how can we make money using this?

Based on Mr. Elliott's theory, we should be expecting a corrective action in the market. We can already see the market moving a bit upward, so this could be our *buy* signal.

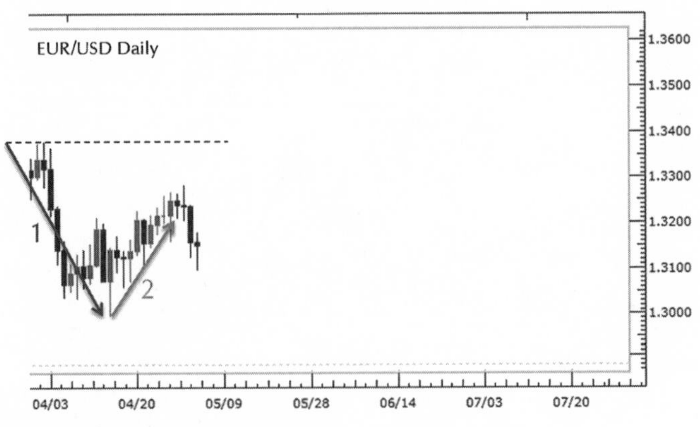

FIGURE 15-11: Two Elliott Waves and Counting

FIGURE 15-12: Wave 3 of Five Elliott Waves Is the Longest Impulse Wave So Far

Let's see what happened next (see Figure 15-14).

Success!!

This was one example of how we can use Elliott wave theory in our trading. Sometimes, after we have identified wave 2 and reconfirmed with technicals and fundamentals, we can ride on a strong trend of the wave 3 and earn some pips.

Obviously, it is now your turn to open your demo account and spot some Elliott waves, whether ones that have already been completed or ones that you suspect are in the process of forming.

FIGURE 15-13: Confirming Elliott Theory's Rule 3: Wave 4 Can *Never* Cross into the Same Price as Wave 1

Contrarian Indicators

Some forex brokers also expose a data-driven indicator based on their client's current positioning on each of the currency pairs. While some big fish in the forex market make their money because they have direct lines into commercial banks like Chase and Citi and into the central banks of other countries, most small traders don't have access to such information. Therefore, the small fish who fail to analyze the market's technicals and fundamentals successfully are usually *wrong*.

Believe it or not, some studies show that more than 70 percent of new small traders lose money. That's probably because they fail to analyze the markets successfully, but

FIGURE 15-14: Elliott Wave Analysis Paid Off in Euro-Dollar Trading

instead trade as if they were gambling. They obviously aren't equipped with the Invest Diva Diamond.

Some retail brokers reveal their clients' positions. We can use this opportunity in our favor and go *against* the majority of the trading crowd. The SSI, or Speculative Sentiment Index, is one of these instruments. The positioning statement, which is the most popular element of the SSI, is a measure of the ratio of the number of traders on FXCM platforms holding long positions in a currency pair to the number of traders holding short positions in the same pair. We can use the SSI as a contrarian indicator and think of it as "fading the crowd," or going in the opposite direction from the majority of retail traders.

The Speculative Sentiment Index can be a powerful tool, but just because it is one of the few leading indicators available to forex traders doesn't mean that it's perfectly predictive. You should still check in with the other points of your Invest Diva Diamond analysis.

One tip in using the SSI would be to first locate strong trends, then filter with the SSI indicator.

As an example, here is an excerpt from my SSI diary for April 2011 on different pairs (see Figure 15-15).*

EUR/USD

In the past week, the majority of traders have been short the pair, resulting in an SSI signal for further gains in the euro/dollar.

» *Price movement result.* EUR/USD has continually gained all week, posting five straight days of gains, totaling nearly 300 pips. A trader would have been successful in this instance had she followed the SSI signal and bought the euro.

GBP/USD

Like the euro traders, the majority of the pound crowd was in a short position for the Pound-Dollar, expecting it to fall. The Speculative Sentiment Index suggested going against the crowd and being long the pair all week.

» *Price movement result.* The pair surged throughout the week, breaking above the resistance at 1.6600 on Wednesday, April 27. Following the SSI signals would have resulted in a successful trade this week, but now it may be too late.

USD/CHF

There has been a sustained fall in the value of the dollar against the Swiss franc, and many traders have been net long the pair for almost a year. Presumably, the thought process might have been that this can't be sustained forever, that the USD/CHF had reached a bottom and prices would turn around soon. However, the SSI has generally been forecasting more USD/CHF losses, including a sustained losing signal in the past week.

» *Price movement result.* The Swissy has fallen for eight consecutive days against the dollar. The pair was below 0.8700 on April 29, after establishing an all-time low at

*Past performance is not indicative of future results.

0.8643 the morning of April 28. The SSI signal was correct in this instance, with the USD/CHF having fallen nearly 200 pips this week.

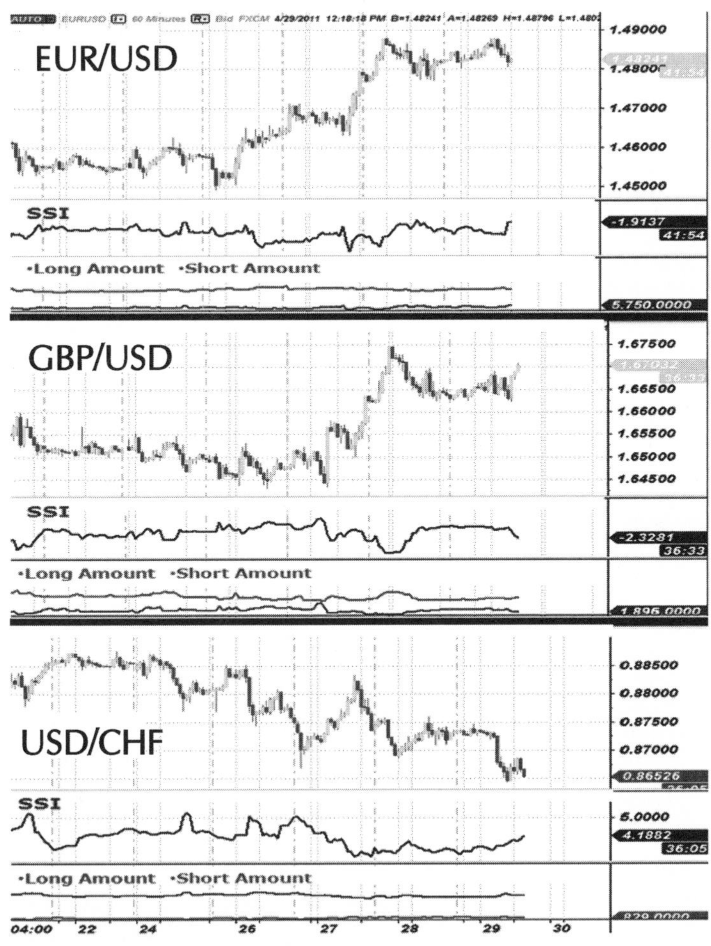

FIGURE 15-15: EUR/USD, GBP/USD, USD/CHF Rates, SSIs, and Long/Short Amounts

PART 3

Winning Diva Stuff

CHAPTER 16

Fundamental Analysis

Fundamental analysis is the second shiny point of the Invest Diva Diamond. It refers to the examination of the underlying forces that affect the well-being of different countries' economies. As with most analysis, the goal is to derive a forecast and profit from future price movements.

Forex Gossip

You probably tune in to E! for the latest entertainment news and celebrity gossip. You also probably check in with the Fashion Police or Style to ensure what people are wearing that is trendy. So where should you tune in to get the latest news, gossip, and rumors in the forex world in order to speculate and confirm your technical analysis?

The answer is, any resource that provides material for fundamental analysis, whether it be the Internet, TV, radio, or even two handsome investors discussing finance loudly on the train or at a restaurant. In Chapter 8, you were told briefly about the importance of fundamental analysis. You were even told how a hot guy is similar to popular and strong currencies. Now let's go into more detail and clarify where you can look for forex gossip and economic news that help the forex puppet master move the currency pairs on the forex dance floor.

Gossip Makers: Whose Speech Moves the Economy?

Are you ready to know the Angelina Jolies and Charlie Sheens of the forex world? They are the people whose words can change the direction of the economy. Thousands of journalists and analysts gather and tune in during their important speeches, interpreting every word or signal that these economic celebrities give away.

The United States has some of the most important economics-related celebrities, but since forex owes its existence to the international community, we have to be aware of foreign economic celebrities as well. Figure 16-1 gives a list of the most influential people in the international economic community as of 2013.

FIGURE 16-1

Who's Who in Economic News

Other than these celebrities, there are tons of other gossip-making organizations and events that make the forex market move. Some of these are given in Figure 16-2. You can compare them to Hollywood, Academy Awards, and Grammy Awards. Every now and then these organizations release a bunch of information and give the journalists something to talk about—while, of course, giving the traders an opportunity to trade!

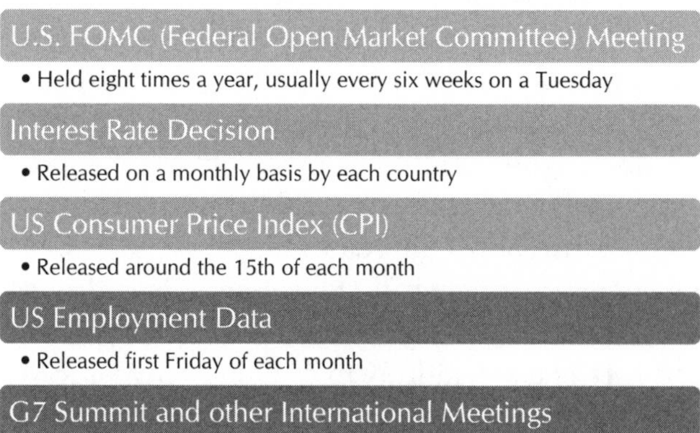

FIGURE 16-2

Gossip Topics: What Are the Hot Figures That Move the Forex Market?

The economic celebrities and organizations talk about different factors that determine the perceived value of a currency. These are called *fundamental data*. By analyzing the fundamentals, you will gain insight into how the currency price action may react to a certain economic event.

Here are some of the most important fundamental data you need to check every time you are trading.

Interest Rates

Interest rates are by far the hottest topic in the forex world. They have a direct effect on the prices of the currencies.

Nothing affects the prices more than interest rates. To sum it up, interest rates are the isht in the forex market!

> When a country raises its interest rates, its currency will strengthen.
>
> When the interest rate falls, it has a negative effect on the currency.

The interest rate is the price that is paid by those who borrow money. It refers to the percentage of an amount of money that was borrowed that is paid to the lender.

Why does a country's currency get stronger when interest rates are higher? Because investors seek more of that currency in order to profit more. The moment a particular country's central bank increases interest rates, investors take this opportunity to shift their money into that country.

Here is an example to make it all easy for you. Let's say that Brad Pitt is a world-known currency investor. Angelina Jolie and Jennifer Aniston are each representative of a central bank, taking care of their own currency (fame). The number of kids can be referred to as interest rates.

It's the year 2005, and Brad Pitt, who is *invested* in Jennifer Aniston, wants to have kids (higher interest rate). Jennifer doesn't want kids (low appetite to raise her interest rate). Angelina Jolie has more appetite to have more kids (appetite to increase her interest rate). Therefore, Brad decides to switch his investment to the one who will ultimately give him more profit: Angelina! And that is how Angelina's assets get all over the media and, for better or worse, her currency rate rises.

Other Characteristics of Interest Rates

- Interest rates dictate the flow of global capital into and out of a country because investors would rather invest in a country with a higher interest rate.
- Interest rates help gauge the status of a country's economy.

Summary: where do you want to park your money? In a country that gives you a higher interest rate! So you start buying more of that currency, and that is how that country's currency gets stronger.

Do Rising U.S. Interest Rates Always Imply a Stronger Dollar?

Here is a catch. The U.S. dollar can be an exception in the interest rate rule for currency values. While we have heard in the past, "The U.S. Federal Reserve . . . confirmed its determination to push U.S. money market interest rates higher to support the dollar,"* according to a study conducted by Douglas R. Mudd, such interpretation may be consistent with short-term analysis but not necessarily always true, especially in recent years and during financial crises.

According to this study, "If the expected rate of U.S. inflation increases because of a sustained acceleration in U.S. money stock growth (while foreign expected rates of inflation remain relatively stable), U.S. interest rates will rise relative to foreign interest rates. The faster pace of U.S. money stock growth also will produce an increase in U.S. spending growth which, in turn, will result in a depreciating foreign exchange value of the dollar.

If the higher expected rate of U.S. inflation also results in an offsetting decline in the expected value of the dollar on foreign exchange markets, no capital inflow will be induced by the rising differential between U.S. and foreign interest rates. Conversely, a sharp deceleration in U.S. money stock growth (not matched by equally restrictive foreign monetary developments) will produce an appreciation of the dollar. In this case, initially U.S. interest rates will rise relative to foreign rates and U.S. spending growth will slow. As a result, the supply of dollars on foreign exchange markets will fall (as U.S. residents reduce spending for foreign goods, services,

*Stewart Fleming and Peter Riddell, "Fed Confirms Aim to Raise Interest Rates in Aid of $," *Financial Times*, July 24, 1979. Also see Robert A. Bennett, "Fed Raises Rates to Aid Dollar," *New York Times*, July 21, 1919.

and securities) relative to the demand for dollars (as foreign investors increase purchases of U.S. securities in response to the higher U.S. interest rate).

However, if the slower U.S. money stock growth is sustained and the expected rate of U.S. inflation is revised downward, U.S. interest rates will decline relative to foreign rates. Further, if the restrictive U.S. monetary actions also produce large upward revisions in the expected future value of the dollar, no capital outflow will result from the declining U.S.-foreign interest rate differential. In this case, an appreciation of the dollar on foreign exchange markets will initially be associated with a rising U.S.-foreign interest rate differential.

Eventually, however, the interest rate differential will decline while the dollar continues to appreciate. So the next time you hear that the United States is increasing its interest rates, don't jump into a buy position for the U.S. dollar. Check in with other points of the Invest Diva Diamond and listen to credible market news analysts before making a final trading decision.

Inflation

Inflation is the reason why your parents paid less than a dollar for a gallon of milk, while you have to pay at least three dollars. Inflation is the general and progressive increase in the prices of the stuff that you buy. Moderate inflation is usually a sign of a strong economy, but you don't want inflation to get out of control! That is why the central bank of each country tries to stabilize inflation-rate indicators such as the CPI (Consumer Price Index).

In fact, inflation rates and interest rates are interconnected. Higher interest rates result in lower overall growth and lower inflation. This happens because when interest rates are higher, consumers and businesses borrow less, save more, and invest less.

When inflation gets high, the Fed (and other central banks) try to control it by raising interest rates. Because of the way inflation affects interest rates, when there is an increase in inflation, this will usually be bullish for the currency of that nation (if that nation's central bank is smart!). The central bank will try to raise interest rates to help stop the increase in inflation. Conversely, if the numbers announced by a central bank indicate a decrease in inflation, this will put downward pressure on the currency because interest rates will be adjusted lower as a result.

GDP (Gross Domestic Product)

GDP is like an annual price tag for a country, showing how valuable the country's economy is and how fast it is growing. GDP shows the overall market value of all the stuff (products and services) that a country produces and is usually gauged on an annual basis. If a country's GDP grows compared to the previous year, that means that its economy has been healthy. It is no wonder that this has a direct relationship to the forex market.

> The country's currency grows stronger when production and revenue (GDP) are high.

Therefore it is important to stay up to date with the GDP for each of the countries whose currency you are trying to trade. Additionally, every time a country announces its GDP, its currency becomes volatile, giving forex traders an opportunity to ride a short-term trade. GDP growth leads to an uptrend in the currency rate.

Unemployment Rate

Yes, even this indicator influences a country's currency rate. The U.S. unemployment rate in particular is a huge forex gossip topic.

How many people do you know who are unemployed even though they are ready and willing to work? I know plenty! This is an indication that the U.S. unemployment rate is high. Beyond the general sense of how unemployment is doing, a more reliable figure is announced on the first Friday of every month, and is closely followed by forex traders. A decline in the unemployment rate means that the economy is doing well and more jobs have been created, which result in a stronger dollar in the United States.

In general, the following holds:

Low unemployment rate = high currency rate High unemployment rate = low currency rate

Nonfarm Payroll

Nonfarm payroll data, also referred to as nonfarm employment change, shows the total number of paid U.S. workers in every business, excluding employees of places like farms, private households, and general government. These data are also analyzed closely because of their importance in identifying the rate of economic growth and inflation. If the nonfarm payroll is expanding, it is a good indication that the economy is growing, and vice versa.

Higher figure for nonfarm payroll = higher currency rate

So how can you use the nonfarm payroll data in trading forex? You first listen to the gossips! Before the actual data are released, a lot of geeky analysts and economists sit together and announce payroll estimates. Then you wait for the data to be announced at around 1:30 in the afternoon (GMT) on the first Friday of the month. If the actual data come in lower than economists' estimates, that usually signals that the U.S. dollar is weakening and that it is a good time to short the dollar (sell it).

Actual nonfarm payroll number > forecast = good for currency

Economic Figures and Forex Trading

Each of the previously mentioned economic figures can affect the forex market. The economic figures are available on many economic news sites, such as Bloomberg, Yahoo Finance, MarketWatch, and ForexFactory. Figure 16-3 provides a summary and a cheat sheet for your fundamental analysis that will enable you to instantly figure out the direction of the currency you are trying to trade.

BUY Signal	SELL Signal
The moment the market expects interest rates to go up	The moment the market expects interest rates to go down
Inflation increases more than expectation	Inflation decreases more than expectation
GDP rises*	GDP falls*
Unemployment rate falls*	Unemployment rate rises*
Higher than expected nonfarm payroll*	Lower than expected nonfarm payroll*

FIGURE 16-3

*Depending on the economic situation, there are exceptions. That is why you should make a habit of listening to reliable analysts such as Invest Diva on a regular basis, and comparing your ideas with other forex traders on the Forex Community.

Currencies and Fundamentals

How does each currency react to fundamental news? Since fundamental analysis is only one point of the Invest Diva Diamond analysis, we should not take a fundamental element's ability to move the market for granted. But experience shows that the major fundamental elements that are capable to move each major currency are as follows (see Figures 16-4 to 16-6):

FIGURE 16-4: USD: The Oprah Winfrey (the Number-One Ranked Celebrity, According to *Forbes*) of the Currencies

Rises When

- Interest rates rise.
- GDP rises.
- Inflation rate rises.
- U.S. nonfarm employment rises.
- And so on.

Declines When

- Interest rates decline.
- Terrorism occurs in the United States or the Middle East.
- Other countries have a stronger economy than the United States.

FIGURE 16-5: EUR: The Jennifer Lopez (Second Most Popular Celebrity, According to *Forbes*) of the Currencies

Rises When

- Eurozone interest rates rise.
- The U.S. economy falls.
- The Eurozone economy grows.

Declines When

- Eurozone interest rates fall.
- One or more countries in the Eurozone are in economic trouble.

FIGURE 16-6: GBP: The Queen Elizabeth of the Currencies (Her Country Is in the Eurozone, but Her Currency Is Too Cool to Join the Euro)

Rises When

- UK interest rates rise.
- Oil prices rise.
- Favorable financial indicator movement occurs.

Declines When

- GDP or other important financial figures fall.
- Terrorism occurs in the UK.
- Middle Eastern relationships weaken.

What's the Schedule Like?

So how are you going to keep up with all these events, announcements, and releases? We all know that knowledge is power, and this remains true when it comes to knowing the schedule of the events that move the forex market. Those are the times you want to check in your calendar and make sure you are trading! A successful Forex Diva pays close attention to the economic gossips because of the probability that what they say will affect the direction of the forex market.

The Kardashians may be entertaining and the media make a lot of noise about the family's every move, but paying close attention to *that* kind of gossip won't make you any money.

The most important information you need on an economic calendar is the schedule of each country's economic figures announcements (duh!). You need a calendar that shows you the previous result of each event and the forecast figure. It is very helpful if the calendar points out the importance of each particular event, as well as which currency or currencies are going to be influenced by it.

For a short-term trade, the moment the actual number of the announcement appears on the calendar, you can decide on the direction of your trade by analyzing the gap between the forecast and the actual result.

"Can I use my Facebook calendar?" you ask. Yeah, there probably is a Facebook app for this purpose out there, but there are also simpler ways. If you just Google (or Bing) the term "Economic Calendar," the windows of endless economic calendars will open in front of you. Different websites offer slightly different events on their economic calendars, so following a number of economic calendars will enable you to get more knowledge, and, eventually, more power!

What Does a Forex Economic Calendar Look Like?

These are the kinds of things you will typically see in an economic calendar's columns (see Figures 16-7 and 16-8):

- *Event.* The event's name, including the data released and the organization that will release them, usually in an abbreviated format.
- *Time.* The date and time of the event. In most economic calendars, this is automatically set to the GMT time zone, but you can usually change it back to the time zone of the city that you are currently in.
- *Currency.* Which currency will be most influenced by these data.
- *Importance.* How much influence these data will have on the currency.

» *Previous.* Data from the last release.
» *Actual.* This number is updated once the data are out.
» *Forecast.* A speculated number by the economists whose job it is to wonder about and predict the markets all the time.

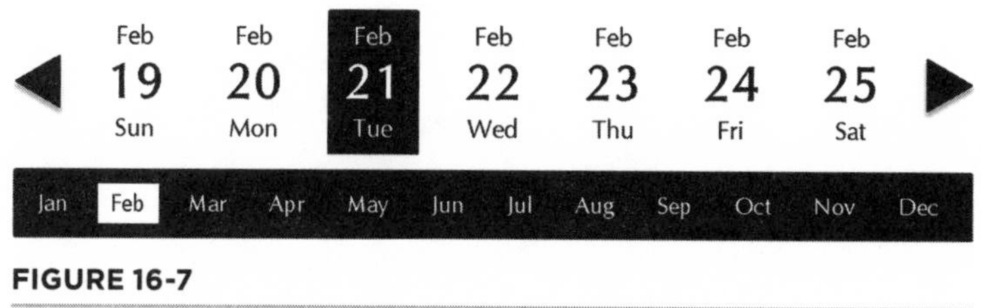

FIGURE 16-7

Time	Currency	Event	Importance	Actual	Forecast	Previous
02:00		NZD Reserve Bank of New Zealand 2-Year Inflation Expectation (1Q)	High	2.5%		2.8%
04:30		JPY All Industry Activity Index (MoM) (DEC)	Medium	1.3%	1.5%	-1.0%
07:00		CHF Imports (MoM) (JAN)	Low	3.6%		8.4%
09:30		GBP Public Sector Net Borrowing (Pounds) (JAN)	Medium	-10.7B	-9.1B	11.1B
13:30		CAD Retail Sales Less Autos (MoM) (DEC)	Medium	0.0%	0.1%	0.4%
13:30		USD Chicago Fed Nat Activity Index (JAN)	Medium	0.22	0.21	0.54
15:00		EUR Euro-Zone Consumer Confidence (FEB A)	Medium	-20.2	-20.1	-20.7

FIGURE 16-8

As you can see from Figure 16-8, even in one day, there are tons of events that affect almost all the major currencies. And this is not even a complete list!

The events may seem to be written in a secret language that only finance geeks would understand. But there's no need to worry. A strong economic calendar will provide an option that expands underneath the title of the event and explains what exactly is going to happen during the event and what to expect. Such calendars even tell you what kind of results will lead to what kind of a movement in the market, so you don't really need to be an economist to use the fundamentals in your Invest Diva Diamond analysis.

CHAPTER 17

Sentimental Analysis

A sentiment is a general thought, feeling, or sense. A popular fashion trend is an obvious example of sentiment: the feelings and emotions of fashionistas concerning a specific design. In free markets, sentiment refers to the feelings and emotions of market participants. In the forex market, all of the participants' feelings concerning a specific currency pair may result in a dominant psychology that is either optimistic or pessimistic. Some hard-core sentiment analysts believe that the price itself is solely a result of where the collective psychology lies in terms of optimism or pessimism. Invest Diva thinks that sentiment is one of the main factors affecting a currency pair's price, but it is not the only one. Sentiment analysis should be carefully added as one of the major points of the Invest Diva Diamond analysis. Especially when you are trading in a shorter time frame and the psychological state of the forex party experiences peaks (bullish extremes) and valleys (bearish extremes), these sentiment extremes can greatly affect the movements of the currency pair.

There are different ways to gauge the sentiment of the forex market. Some sentiment indicators are based on past prices, and some of them show less of a lag than others. While past prices can give us an idea of future prices, it is always good to check in with the current sentiment as well.

How to Gauge the Sentiment

One way of understanding the market sentiment is simply to observe how the market is performing. For example, let's say you are trading EUR/USD based on a continuation pattern around a big event risk. The pair has been selling off for two days, and you also have a short position. You are getting close to the event risk, but the currency pair is not falling enough to reach your target, and it is consolidating. This shows that the momentum is not on your side, and you may consider getting off your trade.

According to Jamie Saettele, author of *Sentiment in the Forex Market*, "Crowds move markets and at major market turning points, the crowds are almost always wrong. When crowd sentiment is overwhelmingly positive or overwhelmingly negative—it's a signal that the trend is exhausted and the market is ready to move powerfully in the opposite direction. Sentiment has long been a tool used by equity, futures, and options traders."

In my opinion, the technical indicators can sometimes also help us understand the market sentiment. Heck, the indicators and patterns were developed (and invented) by observing the habits of the traders that repeat themselves over and over again in any charted market, such as those for stocks, bonds, and commodities. Most of the time, we can use the same indicators in the forex market.

Mr. Elliott was one of the market observers who discovered these underlying social principles and developed the analytical tool called Elliott waves, discussed in Chapter 15.

CHAPTER 18

Capital Analysis

This is the most important point of the Invest Diva Diamond analysis for ensuring a relaxed and stress-free trade. As mentioned before, you should invest only your expendable money in forex. Now, what exactly does this mean? That depends on your financial goals for your life. Is your goal to be a homeowner? Do you have a desperate need to buy a car? Are you able to feed your children healthy food? Are you on track with savings for your children's college expenses? Your expendable money is the money that you can spend on things other than your living essentials. While you may be able to make enough money to buy a house by trading forex, the risk of losing all your savings could be as great. I wouldn't take that risk if I didn't have sufficient capital. Therefore, your forex investment capital is directly correlated with the level of your income and your savings.

It is not recommended that you invest more than 30 percent of your monthly savings in the forex market. That is 30 percent of the money that remains after you have deducted your essential living expenses. With Invest Diva's saving plans, you can also cut down on the money that you would spend on beauty care, groceries, entertainment, or luxury items in order to maximize the potential of a larger return on investment in forex, which will ultimately bring you a greater ability to spend the next month.

To sum it up, you can learn to save. Then you can invest 30 percent of your monthly savings and aim to make money with that money.

This brings us to the next topic, which is finding out how much money you are eligible to invest in forex, if any.

Let's explore the lifestyles of real women and see whether they are eligible to trade and, if they are, the amount of money that is safe for them to invest in forex. We have changed the names of some of our survey participants to protect their privacy. Find the one that you can relate to the most.

Real Women's Trading Eligibility

Lily: An Ideal Forex Diva Candidate

Meet Lily. She is a stay-at-home mom with two boys, 11 and 15 years of age. Her husband, Tom, is the breadwinner, and their annual after-tax household income is $80,000.

That gives them a monthly income of about $6,600. They have both paid off their college loans, and they have no debt. Tables 18-1 and 18-2 give their household expenses, divided into two categories: essentials and extras.

TABLE 18-1: Average Essential Monthly Expenses

Groceries	$1,000
Housing	$1,200
Vehicle	$200
Utilities, fuel, and public services	$390
Housekeeping supplies	$150
Healthcare	$185
Education	$50
Total	**$3,175**

TABLE 18-2: Average Extra Monthly Expenses

Eating out	$400
Entertainment	$50
Apparel and services	$400
Beauty care	$40
Alcoholic beverages	$50
Reading	$30
Vacation	$500
Gifts	$50
Total	**$1,520**

Total monthly expenses = $4,695.

Monthly income > monthly expenses

Lily's total monthly average household expenses are about $2,000 less than her household's monthly income.

Is she eligible to trade forex? Yes.

She can also save some extra cash by following the Invest Diva saving tips. Her family's gross monthly savings are $2,500. She can consider investing 30 percent of their monthly savings in the forex market after gaining her Forex Diva title. That is $600 per month.

Shirley Should Probably Avoid Trading Forex

Should Shirley consider forex trading to earn some extra cash? The answer is no. Here is why.

Shirley and her husband, Richard, are both retired and enjoy taking care of their grandchildren during the day. They lost a large portion of their savings during a financial crisis, and they have about $70,000 left in their bank account. Including withdrawals from their 401(k)s, their annual household income is about $20,000. Fortunately they have no debt, but they are hoping to buy a larger house soon so that they can fit all their children and grandchildren during the holidays. Tables 18-3 and 18-4 give their monthly expenses.

TABLE 18-3: Average Essential Monthly Expenses

Groceries	$340
Housing	$450
Utilities, fuel, and public services	$200
Housekeeping supplies	$150
Healthcare	$0—Medicare paid by government
Total	**$1,140**

TABLE 18-4: Average Extra Monthly Expenses

Eating out	$150
Entertainment	$40
Apparel and services	$175
Beauty care	$10
Alcoholic beverages	$20
Vacation	$40
Gifts	$25
Total	**$460**

Monthly income = $1,600

Essential + extra monthly expenditures = $1,600

Monthly income = monthly expenditures

Should Shirley invest part of their savings in forex? No, because they want to buy a larger house, so the profit that they can take from trading forex can't really help. Now if she wants to trade just as a hobby with a maximum of $50 per month, that should be harmless. She can get together with Richard and enjoy attending a forex party while the grandchildren are not around!

Linda—a Corporate Tax Lawyer

Linda is a 33-year-old corporate tax lawyer. She is currently single, and her gross income after tax is $180,000 per year. She has paid off all her college loans and has $100,000 in her savings account. She is thinking of buying a house in the suburbs in the future, and she is also saving money for her potential dream wedding after she finds Mr. Right (probably not the Mr. Right we talked about when introducing Mr. Elliott).

Is she eligible to trade forex? Yes.

As seen in Tables 18-5 and 18-6, her total average monthly expenses are $7,360, which is less than her average monthly income of $15,000. After getting her Forex Diva title, she is eligible to invest in forex. However, considering her goals of buying a house and throwing a dream wedding, she might want to lower the percentage of her forex investment down to 20 percent instead of 30.

TABLE 18-5: Average Essential Monthly Expenses

Groceries	$100
Housing: taxes + mortgage + maintenance	$5,200
Utilities, fuel, and public services	$60
Total	**$5,310**

TABLE 18-6: Average Extra Monthly Expenses

Eating out	$700
Entertainment	$400
Apparel and services	$300
Beauty care	$50
Alcoholic beverages	$60
Reading	$40
Vacation	$500
Total	**$2,050**

Total monthly expenses: $7,360

Total monthly income after taxes: $15,000

Eligible to trade forex: yes

Recommended monthly forex investment: $3,000

Miriam Gantman, Tutor and PhD Candidate at Columbia University

Age: 29
Monthly income: $1,000 to $4,000
Children: none
Debt: $70,000 in school loans
Savings: Not that much
Future earning potential: High
Future investment desire: Yes

Tables 8-7 and 8-8 give Miriam's monthly expenses.

TABLE 8-7: Average Essential Monthly Expenses

Groceries	$250
Housing	$900
Vehicle	$340
Utilities, fuel, and public services	$60
Household operations	$50
Housekeeping supplies	$10
Healthcare	$650
Education	$0 for now
Total	**$2,260**

TABLE 8-8: Average Extra Monthly Expenses

Eating out	$200-$300
Entertainment	$400
Apparel and services	$400-$600
Beauty care	$50
Alcoholic beverages	$0
Reading	$50
Vacation	It's a once a year thing, so $3,500 per year
Gifts	$0
Total	**$1,100-$4,900**

Minimum monthly income = $1,000 < average essential monthly expenses = $2,260

Maximum monthly income = $4,000 > average essential monthly expenses = $2,260

Maximum monthly income = $4,000 > average essential monthly expenses + minimum extra monthly expenses = $3,360

Depending on her monthly income and monthly savings, Miriam could consider investing 10 percent of her monthly savings in the forex market, with a 2 percent risk appetite.

Real Forex Party Time!

It's now your turn to calculate your eligibility to invest in forex. And no, this time our forex party is not fake. Be as honest and realistic as possibile when taking the forex eligibility test that follows, and calculate the amount of money you can safely invest in forex without endangering your future financial goals. If you need additional assistance with your calculation, just subscribe on InvestDiva.com and apply for a Forex Diva Eligibility Test.

Name:
Occupation:
Age:
Annual household income:
Children:
Debt:
Savings:
Future investment desire:

AVERAGE ESSENTIAL MONTHLY EXPENSES

Groceries	
Housing	
Vehicle	
Utilities, Fuel, and public services	
Household operations	
Housekeeping supplies	
Healthcare	
Education	
Total	

AVERAGE EXTRA MONTHLY EXPENSES

Eating out	
Entertainment	
Apparel and services	
Beauty care	
Alcoholic beverages	
Reading	
Vacation	
Total	

- My minimum monthly income = $__________
- My average essential monthly expenses = $__________
- My minimum monthly income is __________ than my average essential monthly expenses.
  - ☐ Larger
  - ☐ Smaller
- My maximum monthly income = $__________
- My average essential monthly expenses = $__________
- My maximum monthly income is __________ than my average essential monthly expenses plus my extra monthly expenses.
  - ☐ Larger
  - ☐ Smaller
- I am __________ to trade forex.
  - ☐ Eligible
  - ☐ Not eligible
- If answered "eligible" in the previous question, my recommended monthly forex investment is $__________.

So, are you eligible to trade forex? If yes, then welcome aboard! If not, you can wait a couple of years and retake this eligibility test. You never know.

Stop and Limit

One basic method for managing your forex investment is setting stop and limit orders. This means simply "ordering" your broker to fulfill your trade at a specific price and to get you out of a trade if you are losing more than you can afford.

"Do I have to shout, 'stop!' or yell, 'limit!' when I'm on the phone with my broker?" you ask.

You could, especially if you are upset with your boyfriend or husband and are looking for a scapegoat. But there is a much easier, healthier, and more professional method of doing this.

As we mentioned before, you make money by buying one currency low against another currency and selling it high against the same currency. Since the currency pairs are very active, jumping up and down, a Forex Diva calculates her risk appetite and possible profit by going through all the steps of the Invest Diva Diamond analysis. Then, before she clicks on "Place Order" on her broker's platform, she clicks on the "Advanced" button, where she can find the option of setting a stop or a limit order (see Figure 18-1). Obviously we advise you to use both to ensure a more profitable and less risky investment.

Limit order. This order automatically executes your trade when the currency pair reaches the particular price at which you wish to take profit.

Stop order. This type of order automatically closes your position if the currency pair moves against you by an amount that exceeds the amount of your risk appetite.

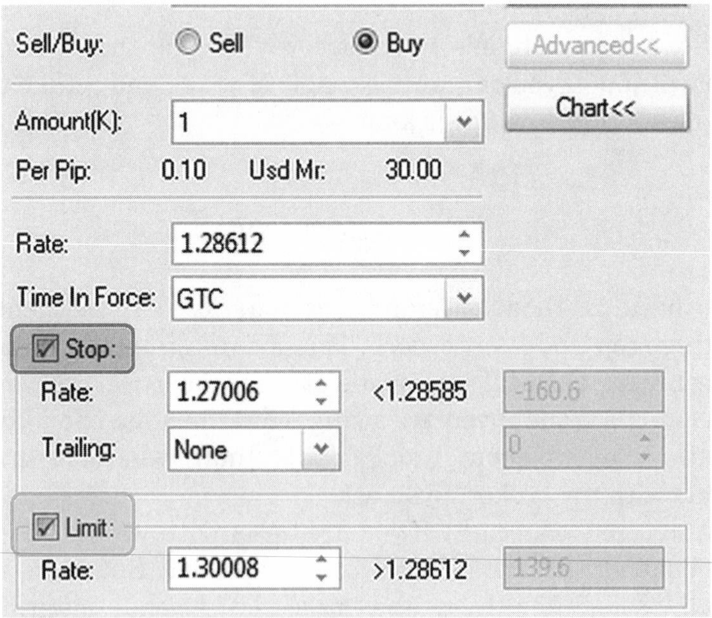

FIGURE 18-1

Remember

If you are entering a *buy* position (going long), your stop order should be smaller than the price at which you enter the trade. Your limit order should be larger.

If you are entering a *sell* position (going short), your stop order should be larger than the current price. Your limit order should be smaller.

How Much Risk Should I Take When I'm Trading Forex?

Many analysts advise that your risk per trade should always be a small percentage of your total capital. A good starting percentage could be 2 percent of your available trading capital. For example, if you have $5,000 in your account, the maximum loss allowable should be no more than $100. By analyzing the market from all points of the Invest Diva Diamond analysis, you can stack the odds in your favor and then manage your risk per trade.

Managing risk per trade literally means setting your stop and limit orders, which we talked about previously.

In order to decide the size of your trade, allowable risk, advisable leverage, and so on, you can simply use the following magic formula:

Loss (or profit)/pips (stop or take profit) = size

Does this look confusing? Let's take it one piece at a time. Let's say you have done all your market analysis, and you are confident that the markets are going to move in a certain direction for a certain number of pips. Now you have two options:

1. Choose your trade size based on the *profit* you think you can make.
2. Choose your trade size based on the *loss* you can afford to risk.

Choosing your trade size based on the possible profit is how men usually trade. They are more goal-oriented and challenge the market to win.

Which of these choices do you think Invest Diva would recommend? If you said number two, you are a true *Forex Diva*! Although it may sound a bit negative, it's always better to be safe than sorry. So as a Forex Diva, we always calculate our investment capital based on risk management calculations.

So here is one scenario. After you are done with your market analysis, it is time for you to decide how much loss you are willing to risk in order to gain that profit. First, you should calculate the size of your trade. What you need to do is to simply put the numbers into the following magic formula and find the size of your trade:

$$\frac{\text{This is how much I'm willing to risk losing}}{\text{This is the distance between my stop loss \& my entry order}} = \text{This can be my trade size}$$

You can also put in any two of the three terms to get the third. In case you don't have enough money to cover for the size, then you can move on to using leverage, keeping in mind that you may lose the exact same amount. Therefore, you need to feel comfortable with investing that amount of money.

In Chapter 21, when we discuss case studies, we will go through a number of trading examples so that you can see vividly how to analyze the market and use the formula just given.

How to Manage Your Tax

Forex taxation and how your gains on investment become your tax liability is something that you should ultimately discuss with your accountant. Every year before tax day, you should make a copy of your trading report for the year, in which you can find all your trades, profits, and losses.

According to Robert A. Green, CPA and CEO of www.GreenTraderTax.com, "Retail spot forex contracts in major currencies may qualify for lower 60/40 tax rates in Section 1256g (foreign currency contracts), riding the coattails of interbank forward contracts—after making a valid opt-out election from Section 988 (foreign currency transactions). The new CFTC forex trading rules . . . may help your case since the CFTC Chairman's 'Gensler letter' implies the term 'spot forex' is a misnomer since it's 'futures-like.'"

Robert continues, "Financial market regulators and their rules are different from the IRS and their tax rules. The IRS may not respect these additional arguments, since regulations don't necessarily set precedent for tax purposes."

Save the Money You Can Afford to Invest

At my workshops, before I jump into forex education, I always assign a 15-minute "money-saving-tips" discussion with my divas, where we share secrets on how to save money while continuing to live a glam life. We continue learning every week. Here are money-saving secrets from real women. Again, we have changed some of the names for privacy reasons.

Naomi: Save Your Life *and* Your Money!

Turn your head to the left, then to the right, when:

1. The waiter offers you the dessert menu.
   - Is the sweetness really worth the extra calories?
2. The bartender asks if you'd like another drink when you're having a girls' night out.
   - According to *The Independent*, the health effects of alcohol go far beyond embarrassing yourself in public or a nasty headache the morning after. It affects almost *every important part of a woman's body*—in a *bad* way!

A woman's risk of *breast cancer* rises by 6 percent for each extra alcoholic drink she has, on average, every day. In the long term, regular heavy drinking can lead to peptic ulcers, inflammation of the pancreas, and cancer, while alcohol impairs the small intestine's ability to process nutrients and vitamins. Alcohol can also damage sperm and *egg production* and the ability of a fertilized egg to implant in the *womb.* The *liver* has to deal with the highest concentrations of damaging chemicals. Excess drinking can also cause hepatitis, which can be fatal. Both hepatitis and cirrhosis can cause the *skin* to become jaundiced, as well as causing anemia, *lower back pain*, and severe swelling of the abdomen. Alcohol can also cause *brain* cells to swell. Permanent disruption of dopamine levels can cause depression and increases the risk of stroke by 42 percent, according to research. Alcohol is the main reason behind a recent steep rise in cases of *mouth cancers*, the charity Cancer Research has warned. Drinking can also weaken muscles and cause pain and spasms in the *arms and legs.* The damage to the body's central nervous system from alcohol can cause permanent tingling or numbness in the *fingers and toes.* Alcohol causes temporary disruption of the body's antidiuretic mechanism, which is why there are always long queues outside the toilets of pubs and clubs. This disruption also means that people who are drinking a lot are likely to sweat more as their bodies try to absorb the alcohol and adjust to the dehydrating effect that it has. You may look shiny and full of color the night before, but the morning after, your body will struggle to rehydrate and will draw fluid from the *top layers of skin*, leaving the surface of your face dry and flaky. In the long term, alcohol weakens the *heart* muscle and its ability to pump blood through the body. It causes high blood pressure, thereby increasing the risk of heart attacks and strokes.

Do you really need more reason to be satisfied with one glass of wine, which can protect against colds, Alzheimer's, and heart disease?

3. The shopkeeper asks if you want a packet of cigarettes like you always do. Do you know how much money you can save by quitting smoking? I'm not even going to get started on the health benefits.

Susan: Gain Your Kitchen Confidence!

1. Get a cookbook that offers 20-minute cooking recipes.
2. Take your breakfast and lunch to work.
3. Invite friends over instead of dining out. (They will return the favor someday!)
4. Start hosting a potluck with your girlfriends every few months.
5. Use a Crock-Pot to make a meal for the week so that you can bring food for lunch every day.

Elena: Pop That Thang

Here is Elena's take on saving money outdoors.

1. Go running with your gal pals instead of grabbing dinner out. You'll meet more guys that way, trust me.
2. Work out at home or exercise outdoors instead of paying for the gym.

Green exercise is actually good for the body and the spirit and is actually a scientific phenomenon that is being studied all over the world. According to Dr. Alan C. Logan, coauthor of *Your Brain on Nature: The Science of Nature's Influence on Your Health, Happiness and Vitality*, a number of clinicians are now prescribing so-called vitamin G for its mind and body benefits. "Any therapeutic intervention that can even put a dent in an individual's perception of stress, while also improving mental outlook, creativity and cognitive function, is surely worthy of consideration," Dr. Logan says.

Elena continues, if you live in New York:

3. Learn how to swing dance and salsa for free in Union Square in summertime.

4. Find a trustworthy promoter who can get you into nightclubs with free drinks and more.
5. Sign-up on www.nycinv.com to receive e-mails about discounts and free Best of New York Invitations.

Maria: Save Some Dough in the Grocery Store

1. Eat a snack before you walk in.
2. Plan a list beforehand to avoid buying unnecessary food that will eventually rot in your fridge.
3. Buy large containers of liquid soap, laundry detergent, dishwashing liquid, and the like for a cheaper price per pound and refill your beautiful small container as needed.
4. Visit the website of your favorite store to see what will be on sale this week.
5. Stay away from convenient packages.
6. Drink tap water and help protect the environment too!

Be More Cautious with Your Gift-Giving Habits

Leah: My daughter is 11, and she keeps getting invited to parties throughout the year. Before I knew it, I was spending more than my budget allowed on gifts for her classmates and for her. That's when I decided to get in charge of my gift-giving habits. Even if others spend more on my child, I decided not to feel pressured to match them dollar for dollar if it's not in my budget. For me, the numbers that work are between $10 and $20 for her regular classmates, and between $20 and $25 for her closest friends.

Helen: Do you really need all the gifts people bring for your kids? Often I get the exact same gift from two different people. In those cases, I save the effort of going all the way to the shop and changing the gift, and simply pass it on to another person. It may not be super personalized, but chances are that the person is going to love it!

Save Money on Mani/Pedis

Kate's secret for saving hundreds of dollars in the salon is very simple: treat yourself to an at-home manicure. She happens to be one of those girls who can't fall asleep if her nails aren't beautifully painted. Her nails haven't seen an unpolished day in years. One reason for this is that she has superweak nails, and the base coat helps enormously in preventing her nails from breaking. You know how much time and money she saves by avoiding the journey to the nail salon? Plenty!

Here are some simple steps you can take to give yourself a manicure while watching your favorite TV show, or as you watch over your trade on your forex account.

1. Remove your old nail polish thoroughly.
2. File your nails before you jump into the shower.
3. Remove your cuticles before you finish your shower, after you have spent enough minutes under hot water for your skin to get softer.
4. Apply moisturizer to your hands. Actually, don't stop at your hands. Did you know that one of the main reasons for developing premature wrinkles is lack of moisture in your skin? Make it a habit to use body lotion and facial cream every time you get out of the shower, before dry air can reach your skin.
5. Turn on the TV, log onto your Facebook account, or open your favorite book (*Invest Diva's Guide to Making Money in Forex*).
6. Apply base coat or nail support.
7. Apply polish or French lines.
8. Apply top coat.
9. Enjoy your TV show, Facebook newsfeed, trade, or book while allowing your nails to dry.

Tip 1. For faster drying, you can use a hair dryer set on "cold" and the strongest power. Five minutes per hand will allow you to leave home immediately without screwing up your nail polish.

Tip 2. Buy high-quality nail polish, base coat, and top coat so that you can enjoy your shiny nails for a longer period before you have to go through the whole procedure again.

Samantha: Let It Last Longer

"When I get a mani/pedi, I always choose a color I already own so that I can do touch-ups myself. Additionally, I always finalize the salon treatment by adding a layer of UV cut top coat and make it last three to four weeks before needing to go back to the salon."

Michelle: Learn from Granny!

1. Always have snacks, an apple, and a banana in your purse when you go window shopping. I'm not cheap, but I'd rather spend more on things that add actual value to my life.
2. Avoid getting that overpriced, delicious-smelling popcorn in the movies. Not only will you save your monthly cash, but you also will do your body a favor by not letting pure fried butter into your vessels.

Tanya: The Magic of My Water Bottle

It's amazing how much money my water bottle has saved me. I'm never without my water bottle, so I never have to stop and buy water. Any fast food restaurant has water in the soda machine, and I just fill up my bottle on the go.

Erica: Fix It

1. Repair your shoes instead of throwing them away. Your closet won't have space for a new pair of shoes that way.
2. Get a tailor to resize your clothes after you lose all that weight by avoiding dessert and alcohol (two birds with one stone, baby!).

Aya: Before You Throw, Put It on the List

Getting cash back for your old stuff? There is no harm in it, and you may actually really help somebody out! After I decide that I'm done using something or when I'm moving, I always take nice photos of it and put an ad on Craigslist, eBay, or my building's board or online listing. Even if I don't end up selling it, I often end up making some new friends!

Jean: Set It and Forget It

Every time I get a paycheck, I transfer a fixed amount to savings, investing, and debt repayment. I also charge monthly utility bills automatically to a credit card (and pay them off the same month) to build a credit history without any manual effort. The set-it-and-forget-it mentality helps me focus on my investments, including the ones in the forex market.

Nicole: Be an Early Bird

1. Many social events and parties offer a discount if you buy tickets in advance. Buy it first and then be the leader in convincing your friends to join you.
2. Buy your airplane tickets early and don't worry about being alone on the plane. Your friends may take forever to make the final decision. Here you have the choice: do you want to save 100 bucks, or do you really need to have someone on the plane with you?

Kristine: Should You Let TV Rule Your Life?

I'm not Amish or old-fashioned, but in my 25 years of life, I have never had a TV. My parents never let me have one, and after I went independent, I never felt the urge to get one. When I compare my lifestyle to that of my friends who have TV, I notice that not only do I save $80 or more per month for cable and $500 or more every four years to upgrade to the latest flat-screen TV, but also I don't let TV rule my life. I never have to rush home to catch my 8 p.m. TV show. I can simply watch the shows I want online by spending minimum amounts on Hulu or Netflix.

Kiana: Never Be in Credit Card Debt

Personally, I try never to buy anything unless I know I'll have the money to pay for it at least by the end of the month. I was amazed to learn that many people just ignore their debt and let it accumulate. This also has become an issue nowadays during the economic turndown. If you don't pay your credit cards in a timely manner, you need to bear more expenses, as you will face many additional charges such as late payment charges, over-credit-limit charges, and finance charges. All these charges will accrue on your balance in addition to your existing fees and interest. The longer you drag out paying, the more debt you need to bear. Furthermore, when you quit or postpone paying your debt, banks may take legal action against you. That's too much drama for simple laziness, I'd say.

Now, I understand that there are always exceptions—situations where you just can't afford to pay off your debt in a timely manner. Maybe your husband is out of a job, you have student loans, you are getting a divorce, or you are a single mom. But more often we simply get into debt by spending more than we are making on things like clothing, nights out, eating out, drinking, cabs, and health expenses.

Here are some tips from real women on how they got out of debt in a short period of time:

- Stay with family for a few months to avoid paying rent.
- Move to a smaller apartment or rent a room in a house.
- Sell your old car and use public transportation until you are debt-free.
- Pay your debt over a long period of time through the snowball method, paying off the smallest balance first, then the next smallest, and so on.
- Move to a less desirable neighborhood.
- Cut cable.
- Limit data on your phone.
- Track all your spending.
- Get a Christmas gift from your parents.
- Read a book on getting out of debt and stick to it.
- Avoid taking vacations and cut back on "fun" spending.
- Make multiple payments each month, regardless of the bill's due date.

» Get creative: get a second job to increase your income! Wait tables, deliver pizza, freelance, babysit, participate in focus groups, clean houses, walk dogs—whatever it takes to get debt-free!

Work It, Girl

Serena: Get Promoted

Don't downplay your success. Know when it is time for a promotion. You are ready to be promoted when you have mastered the position above you. More important, ask for it!

Michelle: Negotiate!

According to the book *Women Don't Ask: Negotiation and the Gender Divide* by Linda Babcock and Sara Laschever, women who consistently negotiate their salary earn at least $1 million more during their careers than women who don't. And 20 percent of women say that they never negotiate at all, even when they know they should.

Sonia: Use Your Employee Benefits

I know it may sound and look lame to go to HR every Thursday and ask for those discount movie tickets, but would you rather have some extra money that you can afford to lose or save face in front of the HR lady who is probably using the perks herself? Many companies offer many trendy benefits, from sporting events to discounts on museums and many other secret ones that you won't know about unless you dig in your employee benefit manual.

Jaclyn: Carpool to Work

Well, I have no driver's license (no joke), so I have no excuse not to carpool. But this lack led me to learn about all the benefits of carpooling, both financial and environmental!

From a financial perspective, not only will you save money on gas by sharing a ride, but you'll also save money that would normally go toward the natural daily wear and tear on your car—its engine, brakes, tires, and so on. Furthermore, many organizations offer reward programs to local carpoolers. You can log your carpool commute with these organizations and get cash in your wallet. Some insurance companies offer discounts to people who rideshare, and sometimes carpoolers receive access to special parking spots.

On the other hand, when you share a ride, you're helping to protect our environment. According to Sightline Institute, the average car with a single driver emits 1.10 lb of carbon dioxide per mile. When you carpool, an average car with three passengers naturally decreases that number by two-thirds—to only 0.37 lb of carbon dioxide per mile.*

Kiana: Learn New Skills

Every new skill can come in handy one day, can help you enrich your lifestyle, and can help you make more money as well. Trading forex is only one of them. All of us are capable of mastering unique skills. Be aware of your skills and be proud of them. Make it your goal to take advantage of all your skills and talents, because, after all, there is a reason why you have them, and you don't want to waste a thing. As the amazing Marie Forleo puts it: "The world needs that very special gift that only you have."

*http://EzineArticles.com/1282448.

CHAPTER 19

Overall Analysis

So, how does it look for you overall? How much money are you eligible to invest in the forex market? Which currency pair should you choose for your trade today? Should you go short or long? Where should you set your stop and your limit? After you've conducted the technical, fundamental, sentiment, and capital analysis, you should review them all before you actually place your trade. This one should be easy. It is just a recap of all the previous detailed analysis from different points of view.

If all four types of analysis point in the same direction (for example, sell EUR/USD, buy AUD/USD, or something else with a specific stop and limit), you should be good to go. Oh, and one more thing. I usually rely on my gut feeling before I actually place the trade. Sometimes, even if the first four points of the Invest Diva Diamond analysis are aligned and confident, something deep down in my stomach prevents me from placing the order, and guess what? It often turns out that I was better off not placing that trade!

Call it women's intuition, the law of attraction, God's guidance, or anything you want. But it won't be enjoyable if you place a trade that goes against your gut feeling. I'm not encouraging you to be a scaredy-cat and not trust your analysis. It's just like deciding on whom to marry, to tell you the truth. You finally meet the perfect guy. His profile and his résumé are all good. Everything matches with all the points you have been adding to your "My Ideal Husband" list. You are ready to say yes and walk down the aisle. Even your family is supportive of him. But suddenly, there's this gut feeling that makes you faint during your wedding planning meeting with your wedding planner, as in many of those Hollywood movies that we love. And you know what? Don't be surprised if you feel like a Hollywood star every time your gut feeling prevents you from placing what looks like the perfect trade. Women's intuition often outperforms men's logic!

Things to Remember Before Ordering Your True Love on Your Forex Platform

1. *Always sell at the* bid *price, and buy at the* ask *price.* If you are trading from a chart, don't forget to switch your chart to the *bid* window when you are selling and to the *ask* window when you are buying. The prices are different, and that difference is the spread. Failing to do so will result in your paying a larger commission fee.
2. *Remember that forex is not an answer to your get-rich-quick quest.* As Martin J. Pring puts it, "There is no such Holy Grail." The saying "patience is a virtue" should be the loudest voice inside the heart of every Forex Diva. It should probably even be printed on a sticker on your fridge, right next to your technical analysis cheat sheets. Let's practice again in a loud voice:

> Patience is a profitable virtue.

3. *Trade to invest, not to win.* Well, as studies show, women in general do obey this one because of their feminine instincts. But still, it doesn't hurt to remind yourself of

it every once in a while. Remember your long-term life plans, your family goals, and your dreams. Never trade to prove someone wrong. In other words, lose the battle to win the war!

This being said, we are not encouraging either fear or greed. Try to be objective in every step you take in your analysis, and avoid trading based on greed or fear—the two destructive mental forces in any investment.

4. *Don't let fear change your gear.* In the overall final analysis, before you place a trade, fear can show itself in two ways: fear of losing and fear of missing out. This can easily change your sense of objectivity, or "objective gear," and push you to make a wrong decision, and it is actually the same in any kind of trading and in all people. All people, both rich and poor, fear losing money; this is especially true if they have had a bad experience in trading because they will fear that the same thing will happen again. When you find yourself in this kind of situation, it is almost always wise to stand aside. Take a deep breath, go out for a walk, visit the Invest Diva Forex community online and have a girl talk with the other forex divas—anything that will help you get back on track and into your objective gear.
5. *Don't let greed change your speed.* Greed is another extreme form of our emotional makeup. In his book *Investment Psychology Explained,* Martin J. Pring describes greed as a result of the combination of overconfidence and a desire to achieve profitable results in the shortest amount of time. Especially when it comes to forex trading, where you have the opportunity to use giant amounts of leverage, the temptation to go for the quick home run is very strong. Change of your investment speed, you want to call it? Well, your wishful speedy investment approach is bound to lead to greater stress and a change in your objective gear. This can also happen to investors who have had a run of success. They tend to be relaxed—in fact, too relaxed and overconfident—and therefore are less likely to question their

investment or trading position even when new evidence to the contrary shows its ugly face.

In the end, moderation is the key to success.

> Too much fear and too much greed can lower your chances to succeed.

6. *When* not *to trade!* "I've become too invested in the forex market and price movements, and I can't stop trading!" Well, this is not an excuse. Forex trading does have addictive tendencies from time to time, but it needs a focused mind and a stable mentality.

   Saying, "It's just a cold! I can totally trade!" is an absolute mistake.

   When you trade forex, you are investing your money with added leverage. Being in your best physical condition is important to enable you to focus, get the timing right, follow the rules, execute proper analysis, make good decisions, and, in general, avoid risk of loss.

No forex party for you when any of the things in Figure 19-1 are true!

FIGURE 19-1

CHAPTER 20

Who Should Host Your Forex Party?

In order to be able to trade forex online, you need to open an account with an online forex broker. So basically, the broker will become the host of your forex party. Now, attending forex parties hasn't always been possible for everyone. At the beginning of online forex trading (the early 1990s), it was available only to superrich people who exchanged humongous amounts of currencies through superlarge banks. Retail forex trading wasn't available to the public until the end of the 1990s, when some smart entrepreneurs took advantage of this new opportunity and started new forex brokerage firms where individuals like you and me could take part in the largest market in the world with a small amount of capital. Recently, even some banks have dedicated a department to retail forex trading.

There are many different retail brokers who offer online platforms for forex trading. Some of them have reliable platforms, and some don't. Some charge a larger transaction fee, and some a smaller one. Some are regulated by reliable authorities, and some aren't. The list goes on. And in today's online-search-aholic society, it is important to remember that some of these brokers pay large amounts of advertising fees to the search engines so that they pop in front of prospective clients' eyes. So you may be asking, how are you supposed to pick from among the many brokers who are trying to host your forex party?

There are different ways to measure which broker is the right one for you, and it all depends on your investment goals and your trading style. You can obviously have different accounts with different brokers to get the best deals on each currency pair as well. We will get into that in a bit.

Ten Things to Check Before Choosing a Broker

1. Regulated or Not

You want to invest your money with an authorized broker. The level of security is the first and foremost characteristic of a broker. You don't want to hand over your hard-earned money to a company that only claims it's legit, right? Invest Diva thinks being regulated by at least two strict international regulatory authorities is mandatory.

Strict international regulatory authorities include the following:

NFA (National Futures Association)	United States
FSA (Financial Services Authority)	United Kingdom
FSA (Financial Services Agency)	Japan
FINMA (Financial Market Supervisory Authority)	Switzerland
ASIC (Australian Securities and Investment Commission)	Australia
DFSA (Danish Financial Supervisory Authority)	Denmark
AMF (Autorité des marchés financiers)	France
BAFIN (Federal Financial Supervisory Authority—in German, *Bundesanstalt für Finanzdienstleistungsaufsicht*)	Germany
FRA (Financial Regulations Agency)	Russia

Brokers that are *authorized* through the MiFID (Markets in Financial Instruments Directive) to operate in more than one country in Europe, but are not regulated through the authorities of those countries, are not considered acceptable!

So the first thing you need to do, before you even think about giving your money to a broker, is to make sure that the broker is regulated by two or more of the bodies just mentioned.

2. Transaction Costs

Every time you exchange money and place a trade on a trading platform, you are subject to a transaction fee, whether you like it or not. These costs are usually the spread or a commission fee, which is, in fact, one of the ways most brokers make money. You didn't think the brokers were hosting a charity party that will give you the opportunity to make money with no costs, did you? But different brokers have different business plans, and therefore different transaction costs.

It is natural to look for the most affordable transaction cost for trading. Some people may prefer a lower transaction cost and accept a less user-friendly platform. Others may prefer a higher transaction fee to ensure security. Just make sure you don't fall into the trap of choosing a high-cost, insecure broker! They *are* out there, and I am not joking.

3. Execution and Slippage

The quality of execution is extremely important to a trader's bottom line.

Under normal market conditions (that is, normal liquidity and no important news releases or surprise events), there really is no reason for your broker not to fill you at, or very close to, the market price you see when you click the "buy" or "sell" button.

A good forex broker will execute your order at your requested price in times of volatility as well. If the broker fails to execute your order, that is when slippage occurs: when a limit order or stop loss order is executed at a worse rate than the one originally set in the order. To be fair, sometimes extreme volatility, perhaps caused by an important news event, makes executing an order at a specific price impossible. In this situation, most forex dealers will execute the trade at the next best price.

Worrying about slippage is especially important if you are a day trader or a scalper. A scalper is someone who trades rapidly and holds a position for a very short period of time. Scalping usually results in small gains (or losses) that add up to a large return (or total loss) at the end of the day. While Invest Diva doesn't usually approve of scalping, some traders enjoy the adrenaline released as they hop from one trade to another, and some actually do end up making money if they play their cards right. The problem with scalping is that you won't have enough time to confirm all five points of the Invest Diva Diamond before placing an order.

One way to test a broker's slippage rate is to start with a demo account, although with most brokers, a good experience on the demo does not guarantee the same on the live. However, it will give you a good idea of how the platform works. Once you are OK with the demo, I suggest that you open a small account initially just to test the live system. If you see that the platform suits your needs, you can just increase your deposit and trade higher volumes.

4. Types of Brokers

There are two main types of brokers:

- Dealing desk (DD)
- No dealing desk (NDD)

No dealing desk brokers can be further subdivided into straight-through processing (STP) and electronic communication network + straight-through processing (ECN+STP).

There is an ongoing debate among traders as to which type of broker is better. While NDD brokers advertise that being a no dealing desk broker is fairer to the customers, many traders believe that whether a broker is a dealing desk or not is unimportant.

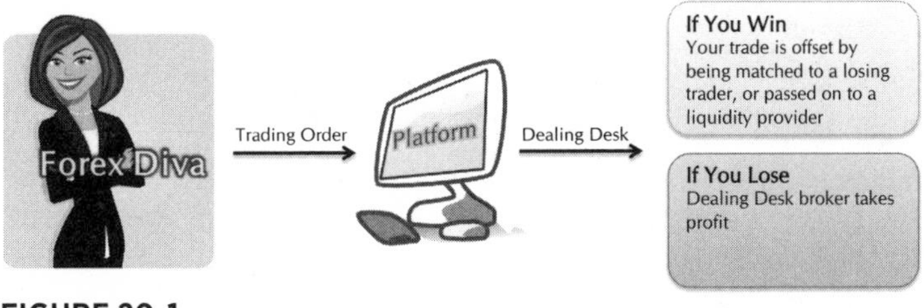

FIGURE 20-1

Dealing Desk Brokers

Also called market makers, dealing desk brokers literally create a market and forex exchange rates for their clients. Market makers provide both a sell and a buy quote, which implies that they are indifferent to the trader's decision.

Clients of dealing desk brokers do not see the real interbank market rates. Since market makers control prices, they are also able to set *fixed* spreads, which can be a great advantage for your trades.

Figure 20-1 shows how a DD broker works. After you place a trading order on your platform, your broker will first try to find an order that is the same size as yours, but in the opposite direction. If you place a buy order, it will be offset by a sell order, and vice versa. Your broker will pass on your trade to its liquidity provider if it can't find a matching order.

By doing this, the broker minimizes risk, as it earns the spread without having to take the opposite side of your trade. However, in the event that there are no matching orders, it will have to take the opposite side of your trade, and since it is a dealing desk, this process is often done by a person and not an algorithm. Different brokers have different risk management policies, so it is important to check with your broker regarding this. Highly regulated firms are held to stringent standards, and price manipulation is strictly illegal in all the jurisdictions in which they operate.

No Dealing Desk Brokers

A no dealing desk broker often passes your trade straight to its liquidity providers, but at times, and in the event that it

FIGURE 20-2

fails to hedge your trade, it will have to take the opposite side of your trade just as a dealing desk broker would (see Figure 20-2). Well, almost. A no dealing desk broker usually does this through an algorithm and not an actual human trader in its office.

No dealing desk brokers can be either STP or STP+ECN. Some brokers claim that they are true ECN brokers, but in reality, they merely have a straight-through processing system.

Forex brokers that have an STP system route their clients' orders directly to their liquidity providers, who have access to the interbank market. NDD STP brokers usually have many liquidity providers, with each provider quoting its own bid and ask prices. The broker's system sorts these bid and ask quotes from best to worst, selects the best price, and shows something similar on your platform. I said "something similar" because your broker adds a small markup to the original price. This is another way of making money for NDD brokers.

True ECN brokers, on the other hand, allow their clients' orders to interact with the orders of other participants in the ECN.

Participants could be banks, retail traders, hedge funds, or even other brokers. In essence, participants trade against one another by offering their best bid and ask prices.

ECNs also allow their clients to see the "depth of market." Depth of market displays where the buy and sell orders of other market participants are. Because of the nature of an ECN, it is very difficult to slap on a fixed markup, so

ECN brokers usually get compensated through a small *commission*.

So to sum up the whole NDD-DD story, as FXTimes analyst and trader Fan Yang puts it: "All brokers have to hedge . . . but that's not defined as trading against the trader. They just have to take the opposite side of your trade sometimes. So with a dealing desk, there are people making those hedging decisions, but without a dealing desk, they have some algorithm that still does the same."

It is important to remember that being a NDD doesn't mean that a broker isn't a market maker. A NDD broker still uses an algorithm to not only match your trades, but also make the market, just as a DD broker does.

5. Minimum Account Size

Especially if you are a new trader trying a real forex account for the first time, it is important that you start with a broker that allows you to open an account of a small size. There are typically three account sizes:

- Micro
- Mini
- Standard (pro)

The micro account is the smallest, followed by the mini account. They both deal with smaller amounts of currency, making them more user-friendly for beginners and those who do not want to risk a lot of money. The gains may be very much less in these accounts, and yet they remain popular with small-time investors and newcomers because of their accessibility. Both mini accounts and micro accounts give traders the opportunity to invest limited amounts of money without fear of being wiped out.

6. Trading Platforms

It is important to choose a broker that offers the most up-to-date and user-friendly platform where you can easily view the charts, execute your analysis, compare currencies, use different indicators, and place orders. Finding the best U.S. forex trading platform is actually one of the harder things to do in the forex world. Many forex trading platforms and brokers do not accept U.S.-based traders, and the list of those that do not continues to grow. However, there are still several out there that do have platforms that accept U.S. traders, and some are even specifically designed for investors that come from the United States.

After going through the previous checkpoints for finding a broker, the best way to decide which trading platform enables you to trade most comfortably is to test the demo platforms. Most forex brokers offer a demo account that operates very much like their live accounts, but where you can trade with fake money. As we have suggested before, it is essential that you test-drive the forex market on a demo account before you actually start to invest anyway, so by doing this, you will be killing two birds with one stone: practicing your forex skills for free and finding the trading platform that you love the most.

Different trading platforms can be suitable for different trading styles, too. Some are better for long-term traders, some for day traders, and some for scalpers. Some brokers get creative and offer a variety of slightly different platforms that they think would match people with different trading habits.

Some platforms can be installed on your computer, but you often have the option of using a web or a mobile platform. Depending on your lifestyle and habits, you can place your trades through your computer, your cellphone, or your iPad with brokers that offer all these options. Alternatively, you can choose one broker for your computer trades, another for your mobile trades, and so on.

In general, the most recently developed downloadable trading platforms include MetaTrader 4 (MT4), MetaTrader 5 (MT5), and Mirror Trader, as of 2013.

MetaTrader

MetaTrader 4, also known as MT4, is a type of electronic trading platform software that is licensed to forex brokers and is widely used by forex traders who use a Microsoft Windows PC. Using MT4, you can write your own trading scripts and robots that can automate your trading.

In 2010 a successor to MT4 was released, MetaTrader 5; however, uptake was slow, and as of early 2012, most brokers still used MT4. The MetaTrader platforms are best known for their diverse technical analysis ability and their ability to run Forex Robots and Expert Advisors.

Mirror Trader

Mirror trading is for traders who don't feel like studying and would rather have a robot make their forex investment decisions. This is not for true Forex Divas who make their own trading decision. In the old school, this is called "copying from your nerdy classmates." In the forex world, it is called mirror trading. The mirror trading method allows you to select a trading strategy and automatically "mirror" in your account the trades executed by the selected strategies. Personally, I prefer monitoring my own trades and not letting a robot do the job for me, but if you select the right strategy, it could make things easier for you.

You can select strategies that match your personal trading preferences, such as risk tolerance and past profits, or basically your Invest Diva capital analysis. Once you select a strategy, all the signals sent by the strategy will be automatically applied to your brokerage account. All the account activity is controlled by the mirror trading platform, and you don't have to do anything else.

The good news is that you can trade more than one strategy at the same time, which will enable you to diversify your risk while maintaining complete trading control of your account at all times.

You can use Mirror Trader's Smart Filters and Real-Time Signals to identify the strategies that work best for you. You can evaluate and build a portfolio of tested strategies, or simply follow individual signals that support your own trading analysis.

What a Mirror Trading Robot Offers

- It highlights which currency pairs are performing best (in the robot's opinion) in the current market conditions.
- It identifies when to enter and exit a trade.
- It allows you the potential to take advantage of market movements even when you are at work or asleep.

You Can Use a Mirror Trader To:

- Manually trade semiautomatic mirroring and automatic mirroring in one platform.
- Use experienced traders' knowledge.
- Control and manage signals generated by other traders and strategy developers.
- Back up your trading decisions with market trends from strategies and users.
- Use other features that are also available on the MetaTrader, such as trading tools, indicators, rates, and market sentiment.

IMPORTANT ALERT

You need to study and educate yourself in the forex market anyway, even if you decide to choose mirror trading. If you don't, you risk copying from a schoolmate who is less qualified than you, and you will simply *lose money*!

7. Deposit and Withdrawal

Good brokers will allow you to deposit funds and withdraw your earnings without a hassle. Brokers really have no reason to make it hard for you to withdraw your profits because the only reason they hold your funds is to facilitate trading.

Your broker holds your money only to make trading easier, so there is no reason for you to have a hard time getting the profits you have earned. Your broker should make sure that the withdrawal process is speedy and smooth. You can test-drive your broker's withdrawal procedure by investing a small amount of money.

8. Customer Service

Reliable and always-ready-to-help customer service is crucial for stress-free and enjoyable forex trading. Most brokers offer 24/7 online and phone customer service. You don't want a customer service operation that pushes you into large investments or into buying the broker's products. You can test your broker's customer service by pretending that you are a forex newbie and asking all sorts of questions about trading, the firm's products, and the company. Brokers may be kind and helpful during the account-opening process, but have terrible "after sales" support. If they sound sketchy, simply move on to the next broker!

9. Promotion

I believe most of us are fans of discounts and sales! Some brokers have discovered this secret, and use it to attract customers. But you have to be careful; every rose has a thorn. Sometimes the brokers use these promotions in order to push new traders into risky investments or into using unreliable products and signals, so it is important that you do your studying and know your broker before you take advantage of a promotion.

There are various different types of promotions:

- Discounts on spreads
- Fixed spreads
- Maximum or minimum spreads
- Discounts on transaction fees
- Free signals
- Cash awards to winning traders
- Unrelated awards, such as phones and other electrical gadgets
- Bonuses upon introducing friends
- Discount food, trips, and hotel rooms to attend their promotional expos

These are all good, but be careful not to fall into the trap of choosing an unreliable broker simply because of its marketing schemes and promotions.

10. Compare

After checking out the previously mentioned nine points and writing down the pros and cons of each broker, it is now time to compare and to choose one or more brokers that best fit your lifestyle and trading strategy. To make this easier for you, we have prepared an A List of strictly regulated brokers on www.investdiva.com. Subscribe for free and look for "Brokers Listing" in the forex section.

CHAPTER 21

Case Study of Successful Investments

Let's look at different scenarios and the thought processes I used when I was placing a successful trade. Here are real blog excerpts that I have posted on www.ForexDiva.com in the past and sent out to my InvestDiva.com subscribers.

August 17, 2012: Trading Australian Dollar Versus U.S. Dollar

I'm liking the way Aussie-Dollar is looking today. Let's take the pair through an Invest Diva Diamond analysis (see Figure 21-1).

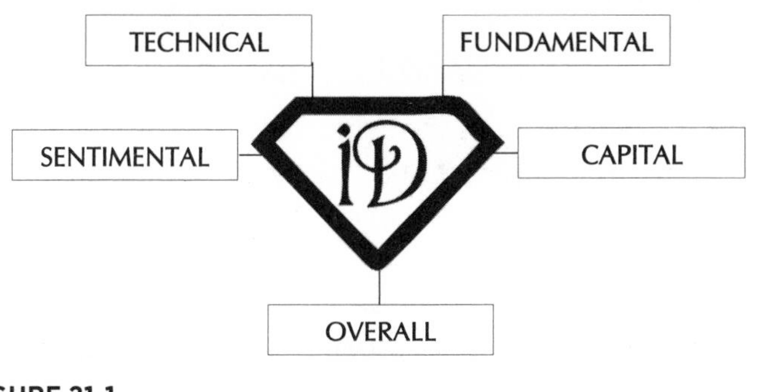

FIGURE 21-1

Technical Analysis

AUD/USD—4-Hour Chart

Will the 50 percent Fibonacci level hold? After a period of consolidation during the uptrend that started July 25, the pair has been moving down today, breaking the previous support of 1.04485 (see Figure 21-2). It is currently showing further bearish movements toward the 50 percent level. Of course, if this strategy works, you would want to buy the pair at the cheapest price. We could wait and see if it reaches the 61.8 percent level.

AUD/USD—Daily Chart

The daily candles are trading above the Ichimoku cloud (see Figure 21-3), signaling more gains. We can expect the pair to be supported at the upper band of the Ichimoku cloud in the 1.02 area.

AUD/USD—Monthly Chart

AUD/USD has been consolidating on a monthly basis in an overall uptrend dating back to 2008. The candles seem to be breaking out of the upper level of a symmetrical triangle connecting the highs and lows of 2011 and 2012 (see Figure 21-4), which can be signaling a continuation of the previous uptrend. A break above 1.06 can open doors to more gains to 1.10749.

This was the first point of the Invest Diva Diamond. A Forex Diva *never* places an order before carefully analyzing all five points.

Fundamental Analysis

Australia's Treasury said that the central bank would be able to ease monetary policy if the currency's gains are hurting the economy. This may have been one of the triggers behind today's declines.

Next week, the Reserve Bank of Australia (RBA) will release the minutes of its August 7 policy meeting, at which policy makers left interest rates unchanged at 3.5 percent.

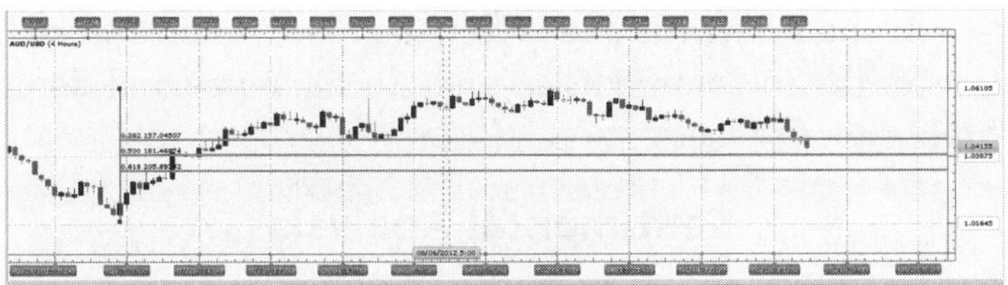

FIGURE 21-2: Australian Dollar (AUD/USD) 4-Hour Chart, August 17, 2012

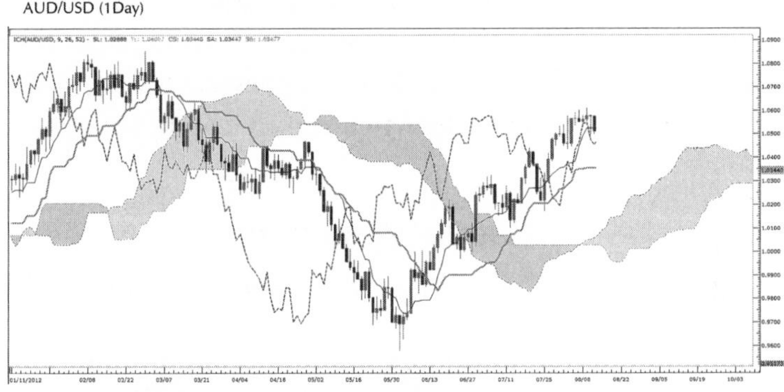

FIGURE 21-3: Australian Dollar (AUD/USD) Daily Chart, August 17, 2012

FIGURE 21-4: Australian Dollar (AUD/USD) Monthly Chart, August 17, 2012

Losses in the Australian and New Zealand dollars were limited, as gains in commodities and stocks supported demand for higher-yield assets.

Sentimental Analysis

Although I have read a few reports and seen that the AUD/USD could be forming a new downtrend, it has yet to be confirmed from my perspective. On the other hand, it is a Friday and many fellow traders may have already called it a week. So a rally over the weekend shouldn't be so intense that it gets out of hand. The smart and conservative target would be aiming to earn just a few pips up at the 50 percent Fib level.

Capital Analysis

Things to check before placing a potential buy order:

1. The spread of AUD/USD with your broker
2. The amount you are willing to risk losing
3. A careful decision on leverage based on the amount of your disposable money

   If you are buying at a 4-hour Fib level:

1. Set your limit, and please don't be greedy.
2. You can take profit at any of the upper Fib levels. If you buy at the 50 percent level at 1.03910, for example, you can look to sell at the 38.2 percent level at 1.04433, and so on.

Size of My Trade and Recommended Leverage

I am trading on a mini lot, where 1 pip is equal to 1 dollar. I have set my leverage at 2:1.

Risk alert: One dollar per pip seems like a small amount, but in forex trading, the market can move 100 pips in a day, or sometimes even in an hour. If the market is moving against you, that is a $100 loss times 2, which makes it $200. Obviously the best thing you can do is either to set your stop and your limit to avoid this kind of loss or to try the trade in a micro account, where each pip would be equal to 10 cents.

August 29, 2012: I Made Money Trading AUD/USD!

I have had my eye on the Australian dollar (AUD) against the U.S. dollar (USD) for a few days, looking for a long-term trade.

Invest Diva is proud to announce that her forecast was correct, and she is now enjoying the dough she made by trading AUD/USD based on her diamond analysis.

Yesterday we had an event that usually affects the AUD trading. I'm talking about the construction work done in the land of Australia. Too bad, the work completed this quarter was 0.2 percent lower than last quarter. We would normally expect a bit more of a drop in the Australian dollar after this news, but it was little changed versus the U.S. dollar. It touched the 61.8 percent Fibonacci retracement and went back up to the 50 percent level today. And that is how I made some money. Let's take a look (see Figure 21-5).

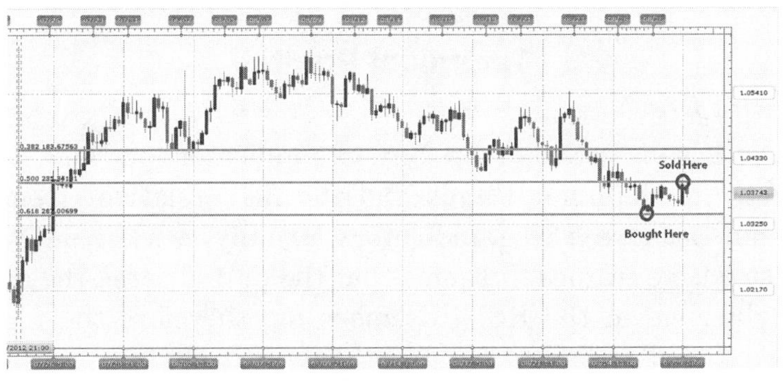

FIGURE 21-5: Australian Dollar (AUD/USD) 4-Hour Chart, August 29, 2012

Now, I know, I could have waited for more potential gains in the pair and made more profit. But Invest Diva doesn't like to take risks. Better safe than sorry, right?

August 22, 2012: The British Are Coming!

Invest Diva is especially excited today because yesterday's prediction of the movement of the British pound against the U.S. dollar (GBP/USD) was correct. Despite what most male analysts were saying elsewhere, the 50 percent Fibonacci level didn't hold, and Pound-Dollar candles are on a rise. Now the question is, should we be expecting a rise all the way to the 61.8 percent Fib level? Let's do our infamous diamond analysis (see Figure 21-6).

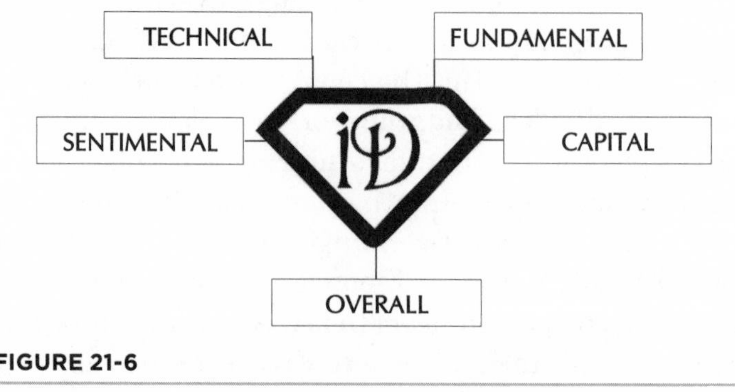

FIGURE 21-6

Technical Points

4-Hour Chart

Invest Diva is getting help from two indicators on the 4-hour chart, the Bollinger Bands and the RSI (relative strength index), because these indicators usually work best with shorter time frames. It seems that the pair entered the overbought zone in the RSI this morning; therefore the prices started to go back down.

The same thing is true with the Bollinger Bands. We know that under normal conditions, we will almost always find the pair within the bands, and more specifically it tends to return to the middle of the bands. This morning the pair reached the upper band at 1.58069 and then bounced back down (see Figure 21-7). For those of you who were up this morning and sold the pair, *good job, divas*!

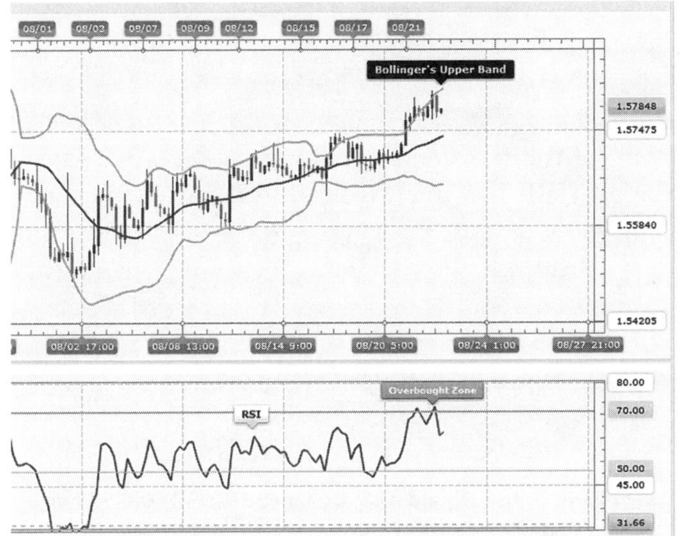

FIGURE 21-7: British Pound–U.S. Dollar (GBP/USD) 4-Hour Chart, August 22, 2012

But I recommend that you not bet on too much of a drop for the pair, and probably set your limit rate somewhere around the middle band of the Bollinger Bands, say 1.574. For the reason behind what I just said, read the rest of the article.

Daily Chart

Not only did the daily candles break above the 50 percent Fib level, but they also broke above the upper band of the Ichimoku cloud (see Figure 21-8). Now this can be bullish! Just to make sure, I also took a look at the daily RSI, and it is in the neutral area, slightly aiming toward the oversold zone. What does this tell me? That the prices have a chance of getting higher, but not too much higher. I think I will aim for a hold at the 61.8 percent Fib level at 1.59103 to sell the pair, and set my stop (always set your stop!) to dynamically follow the movements around the 50 percent Fib level and below. We never want to be greedy, right?

But hold on. Never place an order before carefully analyzing all five points of the Invest Diva Diamond strategy.

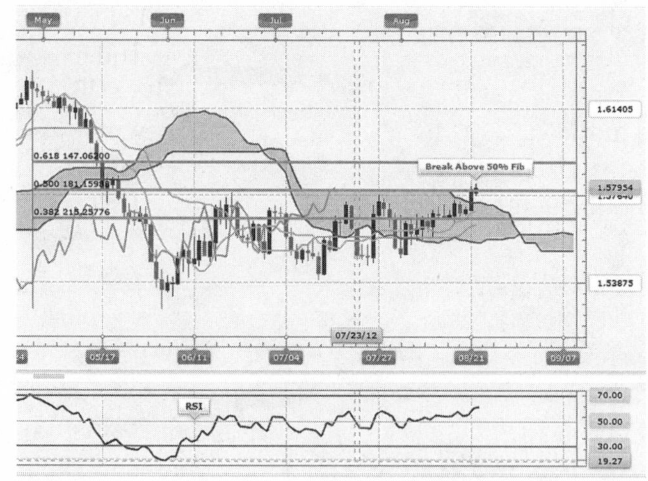

FIGURE 21-8: British Pound–U.S. Dollar (GBP/USD) Daily Chart—Fibonacci, Ichimoku, and RSI, August 22, 2012

Fundamental Analysis

British Pound (GBP)

On Thursday we have two fundamental events that can move the British pound:

1. British Bankers' Association (BBA) mortgage approvals. The forecast for BBA approvals currently stands at 28.2K. If tomorrow's number is larger than this forecast, we could expect more GBP gains.
2. Confederation of British Industry (CBI). The forecast for CBI is 16. If tomorrow's number is larger than 16, we could expect more GBP gains.

Previous numbers of both reports have been lower than expected.

U.S. Dollar (USD)

1. Today we have a major influential event coming up: the Federal Open Market Committee (FOMC) meeting, where the Federal Reserve provides in-depth insights into the economic and financial conditions that influence

its vote on where to set interest rates. And we all know that interest rates are the hottest topic in the forex world.

So I took a look at the U.S. Dollar Index (USDOLLAR) and noticed that it is on an overall downtrend. David Song, a currency analyst at DailyFX, expects the Fed to "talk down speculation for QE3" and sees USD gains during the North American trade.

2. On Thursday we have another major event that can move the U.S. dollar: the Unemployment Claims report. This weekly report gives us a general view of the U.S. economy's health. Recently the numbers have been larger than forecast, which is bad for the U.S. dollar. If this happens again tomorrow, we can expect more losses in the U.S. dollar, which will lead to a drop in GBP/USD.

Sentimental Point

Now let's take a look at the market sentiment. GBP/USD has had a nice, strong, and impressive day! By looking at the speed at which the daily candle is moving up, breaking a resistance level at 1.57954, it seems we could expect the market to continue the uptrend at least until we hear from the Fed with their quantitative easing talks.

Overall/Capital Points

Putting it all together, Invest Diva expects a near-term gain in GBP/USD, which will be followed by a drop. Should anything happen to change the direction of the market and force the pair to pull back, the 1.5700 level seems to be strong enough to act as support.

Things to check before placing a potential sell order at the 61.8 percent Fib level:

The spread of GBP/USD with your broker (don't place a trade if it is too wide)
The amount you are willing to risk losing
The leverage based on the amount of your disposable money

Set the stop without being greedy.
Happy trading!

August 31, 2012: I Made Money Trading British Pound Against U.S. Dollar!

Here is another triumph for Invest Diva! I was away during the week and came back today to find that I made some dough on the trade that I placed last week. In my previous diamond analysis of the British pound versus the U.S. dollar (GBP/USD), I was eyeing a rise all the way to the 61.8 percent Fibonacci level.

I placed a buy order at the 50 percent Fibonacci retracement when the price of GBP against USD was 1.57950 and waited for the market to rise (see Figure 12-9). I had set my limit order at the 61.8 percent Fibonacci retracement at 1.59 and left the GBP/USD room for a week. (It is summer, after all. What else is a girl to do?)

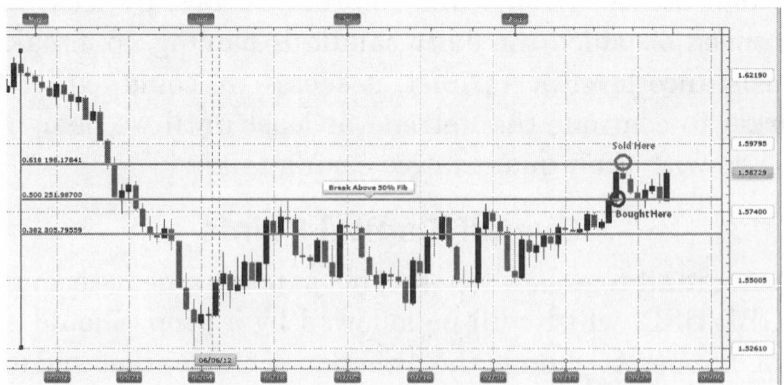

FIGURE 21-9: Invest Diva Made Money Trading Pound-Dollar (GBP/USD)

I came back to find that the prices had reached my forecasted price at 1.59 and my trade had been automatically closed while I was away, leaving me with a good 100+ pips.

Mr. Fibonacci has been so good to me in the past week. It seems that the candles are once again reaching the 68.1 percent Fib level, but I would keep an eye on the fundamentals, especially today's Jackson Hole Symposium. Ready or not, it's Bernanke time. While Invest Diva was away, the rest of the financial world spent the week talking up Fed Chairman Ben Bernanke's upcoming speech, which can move the dollar and therefore its major counterparts, namely, the British pound. Traders are hoping to hear from the Fed chairman an update on whether the Fed is ready to apply further monetary stimulus at its upcoming FOMC meeting. If Bernanke fails to give much clarity on changes, we could see a rally in the dollar, which would translate into a drop for GBP/USD.

September 6, 2012: Euro Is About to Rock'n'Roll

We have a number of scandalous events today that are about to rock a number of forex parties. Here is Invest Diva Diamond analysis, viewing the Euro-Dollar market from a technical, fundamental, sentimental, capital, and overall outlook (see Figure 21-10).

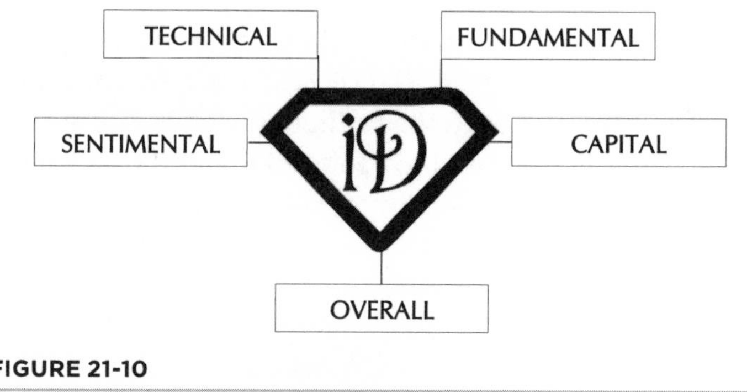

FIGURE 21-10

Fundamental Points

- Bank of England Monetary Policy Committee (MPC) meeting
- European Central Bank (ECB) interest-rate meeting
- U.S. Institute for Supply Management services Purchasing Managers' Indexes

Is the ECB going to rescue the Eurozone's single currency? Well, earlier in the week, ECB President Mario Draghi stated that the ECB will do what needs to be done to preserve the euro, even if this includes unlimited sovereign bond buying. With this backdrop, traders, analysts, stay-at-home moms, college kids, and fashionistas have been anticipating, talking about, and even at times holding a cat fight arguing the destiny of the euro as a result of today's meeting. The media especially have been building up today's meeting as a "do or die" session for the survival of the euro.

But here's a little secret: this is like the gazillionth time we have heard this type of talk. Yet again, the ECB is currently betting on growth. It will fire up the printing presses and hope inflation doesn't hit before growth does.

Invest Diva here is hoping for a stimulation in the currency market that will enable her to make some much needed dough. It's Fashion Week in New York, and we are desperately in need of some extra cash!

Technical Point

Daily Chart

The daily candles have finally broken above the 38.2 percent Fibonacci level (see Figure 21-11)! And not only that, but the candles are trading above the Ichimoku cloud. These two can be bullish signals. Now we have to keep in mind that this could

FIGURE 21-11: Euro-Dollar (EUR/USD) Daily Chart, September 6, 2012

all be because of the anticipation that the ECB will "do something" for the euro. Today's meeting can have the final say.

Sentimental Point

At the broker that I'm trading with today, nearly 66 percent of traders are short the EUR/USD. Experience shows that we can use this as a contrarian indicator and expect more EUR/USD gains.

Capital Point

I have $1,000 worth of expendable money today, and I can afford the risk of losing $200 for a reward of $400.

We know that for all pairs that are quoted as xyz/USD, every pip is worth $100 on a million-dollar trade size, $1 on a $10,000 trade size, 10 cents on a $1,000 trade size, and so on.

Therefore, now that I know that I'm willing to lose $200 and I know my stop distance, I can easily get the size. According to Mr. Fibonacci, it's best to set the stop one level lower than the one we are making the trade on. In this case, it is below the 38 percent Fib retracement level, or a little above 1.25. Let's make it round and say that the stop is 200 points away, at 1.25.

Now we will move on to find out the size of my trade that will manage my risk and give me less than $200 loss and more than $200 profit. Here is our magic formula:

Loss (or profit) divided by pips (stop or take profit) = size

So, [$200 loss/0.0200 (200 pips)] = $10,000.

In other words, I need $10,000 in order to win more than $200 while risking $200. So what do I do? Since I am feeling comfortable with losing $200, but at the same time I have done my Invest Diva Diamond analysis and am confident about my trade, I will go ahead and set a 10:1 leverage to multiply my original investment by 10.

Overall

A conservative buy entry order would have its stop loss set at 1.25 and its limit order at the 50 percent Fibonacci level on the daily chart at 1.27550.

September 7, 2012: I Made Money Trading Euro-Dollar!

Oops—I did it again. I played with your heart and totally won this game! I'm talking to you, Mr. Euro. The Invest Diva Diamond analysis of Euro-Dollar (EUR/USD) yesterday paid off. I earned money. I'm happy.

So here is what happened. As far as the fundamentals were concerned, the ECB meeting came and went in the morning. The big surprise was that Mario Draghi announced that the central bank had cut its GDP forecasts for the EU for 2012 and 2013. All the other bond-buying stuff was as expected. In any event, on the news, the EUR/USD dropped from about 1.2650 to 1.2560. That gave me a good heartache for about two hours. But that move was short-lived, as the market quickly ignored the EU and took its cue from equity traders, who were going bananas over the strong ADP Employment Report and initial claims figures that were released. The news caused the S&P 500 to hit four-year highs. As a result, rather than care about the cut in GDP forecasts, forex traders put their attention on the fact that the ECB was in fact going to expand its bond purchasing program (big surprise!) and positive U.S. news. The change in sentiment triggered an overall rise that gained me 117.2 pips!

Technical Review

As you can see in the chart in Figure 21-12, I noticed that the EUR/USD was trading above the Ichimoku cloud and confirmed a break above the 38.2 percent Fibonacci retracement. These were two strong bullish signals that, combined with fundamentals and market sentiment, set me to place my buy order at 1.26329. I set my *limit* order at the 50 percent Fibonacci retracement because the market usually holds at this level, and also because I don't take too much risk. My *stop* was set at a previous support at 1.24186.

Then I went on taking care of my daily errands, including attending a few Fashion Week parties in the fabulous city of New York. I came back home late, at around 3 in the

FIGURE 21-12: Euro-Dollar (EUR/USD) Daily Chart—Technical Analysis with Fibonacci and Ichimoku

morning, and went directly to my computer to check on my trade. EUR/USD was still rocking it! So I went to bed with relief and woke up this morning to find that my order had hit the limit and had been automatically closed, leaving me with a delicious 117 pips.

It's Friday, folks! If you are about to leave trades open over the weekend, don't forget to adjust your limits and stops carefully, that is, loosen them up a little bit, because at the Sunday open, the prices usually mess around a bit from the original pattern before they get back on track. You don't want to get kicked out of a trade just because of a foolish test of an open market.

APPENDIX

Meet Some Forex Divas

Are you still worrying that forex trading may not be suitable for women? Here is what female traders from around the world have been saying about their experience with forex.

Maiko, Forex Trader from Japan

Q: When did you start trading?
A: In 2007, when the carry trade was at a peak.

Q: Why did you start forex trading?
A: My friends were trading, so I started.

Q: What is your educational background in college or high school?
A: I graduated from a university in the United States with a bachelor of science.

Q: How did you learn about forex trading?
A: Online, by trial and error.

Q: What percent of your expendable money do you invest in forex?
A: Approximately 10 to 15 percent. I also do not plan to invest more than 15 percent in the future because I have learned that I should not trade (invest) more than I can risk.

Q: What is the most that you have earned trading forex?

A: My total gross profit was once close to 1 million JPY.

Q: What is the most you have lost trading forex?

A: I lost 0.5 million JPY in one night. When I woke up in the morning, my account had been liquidated and all of my positions were automatically closed. I think I was way too overleveraged at that time.

Q: Does being a forex trader boost your self-confidence among your friends? How about at home?

A: I feel that I am always up-to-date with news and economic events because I am a forex trader. That is something that I can be positive about!

Q: Do you ever trade with your female friends? How about with your husband or boyfriend?

A: I trade alone because I want to stand by my own trading rule and strategy. Trading is an individual responsibility. I mean that I should be solely responsible for the outcome. It can get nasty if I lose a trade or enter or exit a market too soon or too early by listening to others. I do not want to get feisty with friends or a partner!

Q: How do you spend the money you earn from forex trading?

A: I cannot recall a specific luxury item that I purchased with money earned from forex. But when I win a trade, I buy fancy desserts or drinks!

Kathy Lien

Let me introduce you to one of the giants of the forex industry, who despite her young age has already published four books on this topic. Yes, I said "her." This is a she. Now, I'm not expecting you to write books on this topic or make appearances on Bloomberg TV and CNBC all the time, like she does. I just want to set her as an example of a successful female forex trader. Yes, ladies, we can!

So without further ado, I bring to you an original Forex Diva, Kathy Lien.

Kiana: When did you first become interested in forex trading?

Kathy: Trading in general, I started when I was in college. There were a lot of different investment training programs when I went to NYU. So I started to become interested in the markets at that time, and during my college career, I actually participated in the Market Technicians Association. My mentor and the person who gave me my first internship when I was in college was a technical trader, so he got me kind of tuned into how the stock market worked and how to look at charts and made me much more aware of technical analysis. That's how my interest in trading started to grow. But I didn't really become interested in forex trading until I graduated from college. When I was in college, we had the "dot-com" boom, and day trading of stocks was extremely popular. When I graduated, I joined J.P. Morgan, and it placed me in the foreign exchange trading group. I knew very early on that I wanted to be in a trading program in an investment banking program. So J.P. Morgan placed me in the foreign exchange group, and that is where my career in foreign exchange started, because I joined the desk, I met the traders, and I got the insiders' view of how the market works. I spent a couple of years there and learned how to trade not only FX but also the derivatives of FX, like FX options and interest-rate derivatives, which all kind of relate to the same thing because they are all based on the same story about whether the central banks are going to raise or cut the interest rate and how the economies are doing. So we basically traded many products. To sum it up, trading came from my first internship in college and forex trading came from my first job out of college.

Kiana: You first learned about technical analysis at the Market Technicians Association?

Kathy: I was an intern for one of the directors and the director took me to a lot of the meetings, so I learned a lot through that. On a day-to-day basis, he would teach us how to look at the markets from a technical basis.

Kiana: Now that you trade every day, what is your trading style?

Kathy: I have two styles of trading. But they are both in the center of what I call medium-term trading. Usually I look at whole positions for a couple of hours or couple of days. I have search strategies that I use on a shorter term, and I have search strategies that are more positional. Usually during the daytime, between about 6:30 and noon, I'm looking more for shorter-term trades. And then in the afternoon, usually 3:30 to 5:30, I look at my positional trades that I hold overnight.

Kiana: How do you come up with your trading strategies?

Kathy: My trading strategies are all based on a combination of fundamental and technical analysis. But some of the core trading strategies that I have come from back-testing. The trades that I take are centered around a technical strategy, and I demo trade it, I live trade it, and then I usually take the trades that have a fundamental catalyst. And that is how I combine my fundamentals and my technicals.

Kiana: What are the steps that you take before entering a position?

Kathy: In terms of my positional trades, I first watch the markets throughout the day. So the most important thing is to understand the momentum of the markets—whether we are in an environment where there is a consolidation or whether we are in a trending environment, and whether the market is closing strong or closing weak. That is the first criterion that I move on for trading.

My second criterion is looking at the event risk calendar. I see if there is a piece of economic data that is going to push the trade in my direction. For example, let's say I want to do an AUD/USD trade. What I'll do is look for whether or not there is a piece of Australian data coming out, like the Australian GDP. If there is a piece of Australian data coming out, I'll look at my general fundamental studies to help me determine whether I think the data are going to be strong or weak. If my belief is that the data are weak, we have a negative momentum in the markets, and I have a technical setup that I'm looking for that is also negative, I have three stars lined up: I have the general sense of the market in my direction, I have a possible data catalyst that might push it further in my direction, and then I have a general technical picture in which I use double Bollinger Bands to see whether the trend is in that direction. When these three things are lined up, that is when I decide whether or not to take a trade.

Kiana: Do you believe in intuition in your determination?

Kathy: I think intuition always plays a role. It is basically always a guess: the right guess versus the wrong guess. You are hoping that the reason you are taking this trade is that there are enough factors that have lined up to support the guess that you are making. I think intuition definitely plays a role because you have to have a good feel for a possible trade and have enough confidence that there is room for that trade to move in your direction.

Kiana: How exactly do you manage risk?

Kathy: I have clearly defined stops and limits, and I stick to them. I don't deviate from the stops and limits that I have originally set. There is a lot of blood, sweat, and tears put into the entry and exit of all of my strategies. A lot of back-testing has been done on the exit strategy and on the entry strategy. So given that all that work has been done already, now I just follow these strategies and stick to the risk and reward parameters that I have laid down before the trade. I never adjust my stops at all. It's always a flat stop and that's it. I think that is the biggest mistake that traders make: once the position starts to move against them, they adjust their stops. The only thing that I may do is to use trailing stops once I'm in profit, but I never adjust my stops to give a trade more room.

I think it's fear that causes people to move their stops. Let's say the stop is at 50 pips. When they are down 40 pips, they think, maybe I should move this to 60 pips or 70 pips just to give it a little bit of room. I would never do that.

Kiana: What are your thoughts on leverage?

Kathy: Leverage is a double-edged sword. I actually trade on less leverage. 10:1 is probably the maximum leverage that I use in terms of my overall account size.

Kiana: Have you ever traded at a higher leverage?

Kathy: I have, of course. Especially when I was starting out. The 50:1 leverage was extremely attractive. But I think as time passes, you become more disciplined. My approach to FX has changed as well, and I realized that in order to survive in this market for a long period of time, it is important that you approach it no differently from the way you approach stock trading. This is not a get-rich-quick type of market. Because if you think like that, you are going to get poor very quickly as well. I think it's important not to be greedy and to be satisfied with double-digit return rates, which is already really good. Some people can't even get single-digit returns.

Kiana: How do you react when you realize that you have made a mistake in your position or analysis?

Kathy: There are only one or two things that I would do. I always stick to the stop, but sometimes, when the trade is not working out as I would like, I may take profits early. I won't necessarily adjust myself if I don't feel comfortable with the position and it's not really moving the way that it should be. I trade momentum, so in a set period of time, if it's not really moving in my direction, I may choose to exit early.

Kiana: What is the indicator that you use when you say that you trade momentum?

Kathy: It is not so much an indicator. You obviously could use indicators to gauge momentum, but for me, it is more the prevalent sentiment in the market, and that really comes from watching the market and the prices.

Kiana: How do you decide which currency to trade?

Kathy: It's based on my trading strategies. The setups are there. I use double Bollinger Bands a lot. Let's say I want to trade the Australian dollar and I want to short Aussies, then I would look to see which Aussie pair has my technical setup. I have the strategy that I use, which I have established and have been using for years. Then I look at the calendar to see if there is a piece of economic data coming out. I may have a strong opinion on the GDP numbers coming out every week. And if I have a strong opinion on the GDP numbers, I may be looking to short Aussies. Then I'll have my indicator—double Bollinger Bands—set up on my charts, then I will look to see which pairs are giving me a solid signal. It may be AUD/USD, AUD/JPY, AUD/CAD, and so on.

Kiana: Do you recommend that people start trading together the way you did with Boris at GFT?

Kathy: I actually think it helps a lot. If you have a trading buddy, it makes a very big difference, because being able to bounce ideas off someone else is basically a quality check. It is a very crucial part of my trading success.

Kiana: What is your advice to new traders?

Kathy: Always test before you try. There are a lot of great ideas out there, but you'll never know if an idea is really good until you actually put it into live testing. It could be on a demo account or a small real account. But when you come up with a strategy, you need to build confidence around it. I think you can't just pull the trigger and start trading immediately just because someone has told you that. It's important that you do some visual back-testing by looking at the charts and actually trying to trade the strategy in real life. Because why waste your money and trade your entire portfolio using it when you can work it out in a way that lets you understand the strategy through demo accounts or smaller live accounts?

Kiana: Do you think that women with no financial background can trade forex?

Kathy: Absolutely. I think many people with no financial background trade currencies. Most people approach it from a technical analysis perspective. There is nothing wrong with that. Technical analysis is not too hard to learn. It's hard to make money, and it's hard to come up with a trading strategy, but it's not as complicated as learning economics or monetary policy, for example. I think that if you start from something simple that you can understand, practice it, and try your own enhancements to it, meaning coming up with a trading strategy, there is a path toward succeeding in this market.

Elizabeth Jeanne le Roux

Now I would like to introduce you to Elizabeth Jeanne le Roux. She is no economist, mathematician, or financier. She is, in fact, an international actress (yes, you can find her on YouTube), and she trades in her free time:

Kiana: Elizabeth, can you tell us a little about yourself? Where are you from?

Elizabeth: I'm from Johannesburg, South Africa. I was born in a city known as Pretoria.

Kiana: Can you tell me about your relationship status? Are you single or married?

Elizabeth: I'm single and exploring the universe at this current stage. I do have time for love.

Kiana: Besides your acting career, how do you take care of yourself? Traveling around the world must be expensive, right?

Elizabeth: There are a couple of investments that I'm currently taking care of. I have three real estate properties in South Africa. On top of that, I'm a consultant for an advertising agency. I operate globally, so wherever I am, I can access these things through the Internet. My third investment is forex. I invest in currencies. Because I travel so much, I like to purchase different currencies and sell them at different exchange rates, either over the counter or on a trading platform.

Kiana: What are your thoughts on forex trading?

Elizabeth: As you know, forex is a macroeconomic global market, so you don't necessarily need to have a background [in finance] in order to know what forex is all about. The news is published as publicly known information to anybody, so it's very easy to earn money with the different fluctuations in the currencies that we deal with. But I must be honest with you: you need to keep an eye out. Sometimes the fluctuations can drop without your being notified if you are not trading on a platform where you can set stops and limits.

Kiana: So I understand that you are a beautiful, independent woman and you make more than 50 percent of your income through investing. How do you feel about investing as a woman?

Elizabeth: I think it is stimulating for me to play Monopoly in my private life as well as my professional business life. It's almost like a hobby where you invest in yourself, and you can even have fun with it!

Kiana: It is funny that you said, "invest in yourself." I believe that is a very powerful quote. You invest and enrich your lifestyle, because not only are you making money out of it, but also you have this lifestyle of independence; you become more aware of what is going on in the world, and, as you said, it can even be a hobby, whether or not you make a lot of money out of it. I understand that with forex trading, you are not taking on a lot of leverage and are not investing too much capital, right?

Elizabeth: Correct. Forex trading is more of a short-term investment for me, while real estate is more of a long-term plan. With any kind of investment, I enjoy watching the markets going up and down, and I definitely get excited when I see my capital grow.

Did You Like the Divas?

At InvestDiva.com, we have a *Forex Diva finder* who spots successful traders around the globe to get their take on trading the largest market in the world. Who will be the next guest on our weekly videos? It could be you! So get yourself over to www.InvestDiva.com and subscribe to get *free* updates and to become a winning Forex Diva.

INDEX